Branding Cities

Routledge Advances in Geography

Branding Cities

Cosmopolitanism, Parochialism,
and Social Change

**Edited by
Stephanie Hemelryk Donald,
Eleonore Kofman,
and Catherine Kevin**

Routledge
Taylor & Francis Group
New York   London

First published 2009
by Routledge
711 Third Avenue, New York, NY 10017

Simultaneously published in the UK
by Routledge
2 Park Square, Milton Park, Abingdon, Oxfordshire OX14 4RN

Routledge is an imprint of the Taylor & Francis Group, an informa business

First issued in paperback 2012

© 2009 Taylor & Francis

Typeset in Sabon by IBT Global.

Library of Congress Cataloging in Publication Data
Branding cities : cosmopolitanism, parochialism, and social change / edited by Stephanie Hemelryk Donald, Eleonore Kofman and Catherine Kevin.
    p. cm. — (Routledge advances in geography ; 2)
  Includes bibliographical references and index.
    1. Urban geography.   2. City and town life.   3. Cosmopolitanism.   4. Social change.
5. Sociology, Urban.   I. Donald, Stephanie.   II. Kofman, Eleonore.   III. Kevin,
Catherine.
  HT151.B645 2009
  307.76—dc22
  2008028827

ISBN13: 978-0-415-96526-2 (hbk)
ISBN13: 978-0-415-53670-7 (pbk)
ISBN13: 978-0-203-88429-4 (ebk)

Frontispiece. Man on phone in a Shanghai street, 2008, courtesy project team and Leicia Petersen

Contents

Figures

Acknowledgments

This project has been fortunate in having great support from a number of institutions and individuals. We acknowledge the superb collaboration of the Menzies Centre at King's College, London, for facilitating Dr. Kevin's contribution to the first project conference and to the present volume. We also acknowledge Australia House in London, which hosted the first of the five international symposia that have underpinned the development of this project, and the technicians at Barnet Town Hall, Middlesex University, who helped make the last seminar so successful. Generous financial support for meetings and for the travel of the editorial team and postdoctoral associates has come from an Australian Research Council Linkage International grant; from the Institute of Health and Social Science at Middlesex University in London; and from the Transforming Cultures Research Centre and the erstwhile Institute for International Studies, both at the University of Technology, Sydney and for time to complete the project, we thank the University of Sydney. Many colleagues have been of great intellectual assistance, but we wish particularly to acknowledge Ian Henderson, Panos Hatziprokopiou, Ilaria Vanni, Andrew Jakubowicz, and Bill Marshall. Michael Prince created and maintained our website, and Brett Todd and John Golder have been of great help in the final stages of preparing the manuscript. Many thanks also to our generous hosts in London and Sydney, Fiona and Norman Fowler, Tony Taylor, and Freida Riggs.

The book has been two years in the making and has witnessed the arrival of two small cosmopolitans, Paddy Pablo Lattin-Kevin and Iris Esmé Fowler. We dedicate this book to their future.

1 Introduction

Processes of Cosmopolitanism and Parochialism

Stephanie Hemelryk Donald,
Eleonore Kofman, and Catherine Kevin

PROBLEMS OF EQUIVALENCE

In a recent opinion piece in the U.K. broadsheet, the *Guardian*, Ulrich Beck claims that "European cosmopolitanism" is the way forward for the world. As the model for this answer to global conflicts, he cites the European Union (EU), founded as it was to be the "political antithesis to a nationalistic Europe and the physical and moral devastation that had emerged from it" (Beck 2008). Closely aligned to globalization, his notion of cosmopolitanism refers to the "erosion of distinct boundaries and the emergence of internal globalization or dissolution of the national state in which the 'us' and 'them' of social identities is constructed less negatively" (Beck 2007). Thus cosmopolitan tolerance involves opening up to the "world of the Other" and the "allure of difference" (Nava 2007:19).

Beck's argument is a compelling and reassuring read in Europe, within the European context and construction of how politics work—or don't work—in an idealized democracy with an operational Fourth Estate (the press) and public sphere. Not yet quite the best of all possible worlds, but not a bad place to start; reassuring because apparently there is already a word for the panacea we crave. The entity of Europe is not easily made cosmopolitan by diktat, of course, although it is already cosmopolitan by virtue of the movement of peoples allowed through and across EU borders. This fluidity is not available to those beyond the existing borders of the territories of the EU, although this is constantly being enlarged,[1] and Beck does not offer an answer to the larger question of how conflicts between large, "almost-cosmopolitan" regions and intraregional faith groups, for example, might be addressed through his model. Nor does he acknowledge competing cosmopolitan systems. The *Ummah* is cosmopolitan, albeit bounded by religious principle and allegiance, in that it requires transnational and transethnic commitment to the world of Islam. Yet in practice the Arabization of Islam undermines the cosmopolitanism of the religious project to the extent that certain regional groups are publicly re-asserting the cosmopolitan possibility of faith. The Sisters in Islam advocacy organization in Malaysia is an example of such resistance:

> Sisters in Islam (SIS) is a group of Muslim women committed to promoting the rights of women within the framework of Islam. Our efforts to promote the rights of Muslim women are based on the principles of equality, justice and freedom enjoined by the Qur'an as made evident during our study of the holy text. We believe that for the *Ummah* (Islamic community) to grow and flourish, everyone must have the opportunity to fully participate in all spheres of life. The participation of Muslim women as full and equal partners in the ummah's socio-economic development and progress is the need of the day. We conclude that it is imperative that the female experience, thought and voice are included in the interpretation of the Qur'an and in the administration of religion in the Muslim world.[2]

Beck's *Guardian* opinion piece is based on his longer argument in his *Cosmopolitan Vision* (2006), where he does note the contextual and historical differences between the United States, which he describes as "multicultural" and a "melting pot" and Europe, which he calls the home of "long history" (176). This leads him to underestimate the power of institutional cultures established since the eighteenth century, and to totally ignore the history of indigenous peoples and their relation to a cosmopolitan vision in settled societies (he describes America as "history light" [176]). Given the growing sense among indigenous politicians and activists that their cultural future depends on a politics of what we might call "cosmopolitan indigeneity," the case for Europe is at the great expense of many other cosmopolitan equivalencies beyond its imaginary reach. This omission emphasizes Eurocentric politics in this version of the ideal polity. Indigenous politics are most vital in settler societies, where multicultural populations are overlaid on a much longer-established group, and where the cosmopolitanism of arrival does not account for the dispossession and violence attached to the process of settlement.

There are, of course, many claims on cosmopolitanism that are not easily accommodated into a European viewpoint. Chinese state-rule over the territories of "China" encompasses at least fifty-two nationalities, albeit with an overwhelming majority of Han, but again, it is not a model of equivalence, freedom of expression, or political diversity as required in the EU model suggested by Beck. The United States is extremely cosmopolitan in terms of ethnicity and origins when compared to an average European nation–state, but it remains a nation–state par excellence in its political ambitions and approaches to other parts of the world. Even Martha Nussbaum, whose work on cosmopolitan ideals, *Cultivating Humanity* (1997), has framed much of the U.S. debate, has been justly accused of parochialism in her adoption of the "we" of normativity and the standpoint of judgment, albeit rational and well-intentioned. Indeed, James Donald (2007) has described her as a multiculturalist rather than a cosmopolitan: "[S]he adopts the point of view of a member of the majority society observing otherness from a distance and extracting from it 'universal' commonalities" (303). Given that the free trade agreements of the past five years have signally reminded smaller economies of their place in the pecking order of cultural production and financial sovereignty, Nussbaum's America-centered approach is indeed problematic for many other cosmopolitans. And, sadly, Beck's own vision of Europe is still only a vision, even in the EU. It is now a truism to remind ourselves that the fluid movement within borders is premised on strict control of movement through and across member states by those without citizenship.[3]

So what exactly might we mean by cosmopolitanism in this book, which engages with the ideals of diversity and equivalence in shared space? What interpretive starting points should we claim in order to start the conversation? First, we would insist that cosmopolitanism is a process of the human imagination, that it is an affective disposition that inflects social and political relationships, but that in order to flourish it is also dependent on the state of those relationships. Though the concept has a long history, the present revival derives from a largely European debate on mobility, belonging, and strangeness (Beck 2002; Rumsford 2006; Vertovec and Cohen 2002, on a rethinking of the nature of a global political community (Archibugi and Held 1995) and on the reasonable bounds of hospitality in a mobile world. Now, however, it may be understood as a floating signifier for a number of ways in which people live together (see section on urban cosmopolitanism), visit each other, ideally with respect if not delight. But it is by no means a contemporary discussion between Europeans in response to changing geographies, cultural mixing, and political institutions. While comparative work has side-stepped questions of cosmopolitanism and focused primarily on the relationship between globalization and the nation–state, Kaufman (2003) traces the historical spread of liberal cosmopolitan ideas in the United States and Europe. Since September 11th, foreign policy trends have diverged, leading to more pronounced affirmation of national self-interest. Many colonial and imperial societies were also quintessentially cosmopolitan. Migration and mobility have not suddenly erupted; they defined colonial modernity; cultures of imperial and colonial trading cities depended on the mixing of their populations (see Jakubowicz this volume; van der Veer 2002; Zubaida 2002).

To return to the discussion of contemporary cosmopolitanism, the strangeness of the cosmopolitan should not be forgotten, however, as it is as much part of the dynamic of the travelling mind as is the willingness to make empathic gestures between cultural and social lifeworlds. That strangeness might be dispersed among various scales and levels of cosmopolitan actor (we are not all of us cosmopolitan all the time), but it is the grit in the oyster that both provokes the attraction of difference and threatens the local status quo. To put it in the terms of some of the contributors to this volume, strangeness resides in the resistance of local power elites to accept the absolute incommensurability of another's belief systems (see Jakubowicz on the Chinese State's refusal of Judaism); or it lurks in the tainted histories of place identity, where economic prosperity has been premised on the subjugation of others (see Marshall on Nantes; S. H. Donald on Liverpool this volume); or it can even be found in the everyday social networks of new Londoners, Berliners, and Mancunians, where migrants find the aura of cosmopolitanism belied by the ineluctable separateness of British/German lives from their own forms of Britishiness and Germanness (see Hatziprokopiou; Kennedy; Kosnick this volume).

Second, we would deny therefore that the methodological impulse to organize the world "better" (*pace* Beck) is in itself a grounded cosmopolitan approach to difference and difficulty. That a better world is to be desired is, of course, the case, but that we might be able to proscribe it and maintain a dynamic and agonistic cosmopolitan process is less obvious (Skrbis, Kendall, and Woodward, 2004). A better—more peaceable, fairer, happier—system may be a side effect in certain circumstances, but, given that we are dealing with a disposition rather than a system, we cannot make idealized ambit claims for the world's future. It is not in our control, whoever "we" are. Skrbis and Woodward (2007) offer a generous interpretation, which is somewhat more realistic, whereby globalization is neither a "sufficient nor necessary condition for the emergence of cosmopolitanism" (731), where nationalism is a local constraint rather than an alternative system (a point Craig Calhoun also makes in his recent book, *Nations Matter*), and where "people in place" (which we offer as a gloss on *parochialism*) make choices based on opportunity, knowledge, and empathy.

Third, we have deliberately tied the notion of cosmopolitanism to the parochial and elected to look at both through the prism of brand identity. The empirical and theoretical bases of the idea of "grounded" or "actually existing" cosmopolitanism leads us to this connection, in so far as place and space are at the core of principles of place branding and contemporary urban development strategies. The latter tend to aim for systemic and ideal solutions to the problems of everyday life, but are generally confronted with the messiness of human wants, concerns, and behaviors. Ideal cosmopolitanism also grounds itself in highly systematized approaches, which are extremely hard to test against the affective impulses of actual human beings. While it is fair to argue, as Beck has done, that in recent years many Europeans really have moved forward in their acceptance of one another as political *confrères* and in the moderation of patriotism (see Tan 135), that does not prove that a larger cross-regional grouping, or even the current expanded EU, will address the undeniable internal conflagrations of difference, or offer sufficient affective ties for people to imagine togetherness as a political reality. While, for example, there has been widespread revulsion at the revelations of the Guantanamo Bay prison camp, the active engagement from nationals in both the United Kingdom and Australia has been to fight for the release or fair trial of "their" prisoners, their compatriots. Conversely, the competing cosmopolitanisms of postcolonial family networks stretch way beyond the EU, and it is perhaps the sharing of local, parochial affect that is missing from certain parts of European consciousness?

As a coda to this volume, Jeff Malpas addresses a similar quandary, when he traces the failure of parochial cosmopolitanism in suburbs on the outskirts of Sydney as evidenced by the riots of 2005. Had the people of Cronulla been a little more cosmopolitan in their outlook on male behaviors, might their parochial relations have been better managed? And, conversely, if both the Cronulla residents and the second-generation Australian migrants they attacked had been better informed about the sensitivities and points of passion among people in and out of the "shire," which is both a local political unit (a county or district in other zones) and a byword for old "White" working class Australian values, would the beachside tensions have erupted so calamitously? If "globalization is not a sufficient or necessary condition" for cosmopolitan dispositions, then perhaps we should also point out that parochialism is not necessarily a detractor from a wider cosmopolitan disposition, but rather, at its best and most humane, it operates as a scaled down but emplaced cosmopolitanism; the successful parochial must have the courage of kindness and self-doubt among strangers and neighbors (see also Morris 2005; J. Donald 2007).

This particular inflection in an understanding of the Cronulla events brings us to the question of the relationships between colonialism and the cosmopolitan; between postcolonialism and the successful parochial. In 2000 Ann Curthoys posed the question: is postcolonialism a prerequisite for Australian multiculturalism (Curthoys, 2000, 21tt)? Kosnick makes the important distinction between multiculturalism and cosmopolitanism, positing the fostering of "transcultural exchanges," rather than just multicultural diversity, as the mark of a city's cosmopolitanism. Can Australian cities make genuine claims to cosmopolitanism, to living comfortably with the presence of the global in the local, while Indigenous Australians—the first locals and a minority culture—continue to suffer substantially higher levels of morbidity and poverty than non-Indigenous Australians? On February 13, 2008, the Prime Minster of Australia, Kevin Rudd, offered a clear apology to Indigenous Australians for past wrongs done and the ongoing suffering caused, which made the possibility of solving problems of inequity and opportunity and of initiating transcultural exchange in Australian cities and rural areas, much more likely (Rudd, 2008). However, we would like to draw attention to representations of Indigenous Australians in relation to the global and the local. Australian brands such as Qantas and the Sydney Olympics have used traditional Aboriginal art, dance, and music to sell their products. The point of this approach to Australian place branding has been that the distinctiveness of Australia, and of Sydney, lies with this traditional, first culture. The preservation of the content in indigenous cultural forms, its particular immunity from colonial forces, and its capacity to represent something distinctly local has been foregrounded by these branding strategies.

It is important to recognize, mark, and share histories that are different and that interlock. In these essays there are stories from cinema, from family histories, and from the observations of layered and multiple-migration sites. Mark Shiel draws on aesthetics to explore the separate histories of modernism and modern representations (such as branding), which are both temporally and spatially overlapping and yet antithetical in tone and depth. The complicated histories of urban belonging and exclusion are at the heart of the branding paradigm, as they are in film, and in the working through of cultural policy on the ground. To see brand narratives as political strategies as well as commercial necessities makes other political possibilities and blockages visible. Complexity is not only relevant to the engendering of successful parochialism and the fostering of "transcultural exchanges," it is also crucial to the processes of decolonization that will bring Australia to a place of genuine postcolonialism, which will, in turn, enable a cosmopolitanism that does not skate over the vagaries of a settler-colonial past, that does not panic in the face of perceived threats to Anglo-Celtic dominance, and that can sit comfortably with the receptive and hybrid aspects of Indigenous Australian cultures and identities. Similarly, different understandings of the connections between parochialism and cosmopolitanism need to be recognized in the processes of contemporary branding of European cities in which migrant cultures may be both exploited and marginalized by urban elites (Chan 2006; Kosnick this volume).

BRANDING

Here, Malpas takes extreme issue with the practice and function of place branding, which for him only serves to highlight the dissonance between achievable goals of lived experience, and the gloss of corporate and governmental claims on place identity (and, by default, the identity of those who inhabit place). On the other hand, Simon Roodhouse gives us a candid report on the process, benefits, and drawbacks of cultural quarters, which rely absolutely on defined brand characteristics to stake an economic and cultural claim for a certain place and a particular economic activity. The brand is not intended to implicate the population in excellent cosmopolitan relations, but it does aim to support a set of employment possibilities which may, if the provincial attitude in that region is sufficiently nuanced towards the neighbor and stranger, make a cosmopolitan disposition more affordable and attractive. Likewise, while Lindner is inherently skeptical of the brand strategies of London and the London

Eye, his analysis of recent London films notes that the city as a visual object is saturated with affective residue that characterizes both cultural memory and contemporary "cool" and is thus re-presented to the contemporary population by brand campaigns as a way of negotiating London as a space that offers collective status and meaning.

Branding is both mundane and extraordinarily ambitious. It is a product development and marketing activity, which ascribes products with unique characteristics or reasonably unique bundles of characteristics. These are designed to define the product for its intended consumers, and to give the company a basis from which to develop further products. Companies themselves may also be significant brands, in which case their product range is assigned a part of that aura. Brands are not static: as with any aspect of dynamic business practice, they must be refreshed, maintained, tested, and reviewed. However, they are somewhat delicate and cannot be easily changed without careful thought being given to the emotional impact that a change of a familiar aspect of everyday life has on consumers. This is particularly true when a branded product is closely attached to a city, a locale, or a type of lifestyle, so that it is attached to a parochial sensibility that is inherently fragile.

Brands have tended in many cases to trade on national identity (real or imagined),[4] to the extent that Simon Anholt, whose 2005 GMI brand index is referred to in Malpas's chapter, and who is possibly the most prominent "brand guru" on the circuit, has argued that nations can claim cosmopolitan justice by building their brands in the global market (Anholt 2003). The relationship between global reach, national exceptionalism, and an ideal of cosmopolitan justice premised on market activity is somewhat confusing in his argument. It does demonstrate, however, on a rather less precious level than that of moral cosmopolitanism, that making ideas, structures, and behaviors connect is never without contradiction. Anholt is, of course, building his own brand as the voice of place branding, and does indeed seem to hold the centre in this sphere of influence. The discussion rages in his journal *Place Branding and Public Diplomacy* (first issue 2004). The journal's theoretical premises do not tend to challenge the premise that branding will happen, but it is a useful source for gauging the sheer pragmatism of brand analysts and those in the business of brand management. A brand manager from Icelandic USA (Gudjonsson 2005) does not dispute that nations are subject to brand manipulation, and that this is premised on a selective exploitation of so-called national characteristics, including economic, cultural, social, and political themes. His particular concern is how Iceland might be able to utilize these methods and leverage competitive advantage (296–97), even though many of its products (especially IT components) are not really attached to nationally focused place recognition. Nation branding has therefore the odd task of creating a limited patriotic identity, which must be sold to nonpatriots wherever they reside and for as long as they have influence on the likely prosperity of companies and people attached to the locale. The process must be globalized in reach and understanding of the influential world elites, cosmopolitan in its appeal to sophisticated observers of difference, and parochial/patriotic in its accurate reflection of a local sense of being and belonging.

The same paradigm applies to city brands (see an extended discussion in S. H. Donald and Gammack 2007), where every cultural and social shift affects the way in which a brand is "bought" or derided, and where even alternative cultural forms may well create "brand advantage" or dissolution. Banksy is an internationally famous graffiti artist, based in London, but with copycats all over the urban circuit. His graffiti are, of course, particularly apt in London, where his witty stencils and visual puns have done the city's image of "cool" and cutting edge no harm at all. Indeed, inner-city councils are rumored to protect his work from over-enthusiastic cleaning staff, while a pub landlord has deliberately preserved a "Banksy" for his customers to discuss.[5] Arguably, without the success of cool London, both in the 1960s and now in its revised, expensive format, it would not have occurred to him to do so. Branding can create urban dispositions of a somewhat cosmopolitan nature, as the promotion of Chinatown has sought to do in proclaiming a city's diversity and connection with other cultures and economies (see Sales et al. this volume).

Making a connection between place branding and the processes of cosmopolitanization is thus a provocation, insisting that we look at diversity, pragmatism, and cultural reflection as components of urban belonging and strangeness, and that in so doing we take our own cosmopolitan advice and encounter the familiar terrain of theory from the perspectives of the less familiar world of "competitive advantage." In retrospect, we could also say that we have been thinking on similar, if not identical, lines to Bronislaw Szerszynski and John Urry (2006), who also see a close connection between visuality, mobility, and cosmopolitanism, and who also locate it in the symbols of belonging and identity: "[V]isual symbols are frequently used in totemic fashion to signify membership of a civic or political community. [. . .] Some are official and formal (flags, coats of arms); others are unofficial and arise informally (graffiti, bumper stickers, modes of dress)" (118). We agree with these observations, but suggest that the next stage of enquiry is to interrogate the nature of symbols that are created for the city or nation's brand status, but which are yet claimed by, or for, its people. We also contend through the various perspectives offered in this book that cosmopolitanism is a process, not an absolute condition (Skrbis et al. 2004; J. Donald 2007; Skrbis and Woodward 2007), and therefore that it entails the democratic paradox discussed by Chantal Mouffe (2000), as well as the pragmatic compromises and negotiations between bureaucracies and people, sojourners, and indigenes; concerning history, future, and the present.

URBAN COSMOPOLITANISM AND THE NATION–STATE

With the popular and intellectual adoption of cosmopolitanism as place branding and cultural disposition, the concept has increasingly been reduced to a cultural characteristic and, to a lesser extent, political offshoot of globalization. Much cultural and political writing on cosmopolitanism explicitly and implicitly positions the subject against the nation–state, largely assumed to be the container of social processes, yet in reality weakened, transcended, or undermined by global processes (Beck 2002; Urry 2000). Calhoun (2002) has written on the need to critique cosmopolitanism as a celebration of privilege and as a defense not against the nation–state, but in defense of a world order which privileges certain national states and regions over others. Calhoun's pragmatic acceptance of a necessary relationship between the national order and the cosmopolitan disposition has continued in recent work (2007). Though the attack on the state as a container of society and sociocultural analysis has been attenuated in the past few years as states have re-asserted their national identities and values (Kofman, 2005a, 2005b), the criticism of abstract and cultureless individuals who populate a cosmopolitan global world remains pertinent.

A growing interest in the nature and different forms of belonging (Yuval-Davis 2006) has drawn attention to the attachment of particular social groups to places. The politics of belonging or the "dirty work of boundary maintenance" (Cowley 1999: 22) leads to quite complex and ever-changing boundaries being drawn within, coterminous with, and beyond the state. Cultural politics within national borders are not the same as the cultural and intranational politics of difference that challenge national mores and sovereign expectations. Yet, cultural borders within states and nations are also the sites on which cosmopolitanism may be assayed and enjoyed.

Nation–states are not the only spaces in which claims to belonging are being formulated. The opposition between cosmopolitanism and nationalism (for critique, see Kaufman 2003) obscures the rich body of work on cosmopolitanism as urban experience. Leonie Sandercock (2003) refers to the mongrel cities of new urban differences that have emerged at the end of the twentieth century, encapsulating otherness, fragmentation, splintering, and heterogeneity. This can be compared to the earlier period of postwar immigration to and within Europe and to traditional settler societies (Australia, Canada, New Zealand, the United States), when specific groups of European settlers populated major cities, often living in their own distinct neighborhoods (on Montreal, see Germain and Radice 2006). Since the 1970s, and the ending of overtly racist immigration policies in settler societies, and the phenomenon of large numbers of asylum seekers and labor migrants (legal and undocumented) in Europe from the 1990s, these patterns have become more diversified. Super diversity (Vertovec 2007) now characterizes the spectrum of socially differentiated and legally stratified migrant groups who increasingly populate not just the major cities, but also and increasingly, regional and provincial cities, small towns, and rural areas that had hitherto been left out of the waves of immigration. Hence there is clamor by a range of cities to be recognized as cosmopolitan (Kennedy this volume; on Manchester, Young, Diep, and Drabble 2006), and thus to receive the full panoply of rewards to be bestowed by globalization. For many cities this has meant demarcating spaces of difference (Binnie et al. 2006) to demonstrate their cosmopolitan credentials.

For some (Keith 2005), the messiness of cities challenges the certainties of the nation–state as building block. Cities more than any other social space raise most acutely issues of how strangers and neighbors coexist and live together with differences in shared spaces (see Hatziprokopiou this volume; Amin 2002; Binnie et al. 2006; J. Donald 1999; Hiebert 2002; Sandercock 2003; Sennett 1970, 2002). Cosmopolitanism denotes far more than individual cultural dispositions of openness towards objects, ideas, and people in response to global processes. Scholars of situated and grounded cosmopolitanism rather seek to explore how social locations and institutions facilitate interaction that goes beyond a tolerance that may signify no more than indifference to difference (Walzer 1997). Hence the cosmopolitan and the parochial come together in the variegated sites and micro-publics of the city, such as schools, workplaces, leisure centers, communal gardens enabling social engagement in particular places (Amin 2002). It is in these places of everyday lived experiences that we maintain human contact and connect with abstract rights and obligations and with local structures and resources. It is not assumed that cosmopolitanism is an end state or seemingly inevitable outcome of globalization, but rather that it is a project to be constantly renewed and renegotiated. People may become cosmopolitan and then cease to be so (Hiebert 2002). Urban cosmopolitanism does not simply refer to the capacity and skills of an individual to be detached from their local concerns. It is more about living with difference than about moving between different contexts (Bridge 158). At the beginning of the twentieth century, Mary Parker Follett, a middle class urban local activist in Boston, had asked why provincials who had taken advantage of their opportunities were not more interesting than cosmopolitan people who, in seeking out homogeneous social situations, are all alike (159). Contentiously perhaps, we suggest that branding does not need to focus on the fixed and the particular, but could boldly consider the shifting processes of representation created as people, cultures, societies, and ideas move across and about the space that they inhabit.

Cosmopolitanism as outcome depends on certain kinds of interaction between agents, in particular, social locations and where, as Simmel (1950b[6]) noted, the far is brought together with the near. For Sandercock (127), cosmopolis means "an acceptance of connection with respect and space for the stranger, the possibility of working together on matters of common destiny and forging new hybrid cultures, urban projects and ways of living." Yet Richard Sennett (1970), drawing on his study of New York

City, concludes that the various ethnic cultures do not share a common destiny and that this poses the challenge of living together not in indifference but in active engagement. In a portrait of London as a world in one city where 300 languages are spoken and at least 50 communities with populations of 10,000 or more live, Leo Benedictus found that many people he interviewed said they had no problems with their neighbors. What emerged was a broad picture of tolerance in a context of indifference. As one young Polish respondent commented:

> People here don't know their own neighbours, and they're like that their whole life. When I meet English people, which is not very often round here, my experience is that they are lost, really miserable people, sometimes with emotional problems. They don't know how to speak to you. They are surprised you are open and nice to them.

London's cosmopolitanism, like that of other global cities, cannot be encapsulated by branded spaces. It offers instead a myriad of ordinary spaces populated by heterogeneous groups of strangers with diverse attachments, forced, and voluntary, to place (see Hatziprokopiou this volume). Of course, the ability to choose ones neighbors varies considerably according to class and immigration status. The asylum seekers, dependent on the state and their own local and religious community networks and resources, were far more place bound than the young skilled with cultural capital. In many Western countries, asylum seekers do not have the right to choose their residence and thus do not have the right to the city. When Henri Lefebvre (1996) coined the term *the right to the city* at the end of the 1960s—*Writing on Cities* was first published in 1969—it was a period when the historic centre of Paris was beginning to undergo gentrification and the old working classes were being expelled to the suburban periphery. The right to the city referred to the right to difference, the right to inhabit, and to participate in the city as a citizen, and it was not reserved for the privileged few.

Today it is not only about the physical presence or the right to inhabit, but the right to be included in the present and future narratives of the city. Even if still inhabiting the city, those deemed marginal to the projects of the urban elites may be expelled from the branding of the city and its narratives of success. While the Turkish in Berlin represent an earlier urban multiculturalism, they no longer figure in the postreunification élite's cultural strategy based on "high culture" consumption (see Kosnick this volume). They have been discarded at the same time as multiculturalism has been challenged (Joppke 2004) and deemed inappropriate and too closely identified with national politics.[7] The Turks are now seen as left-over problems and are not regarded in the same light as the dynamism and fluidity of global processes. This is despite the fact that imagining cities and their diversity can in itself be taken as a sign of progress. The examples of migrant artists' strategies to engage with and contest dominant versions of urban branding in Berlin suggest that official cosmopolitan branding efforts can both coexist with multicultural paradigms of managing urban cultural diversity, and may present even greater challenges to counterforms of symbolic exclusion from the city. Business people and migrant professionals, unlike migrant workers, conform to the desirable image cities seek to project (see Kennedy this volume).

As urban elites seek to brand their cities within the flows of global networks, they have turned to the cultural dispositions largely embodied in those with social and cultural capital who are able to take advantage of the full potential of globalized consumption of objects and places. A captivating diversity is held out to attract investment and major cultural and sporting events such as the Sydney (2000) or London (2012) Olympics. The slogan "The world in one city" was adroitly deployed in London's successful bid against Paris, which relied on its typical French qualities. London, ranked second in 2006 behind Sydney in the list of cities with the most positive perceptions, put itself forward for the 2012 Olympics in terms of "Our multicultural diversity will mean every competing nation in the Games will find local supporters as enthusiastic as back home."[8] The London committee had obviously read the social integration question asked in the survey for the Anholt City Brands Index (2006): "Do you think you would find a community of people who share your language and culture, and with whom you could fit in?" Diversity can represent the single attribute of a successful city, but real diversity is likely to be too messy for the narrative. In light of China's recent refusal to release tickets to the families of foreign athletes in 2008, the meaning of that parochial cosmopolitanism in the Sydney bid strikes home.

This collection of essays is organized into sections; settlement and migration issues, selling and branding, cinema and the modern, and family narratives, all of which derive from disciplinary approaches to the central themes, and each of which depends on a conversation between the apparently polarized notions of the cosmopolitan and the parochial, belonging, and branded identities. Each essay is also concerned, if only by juxtaposition, with the seemingly intractable problem of comparison across cultural borders. European, Asian, and Australian cities are discussed as zones and sites of equivalence in which the meaning and occupation of space and history are constantly, and necessarily, under negotiation.

NOTES

1. In *Second World: Empires and Influence in the New Global Order* (2008a), Parag Khanna notes that the European strategic expansion to the east drawing in an increasing number of states is a gamble that is paying off: "Europe's growing diversity makes European-ness a gradually attainable ideal rather than a mythical Platonic form, transforming Europe; identities from tribal to cosmopolitan" (28).

2. <http://www.sistersinislam.org.my/mission.htm> (accessed February 1, 2008).
3. Indeed, there is a continuing conflict between, on the one hand, those who want to open up to non-EU migration, especially to the skilled of the Third World, for example the implementation of a Blue Card announced by the Commission on October 23, 2007, and on the other hand, other states, such as Austria and Germany, which remain wary. The United Kingdom also has closed its borders to lesser-skilled non-EU migrants on the premise that the continually enlarging EU will satisfy all their labor needs. http://ec.europa.eu/news/employment/071023_1_en.htm (accessed September 10, 2008).
4. Europe is also being branded. Khanna (2008a) comments: "[E]ven as some west Europeans fear the dilution of their elite brand, Europe's evolution is giving the term Europe a positive meaning" (28).
5. http://www.thisislondon.co.uk/arts/article-23409115-details/Smile+please,+it's+a+Banksy/article.do (accessed January 31, 2008).
6. Simmel's essay, "The Stranger," was originally published in 1905.
7. More interesting, Jan Nederveen Pieterse (3) sees multiculturalism as work in progress, in which global inequalities are being played out and which, though originating in Western societies, is being adopted in a number of countries in the global South.
8. <http://www.london2012.org/en/city/onecity> (accessed March 6, 2008).

2 Strangers as Neighbors in the Cosmopolis

New Migrants in London, Diversity, and Place

Panos Hatziprokopiou

LONDON: DIFFERENCE, DIVERSITY, AND PLACE

In another chapter in this book, Rosemary Sales and her colleagues discuss issues of space and place in the cosmopolitan city, focusing on London's Chinatown. Chinatown and the East End's Brick Lane constitute perhaps London's most recognizable sites of "branded difference" in a general trend of "ethnic" neighborhoods being transformed into places of leisure and consumption (Shaw et al. 2004; Rath 2007), a trend that reflects broader developments associated with contemporary dynamics of urban restructuring, especially in global cities (Sassen 1991). Yet both these areas emerge as "signifiers" of difference "inscribed in urban landscapes" (Shaw et al. 1983) and have come to represent visible loci of multiculture in Britain's capital, featuring as emblematic, celebratory examples of its diversity and as spectacles of its cosmopolitan appeal.

This may appear contradictory at a time when the concept and content of multiculturalism is being rethought and the management of difference retreats towards assimilatory views (Grillo 2007).[1] The celebration of diversity in mainstream discourses reflects of course a sort of political correctness drawing from the liberal tradition, the legacy of antiracist struggles and the politics of multiculturalism. But "the production and reproduction of the 'cosmopolitan city' involves a symbolic and material territorialisation of difference, involving a 'normalised' fixing in place of 'acceptable' and 'unacceptable' difference." (Young et al. 2006: 1689). The former is encountered in those spaces of "packaged" diversity and complies with "neo-liberal and entrepreneurial forms of urban governance" (ibid.: 1690). The later is found in spaces of exclusion and neglect concentrating the new multi-fragmented ethicised working classes, where difference is equated to poverty and anomie and is not part of the cosmopolitan imagery of the city. Hidden behind celebratory portrayals of "the most successful world city" in which diversity features as a politically neutral creative force,[2] London's emerges as a deeply unequal city, divided in lines of ethnicity, race and class, much of which are manifested upon its space (Amin 2002; Hamnett 2003; Hall 2004).

Nevertheless, decades of coexistence in the postcolonial state gave way to hybrid cultures and some degree of normalization of difference, particularly sensible in everyday realities of sociocultural symbiosis in shared spaces. This chapter is concerned with areas where 'multi-ethnicity has not resulted in social breakdown' (Amin 2002: 960) and which represent "the emergent multicultural Britain that exists, largely unnoticed and always unvalued, alongside its better known, official counterpart" (Gilroy 2004: 148). Following a "need to explore and investigate how cosmopolitanism is formed and reformed in particular locales and everyday spaces" (Binnie et al. 2006: 12), this chapter reflects on the cosmopolitan city by considering areas that are not characterized by a single, dominant ethnic group (however diverse and heterogeneous these may be), and by considering districts that are not already branded or in the process of gentrification. These nonbranded and nonideal places are currently deemed problematic, but are nonetheless part of the story of the cosmopolitan city in process and should therefore be considered within a wider narrative of cosmopolitanization. Drawing on examples from a case study of a North London neighborhood, the chapter explores some grounded aspects of such everyday realities in ordinary spaces, accounting in particular for new migrants' experiences and perceptions of place, diversity, and difference in the cosmopolitan metropolis.

Accelerating migration processes came to epitomize the West's worst fears about globalization, and public concerns over integration and social cohesion refer to the implications of living together in shared spaces. In Britain, especially London, new migration accounts for much of what has been described as the diversification of an already-existing diversity (Vertovec 2007) resulting in a complex ethnic, cultural, and social mix that goes far beyond the postcolonial order. However, "the spatiality and sociality of immigration" (Sandercock 2003) remain poorly understood. How do new migrants "fit in" with London's diversity? How do they perceive it, see themselves in it and negotiate their lives in that respect? What are the elements of contact or friction in their experiences of living together in cosmopolitan space? These are the broader questions inspiring this chapter. I want to begin by sketching a conceptual framework that draws on the notion of the stranger as neighbor. I shall then describe two concrete examples from a case study that involved new migrants and refugees in Finsbury Park. I shall end with a discussion of these using an approach that builds on the multiple relationships acknowledged by strangers and neighbors in the everyday spaces of the cosmopolis.

STRANGERS AND NEIGHBORS IN THE COSMOPOLIS

Simmel's (1950b) delineation of the stranger as someone "who comes today and stays tomorrow" encapsulates the "unity of nearness and remoteness" that makes the Other simultaneously an "objective" outsider and an "element of the group itself" (402). This simultaneous "nearness and remoteness," however, is also a feature embedded in the urban condition, marked by uprooting and resettlement, proximity and distance, anonymity and mutual indifference ("blasé attitude"): the city is a coming together of strangers and a site generating estrangement (Simmel 1950a; Papastergiadis 2000; Iveson 2006). Until now, the stranger has not necessarily entailed difference, but abstractly has represented the unknown; in a sense, we are all strangers (Kristeva 1991). The public space of the city is the place where strangers come into contact and interact with each other (Vaiou and Kalandides in press). The tensions between public and private and the very anxieties of life in the metropolis, entailing both mechanisms of enslavement and the potential for freedom along with the pace of social change, are to an extent manifested in the fear of living together (Papastergiadis 2000; Ruggiero 2003; Sandercock 2003, chap. 5). The figure of the stranger is thus not that of a distant Other; it appears before us as soon as s/he becomes a neighbor. Place, then, as socially constructed and meaningfully articulated space (Lefebvre 1996), may be seen as the concrete terrain upon which strangers become neighbors, the social locus where they organize their life in the private sphere, where their presence attempts to make a claim on public space and where they engage in various forms of exchange with others.

Strangers, however, are constructed as such through power relations. As Bauman (1995) observes, '[A]ll societies produce strangers; but each kind of society produces its own kind of strangers' (1). The migrant, of course, is a particular kind of stranger, produced by borders and the politics surrounding them (Balibar 2006). Constructing ethnic and cultural Others has been an integral feature of the making of the modern world, the expansion of Europe and the consolidation and spread of the nation–state. However, these forms of alterity became primarily a concern of today, inevitably associated with the postcolonial (re)discovery of the Other here and among us; the complex mobilities and flows of globalization; the insecurities brought by the multiple challenges facing the nation–state as it overcomes its historical role; and the retreat of formerly universal points of reference. As migration involves at the same time processes of displacement and resettlement, the migrant has a specific relationship to place marked by the ambivalence of "here" and "there" and the crossing of boundaries. Therefore s/he epitomizes the figure of the stranger, not simply by being "faraway so close," but crucially by becoming visible when constructed and recognized as different. The processes by which strangers become neighbors in the everyday spaces of living together are what grounds and gives depth to the abstractions of the nation–state and its internal others. It is on the streets of Finsbury Park, for instance, that contact with difference becomes unavoidable, challenging established norms, practices, and politics of belonging, as well as negotiations between private and public and the respective codes of social interaction (Vaiou & Kalandides in press). The notion of the neighbor thus is important here also because it illustrates the contradiction between, on the one hand, the biblical plea to "love thy neighbor as thyself" and, on the other, its Freudian critique as employed recently to challenge official talk on social cohesion that moralistically calls for embracing the Other (e.g., Gilroy 2004: 71–72; Fortier 2007).

The concept of the stranger crystallizes the interplay between the abstract Other, the migrant as a concrete form of otherness, and the complexities of urban life in (late) modernity. As the editors suggest in their Introduction, the poly-faceted and multistratified relationship between the stranger and neighbor, and the everyday modalities of living together in cities of difference, provide the frame in which to ground cosmopolitanism as urban experience. In her seminal work on (planning for) the twenty-first century's "mongrel cities," Sandercock (2003) defines *cosmopolis* as a "dreamed" city, "in which there is an acceptance of, connection with, and respect and space for 'the stranger'" (127). Others have used the term simply to describe, in the case of London, its demographic mix (Storkey and Lewis 1996). But beyond utopian notions of the "good city," or simply the composition of the urban population, the "actually existing" cosmopolis—the cosmopolitan, multicultural, global city of today—brings together, accommodates, but also produces, strangers of various kinds (see Iveson 2006).

My own use of the term is rather methodological, because of the various points of reference it entails. First, it offers an acoustic parallel to *metropolis*, which has a dual sense: the conventional understanding of a wide political, economic, and territorial urban structure, its organization, dynamics, and governance; and a centre, a core, a capital city, as assumed by the prefix *metro* (deriving from μήτρα, μήτηρ, meaning "mother"). Then, literarily translated from Greek as "world-city," it assumes, on the one hand, the international character of the city in today's context of globalization, for instance with respect to the international political economic processes associated with global cities. And on the other hand, it refers to the demographic—but also the social and cultural—composition of the urban population, the diversity of which embraces individuals, whether settled or transient, from virtually the entire world. This aspect of the urban, expressed in economic, social, and cultural practices, as well as experiences and uses of space, and structured by class, gender, and status, reveals the city as a container of many worlds, some visible, others less noticeable, within its vast and diverse metropolitan space. Last, because the term obviously derives from the word *cosmopolite*, which in its essence contains a political element since the Greek *polites* equates to *citizen*, it suggests the existence of a public sphere that raises questions of membership (participation, belonging), both external (related to international/ist or transnational/ist ties associated with the openness of the city to the world) and internal (applying to the members of the *polis*). Thus, the concept refers to different aspects of the relationships between globalization, migration, diversity and the city, and may also capture the persisting relevance of class—how is the *polis* stratified by reflecting and reproducing the inequalities of the *cosmos*, however arbitrarily it might be defined in global capitalism, and in however complex a way it might be intersected with race or ethnicity in the cosmopolitan city.

NEW MIGRANTS, DIVERSITY, AND EXPERIENCES
OF PLACE IN FINSBURY PARK

Finsbury Park is in North London, at the intersection of three boroughs (Islington, Haringey, Hackney) and several wards. It is characterized by relatively mixed land use and economic activity, with the park itself located almost at its heart. All this makes for an extremely diverse landscape— from the urban chaos outside the station to the calm of the park; from the massive and impersonal Andover estate southwest of the station to the tree-lined streets of Stroud Green to the northwest or Highbury to the south-east. Regeneration in the area dates back to the 1980s, with the Finsbury Park Community Trust having been described as a "pioneering" local part-nership (Jacobs 1992: 241). This was later succeeded by the £25m Finsbury Park Partnership, which was replaced, in July 2005, by the FinFuture Local Development Trust, one of whose aims, as recorded in its "vision" state-ment, was "to encourage the Finsbury Park communities to feel proud of and celebrate their diversity" (FinFuture 2006: 5).

The area is not characterized by a single ethnic group. The *Guardian*'s "A World in One City" maps (Benedictus 2005) identified concentrations of Caribbeans and West Africans along Stroud Green Road, west of the station, Algerians on Blackstock Road, to the east of the station, and a Cypriot and Turkish presence on Green Lanes, north of the park. Indeed, this is what captures the passerby's eye on those sites. The streets derive character not only from the people who inhabit them, but from the multi-lingual signage in so-called ethnic stores, and from the goods, tastes, and styles of packaging that refer the passer-by to a world beyond mainstream London. Walking along its streets, the diversity of businesses is impressive. According to the 2001 census (ONS, 2008),[3] the majority of Finsbury Park residents are single and relatively young, with rates of unemployment and inactivity slightly higher than those for London as a whole and with a high proportion of the population living in social housing. The proportions of non-White British and of foreign born are above the average for London as a whole, as is that of Muslims—though this is not the case for any other religious group. The area is home to various churches, a synagogue, and two Islamic institutions: the Muslim Welfare House and the formerly (in)famous Finsbury Park Mosque (now the North London Mosque, once the place where extremist cleric Abu Hamza preached).

This exploratory case study was based on a number of interviews with twelve key informants from local community organizations as well as with eight individuals who had recently arrived in London and had some connec-tion with the area. The interviews were conducted over a period of about ten months in 2005–2006, during which several field visits were made, involving observation, informal chats, and the collection of gray sources. Not all the material gathered has been used, although it largely informs the examples that follow. These build mainly on the testimonies of two groups of individuals, which focus primarily on narratives of home, belonging, daily practices, experiences of place, perceptions of Finsbury Park, London, and diversity.

DIFFERENCE IN COSMOPOLITAN SPACE: NEGOTIATING PUBLIC SPACE IN THE STREET

The first example draws on the testimonies of four refugees from Algeria: Ali, Farid, Mohamed, and Salim. These men had "to be out" because of "political problems," which made their return home unthinkable: their lives had been in danger and they had fled their country to claim asylum in Europe. Two of them had already been granted indefinite leave to remain, and the other two had only recently arrived and applied for asylum. Each of them had been through similar experiences of difficult travel, illegal border crossings, arrest, detention, and harsh conditions. None of them had had any prior contact in Britain. None had completed high school; their English was generally poor, and none was working at the time of the interview. All of them were either receiving income support benefit or were in the process of applying for it.[4]

Their narratives were marked by sentiments of limited control over their lives. As refugees and asylum seekers they lack a voice and public presence and their overall experiences are structured through multiple layers of "confinement," including space. They had no choice regarding their residence, and they were dependent on the hospitality of acquaintances or the authorities' decision over council accommodation placement. Moreover, they were dependent for language and welfare support on a community organization based in Finsbury Park, the Arab Advice Bureau (AAB; formerly the Algerian Refugee Council). Although not all of them lived locally, they would gather in the area on a daily basis because their social networks, mostly comprising of fellow Algerians, are located there as well as the two Islamic institutions. One may talk of a small but vibrant community, whose presence is particularly noticeable on Blackstock Road, just across from the station to the east, where numerous ethnic businesses are concentrated (cafes, patisseries, groceries) and men "hang out" in the street, alone or in small groups:

> Because we are based at the heart of our community . . . if you go just to Blackstock Road . . . you see the people congregate and hang around this area. . . . Finsbury Park is a main area, because . . . if you walk in Blackstock Road, you will see many Algerian and North African shops

> . . . people come to socialize . . . as there are two mosques as well. (personal communication, AAB key informant)

Notions of community featured strongly in the interviewees' stories, not only regarding their perceptions of place, but more generally with respect to the organization of everyday life in London. "Hanging around" locally is for them a mundane daily practice, a way to organize free time that allows public presence in a microsocial space. The street and surrounding area become a meeting point and welfare space, and therefore, a public sphere structured around informal socialization, recreation, exchange of information, access to services, and spiritual fulfillment:

> I like this area . . . because you know I've got some community. . . . I go to mosque . . . I go to coffee shops . . . During the week, I go to play football . . . I spent my time with my wife, go to the park . . . Sunday or Saturday we meet at the coffee shop, talk about the life, or something like that, how are you, what do you do. (Farid)

> Mostly I hang around in this area, sometimes I stay indoors, depends. . . . Mostly I come because there is a mosque and there is our community. (Ali)

> We meet with members of my community and we have a coffee and we sometimes just go out, hang around . . . playing football . . . Staying locally, most of the days. (Mohamed)

> I hang around a lot. Not all the time, sometimes play [I] football as well. (Salim)

Hanging around may be seen as a form of appropriation of the open urban space that has both a "strategic" and a "tactical" dimension (de Certeau 1988): the former refers to strategies of survival, the latter to practices related to the organization of time. Through such an appropriation, they are able to orient themselves by inscribing reference points in their cognitive map of the city, to renegotiate their identity, to belong. Belonging becomes meaningful through the reconstitution of a sense of familiarity, which partly reproduces social and cultural practices that are common "back home," with respect to social activity that traditionally takes place in the open public space of Mediterranean societies (Leontidou 1997). Having once established themselves in a space, they make it "their place," with feelings of identification going beyond the limits of their community to touch vernacular signifiers of local identity, such as support for Arsenal, the local team.

This social space and public sphere is however, highly gendered, as the people who hang around are almost exclusively men. This may once again resemble uses of public space in the country of origin (on the gendering of public spaces in southern Mediterranean cities, see Leontidou 1997), but certainly reflects patterns of migration and the composition of the Algerian population in Britain (more than 70% of the U.K. Algerians are male, according to Collyer 2004). This aspect, combined with the very practice of using the open urban space in ways that are largely unfamiliar to locals, generates suspicion, fear, and prejudice stemming from the public visibility of difference, which may or may not be informed by what such difference represents. A look at internet blogs and online discussion forums about Finsbury Park is revealing:

> The junction of Blackstock Road and Rock Street can be pretty weird if you are female and alone, but only because of the bizarre hissing noise the men who hang around there outside the cafes make. . . . New influx of Algerians . . . I'm not racist but they spit a lot and leer.
> Towards Finsbury Park, the coffee shops on Blackstock Road are always full of men from Eastern Europe (but there are never any women).[5]

Reactions of this kind question the refugees' social uses of space and generate contestation over the social space of the street. Their public existence is challenged, as community leaders comply with and adopt what emerges as a dominant discourse at the local level by actively undertaking the role of the mediator in order to eliminate the "loitering" habit:

> People from my community like to have a coffee and hang around on the street, but local people are complaining and are saying that they are getting intimidated by the people who hang around. It's like looking [at] the girls, and staring at their daughters or their sisters. And we are trying to explain . . . to our community that . . . they shouldn't congregate. . . . Some people are saying this is our culture, but in fact it is not our culture . . . this is a habit. (personal communication, AAB key informant)

TRANSITING COSMOPOLITAN SPACE: PERCEPTIONS OF PLACE AND DIVERSITY IN THE CITY

The second example draws on the narratives of three young Eastern European professionals: Nora from Bulgaria, Lucas from Poland, and Luan from Albania. What these very different individuals have in common lies in their comparable life trajectories: all of them arrived in London in order to study without clear settlement plans. Their migration has been more a matter of career choices and lifestyle options, while the possibility of returning home remains open. They have similar employment histories, passing from part-time work during their studies, to temporary agency work after completing their degrees; all are now in permanent professional posts matching their

skills and expectations. None of them is in contact with community organizations and their personal networks consist of both compatriots, usually
friends from their hometowns also living in London, and people of various
nationalities, mostly met through university or work. They all have lived
for a period in the area, but have eventually moved out due to work circumstances and housing market considerations as well as out of choice when
their conditions improved.[6] Reflecting on their memories of Finsbury Park,
they articulated their perceptions of its diversity through notions of a local
'community' and images of its vibrant streets and ethnic businesses:

> We are kind of used to the area . . . there are a lot of shops . . . with
> goods from even our own countries, like all those Turkish shops where
> they sell all this fruit and vegetables I cannot live without. (Nora)

> It was a bit better in Finsbury Park . . . there was more kind of a commu-
> nity, because there were children and . . . there were playgrounds, it was
> more humanized, I would say. . . . Finsbury Park is also more . . . minori-
> ty-orientated . . . on Stroud Green Road, some of the greengrocers . . . the
> vegetables that they have I have never seen prior of coming to London and
> it's mainly because there's quite a big African population. (Lucas)

> Finsbury Park, I mean, I know Seven Sisters Road quite well, I like busy
> streets . . . with people doing activities . . . selling, or meeting people,
> or having shops around, it's brilliant; I mean it shows the vitality. Seven
> Sisters Road is full at the weekends, so it's very nice . . . you could find
> nice food and fruits and vegetables. . . . So if I refer to my culture back
> to my country, that street was quite familiar. (Luan)

Their overall impressions of the area however, were rather negative, revealing issues of class and inequality. At the abstract level of opinion, these may
reflect personal aesthetics, media discourses, and internalized stereotypes
about difference, crime and inner-city life; at the concrete level of the lived
experience, however, they are marked by accounts of shared spaces in over-
crowded estates:

> We were renting a room in a two-bedroom flat which was in Manor
> House, just next to Finsbury Park. . . . It was . . . one of those housing
> estates . . . I mean, it wasn't bad, but . . . there was this gangs of kids,
> you know, moving around, so you don't feel very safe . . . being on your
> own, let's say late at night. . . . They were often hanging around on the
> staircase. (Nora)

> Andover estate is absolutely, it's a shithole. . . . On an estate, people
> they just don't think; they don't live among other people. . . . It creates
> crime as well because of the design . . . violence, abuse. . . . There is a

huge difference in economic status. . . . It's also the amount of people that go through that place . . . it just creates problems . . . it just attracts . . . muggers and that kind of people. (Lucas)

Dodgy . . . in terms of personal experience I never had any problem in that area. . . . But there had been in the newspaper . . . that someone had been killed around the area, someone had been robbed . . . you'd see sometimes the hoodies . . . you'd see the illegal people selling cigarettes around the Holloway area. . . . Housing quality in Finsbury Park, maybe it's a bit poor. . . . Maybe not as quite [safe] . . . especially Friday nights . . . there are drunk people around. . . . So I think it's a nice area, but maybe there are the dodgy bits, with this category of people who could create some trouble sometime. (Luan)

Their cultural capital, employment, and residential trajectories position them as free-floating professionals moving with relative ease around the city. Place for them acquires functional and aesthetic qualities and becomes a matter of private choice, depending on circumstances and subjective considerations. Feelings about life in London in general were mixed. While all three praised the opportunities available, primarily in the employment field, their stories also reveal the chaotic side of the metropolis: the costs, distances, haste, and anonymity that make urban life anxious, impersonal, and less spontaneous. However, they all valued London's cosmopolitan character, not simply for aesthetic reasons, but, most important, because it eased adaptation and allowed belonging. While they may think of themselves as "foreigners," this is not understood as a disadvantage, due to the city's multicultural and international ambience. London's diversity accommodates notions of "home" and this very characteristic allows sentiments of identification with the city.

It's not the best of lifestyle you can have because too great distances, difficult to meet your friends . . . could be very expensive as well. . . . And things are not very spontaneous. . . . It's cosmopolitan, it doesn't make you feel like you have to stand out . . . there are so many foreigners around that the feeling of being other nationality is not too much in your head . . . it's very accommodating to people from different nationalities and that's what I like. (Nora)

London is basically . . . a huge metropolitan city, and that's what attracts me . . . I think, because London is so multicultural, it's very, very different. . . . I've never experienced anything bad with . . . being Pole . . . I feel like at home, I feel actually like better here than in Poland . . . it's very easy to fit in . . . I've been here for four years . . . I've been through the 7/7 bombing, you know, you do associate. (Lucas)

London is . . . very cold . . . you never talk to neighbors . . . people
move very often and you find that your neighbor changes every three
months. . . . This kind of individual life is the thing that sets people
apart. . . . Here lots of things are very formal, you have to set up ap-
pointments for everything. . . .When we came . . . we had that image
of London maybe of the 70s or 60s . . . world class, aristocratic, very
clean, very organized, very polite everyone, shiny. . . . And what we
found is a normal London, having the shiny part and the dirty part,
having the good side and the bad side, having locals and internationals.
Sometimes you are in a bus and you never hear English. Which is . . .
very good, in a way it also made us feel home because we didn't feel
as foreign as we thought we would. . . . London is somehow home for
internationals, and you can feel comfortable . . . that's a special bit of
London. (Luan)

CONCLUSION: STRANGERS AS NEIGHBORS
IN COSMOPOLITAN LONDON

Of course, what the individuals in the above examples represent has to do
with significantly different positions in terms of class, status, migration
trajectories, and so forth. With respect to place and diversity in particular, their testimonies articulate contrasting figures of the stranger in the
cosmopolis, constructed along binaries of visibility/ invisibility, difference/
indifference, public/ private, acceptability/ unacceptability.

In the case of London, the narrative of the multicultural, cosmopolitan
city reflects a powerful imaginary, perhaps still in the process of taking
shape: diversity and multiculture emerge as aspects of the city's identity,
both official and from below, through the market and through everyday
experiences of living together. New migrants are reaching a shore that many
others reached before them, and their copresence features strongly in both
its landscape and its ways of understanding itself. This very fact smoothes
their estrangement as Others, although estrangement might remain an
important element of the subjective urban experience in the alienating
metropolis. If the blasé attitude in the metropolis refers to anonymity and
indifference, in the cosmopolis this extends to indifference towards difference (Iveson 2006). The visibility of strangers is reduced, since they are not
alone in this city of Others, but rather surrounded by difference at large.
After all, with "super diversity" (Vertovec 2007), clear-cut categories of
difference (race, ethnicity, culture, religion) are no more: notions of Whiteness and Blackness, and minority categories as constructed in the postcolonial context and in the premises of multiculturalism, are blurred. The
individuals of the second case expressed this quite clearly: in their experiences of transiting the cosmopolitan city, their difference is lost in its

multicultural anonymity; they are the neighbors we never came to know. Moreover, they move through London's diverse space since they have the rights and means to do so, although these are reduced to the private sphere: home, work, studies, consumption, and entertainment. Their experience of the city becomes a matter of private choice and does not entail direct claims on public space.

But, as the first case shows, not all Others become less stranger in the city of strangers. This contradiction in itself suggests the complexity of the existing cosmopolis and constitutes one of its major paradoxes (see Binnie et al. 2006). Conventional accounts of cosmopolitanism, multiculturalism, and diversity—even those that take a critical stance—often place excessive emphasis on culture and identity (i.e., the play of ethnicity, race, religion, etc.) and overlook or neglect primary forms of domination such as class and the state and the ideologies and politics around them. The cosmopolis is not simply a site shaped by global economic, political, and ideological forces, but it is also a place that of itself replicates, fashions, and sustains the processes by which such forces take shape and unfold. So, not all kinds of strangers are constructed as different nor are all forms of difference deemed to produce strangers; rather, strangers are produced as outsiders, internal Others, or enemies (Balibar 2006) to the extent they come to represent all that is dangerous in the present geopolitical and economic order. The figure of the asylum seeker portrays the Third-World poor, who arrive to take advantage of our (changing) welfare state; that of the Muslim masks the potential terrorist who threatens our stability. Moreover, concrete, visible difference is also constructed in class terms. What also estranges is the visibility of poverty and of unacceptable approaches to time and space. Deprived of rights in the public sphere and confined to locality because of need, the refugees in the first example negotiate their own public space through vernacular practices of resistance. By doing so, they informally claim their "right to the city" (Lefebvre 1996) in a manner that increases their visibility by establishing alternative uses of the open space. Their attitudes towards space deviate from the emerging norm of acceptable public places mediated through the market and are therefore being contested. They thus become the neighbors envied for being too close and so obviously different.

What this case study further reveals is that contrasting forms of difference may not be simply territorialized across the space of the cosmopolis in clear-cut, segregated ways, but they interplay simultaneously even in ordinary localities, as earlier defined. As "open and provisional" syntheses "of social relations, individual and collective practices and symbolic meanings" (Vaiou and Kalandides 2009, forthcoming), the city's everyday spaces of diversity are themselves fragmented, complexly stratified, accommodating overlapping worlds and transcended by conflicting negotiations of public and private. So the "vernacular" cosmopolitanisms of "nonelite" places (Werbner 2006, 497) involve power relations and inequality structures that also shape the mundane level of lived experience and everyday practice.

London's position and role in the global economy, its function as a hub in global circuits of capital, goods, information, and people; its continuous attractiveness to various types of migrants and the ever-increasing diversity of its population (Eade 2000; Hamnett 2003; Greater London Authority 2005) suggest its emergence as a cosmopolis. Its peculiarity, however, should be traced in both time and space. There is thus, first, a historical dimension, for it has been for centuries a "promised land" as various populations have fed its bloodstream (Kershen 1997). The narrative of a historically "cosmopolitan London," with the "signs of the immigration which have become merged into its history" traceable in its landscape (Holmes 25), might be partly invented in search of an identity fitting to its present. But it also entails a degree of continuity in constant mobility, flows, and processes of assimilating difference and in multiple-transnational ties and international connections over its long trajectory "from imperial capital to global city" (Eade 2000). Second, geographical comparisons are important: provincial British cities, not so deeply affected by earlier and current waves of immigration and settlement, brand themselves as cosmopolitan as part of broader regeneration projects (on Birmingham, see W. Chan 2005; on Manchester, see Young et al. 2006). In the case of London, by contrast, the whole city is multicultural and this multiculture goes beyond both "branded" and "problematic" difference as it very much concerns daily experiences of quotidian symbiosis.[7] So, while the central problem of the cosmopolis Sandercock (2003) identifies is that of "coexisting in shared spaces of cities of difference," one of the key questions she asks about how migrants can be integrated into cities "unused to thinking themselves as multicultural" (127) is rather irrelevant here. Migrants in London enter a space that is not only already marked by diversity, but also understands itself as such, albeit in an interplay of exclusion and inclusion that produces acceptable and unacceptable forms of difference and constructs various categories of strangers.

At the dawn of the millennium, migration emerges as the new specter haunting Europe (and other parts of the world), and its supposed pressures on labor markets and the welfare state legitimize restrictive policies, tightening controls, and a general hostility towards the Other. The migrant, the asylum seeker, the Muslim, are constructed as new strangers, who come to take advantage of our hospitality, take away our jobs, abuse our system, threaten our security, and alter our national cultures—in other words, embodying all the fears associated with (neoliberal) globalization and accelerated social change. In this structural and institutional context, individuals and groups move through the cosmopolitan city, organizing their lives at the mundane level of everyday practice, which inevitably attributes meaningful attachments to space in order to make it their place. Yet those strangers who become new neighbors in a city like London do not settle in a homogeneous entity. Emerging communities add to the city's multiculture, while existing ones are themselves transforming and diversifying, in ways that go beyond conventional ethnic-minority categories. This growing diversity impacts on urban structures and landscapes, in notable or less visible ways, and certain districts become vibrant examples of the cosmopolitan city where diversity manifests itself in the daily experiences of urban life and coexistence at the local level. Since diversity is the norm rather than the exception, questions related to the ways in which it is perceived and lived, how it works on the ground, and how—and with what effect—new dynamics are emerging in multicultural settings, become central. Drawing on the concept of the stranger who becomes a neighbor, this chapter has reflected critically on ways to think about the position of new migrants in the cosmopolis' everyday spaces of diversity and difference. The cosmopolitan city accommodates and at the same time produces different kinds of strangers who move ambivalently through its multifragmented space by crossing boundaries between visibility and invisibility, private and public and so forth, but remain bound in the dynamics of class and status that construct acceptable and unacceptable forms of difference.

NOTES

1. Although reflecting trends common across Europe, recent events in Britain—e.g. the northern town riots of 2001, the moral panic over "bogus" asylum seekers in the 2000s, migration from the new EU member-states of central and Eastern Europe since 2004, the July 2005 London bombings, etc – gave rise to concerns about "parallel lives," "excessive" diversity, or "sleepwalking to segregation" (see Grillo, 2007).
2. Mayor of London, "State of London Debate: London, the Most Successful World City," press release, May 11, 2007, <http://www.london.gov.uk/view_press_release.jsp?releaseid=11934> (accessed on Sept. 27, 2007).
3. The weblink given in the bibliography is the general ONS website, other information derived from author's analysis and census data.
4. Their characteristics do not seem to fit the overall profile of Algerians in Britain (Collyer 2004). The absence of established networks in Britain, however, confirms Collyer's finding (2005) about Algerian asylum seekers not being directed to traditional destinations with established communities (as e.g., France), due to the changing character of community relationships or broader political and economic factors.
5. The first of these quotes comes from "The Knowhere Guide, Best and Worst in Finsbury Park" at <www.knowhere.co.uk/3689.htm>, the second from "Stressqueen: Only three missed meals from anarchy" ("The Multicultural Myth, Sept. 28, 2005), at <Stressqueen.blogspot.com/2005/09/multicultural-myth.html> (both accessed Sept. 27, 2007).
6. Their profiles differ from those of the majority of migrants from the respective countries in Britain (e.g., Ryan et al. 2007; Markova and Black 2007). Taking into account the complications to their mobility related to their status, and certainly the socioeconomic and political context of their countries (with significantly different variants of "actually existing socialism" and different pathways of transition), their experiences can be paralleled with those of the French professionals in London studied by Favell (2006).
7. I owe this part of the argument to the editors' comments on an earlier draft of this chapter, particularly a relevant discussion with E. Kofman, for which I am grateful.

3 Conflicting Mobilities
Cultural Diversity and City Branding in Berlin

Kira Kosnick

Representations of urban cultural diversity have become a staple of city-branding strategies for metropolitan centers across the globe. The "rich mix" (Evans and Foord 2004) that many cities can offer figures prominently in contemporary place marketing, most important against the background of growing interurban competition for tourism, creative talent, and investment. In many locations, ethnocultural diversity has come to be accepted as a key asset and requirement for urban development by city officials, business executives and planners alike. "An attractive place doesn't have to be a big city, but it has to be cosmopolitan"—as Richard Florida (2002) insisted in his influential *Rise of the Creative Class* (227)—has certainly been taken to heart by urban-marketing strategists. Urban ethnocultural diversity, as Florida and others have argued, contributes to the climate of openness and tolerance in which innovation and creativity can flourish, and thus translates into economic success in a postindustrial era. Economic growth now depends on cities being able to share in the flow of the "creative classes," and the new human motors of growth will be both attracted by and contribute to a city's diversity.

Despite this positive evaluation of immigration and diversity as economic growth factors in urban environments, the headlines made by urban immigrant minorities in the European mass media over the past years hardly contribute to the positive cosmopolitan image that many cities would like to convey. The large immigrant minorities that have taken up city residence as a result of labor migration in the 1960s and 1970s—as refugees fleeing violent conflict or in the aftermath of colonialism—are more often than not publicly associated with threats to the very values of tolerance, openness, and enterprise that are regarded as central to cosmopolitan success. What is more, these population groups are disproportionately affected by rising unemployment, poverty, and educational failures that characterize the increasing socioeconomic polarization of urban spaces across Europe. Mass-mediated "moral panics" in the wake of the London Transport terror attacks of July 2005 and the French *banlieue* riots of November that year have connected immigrant minorities with both Islamist fundamentalism and violence. When, in response to the French riots, the then-Minister of the Interior Sarkozy[1] referred to the immigrant youths as *racaille* (scum) and promised to deport young offenders regardless of their legal residence status, he contested not only their right to belong, but also their potential to contribute to the future of European cities.

Variants of city branding that seek to market a cosmopolitan image for urban spaces containing substantial immigrant populations face a potential problem: how can immigrant minorities be accommodated in cosmopolitan representations of urban space that have the idea of tolerance, openness, and cultural enrichment at heart, when dominant perceptions are that particular ethnic and religious minorities constitute problem populations? And how can immigrants and their descendants themselves develop alternative forms of place branding that do not exclude them?

This chapter examines these problems as they have arisen in Berlin, with the uneasy accommodation of immigrant minorities as part of the city's cosmopolitan branding efforts. It traces the transformation of urban diversity brandings from multicultural city to cosmopolitan metropolis, with a particular focus on popular and high cultural practices relating to the performing arts. The cultural sector is currently playing a pivotal role in efforts to market a city that has effectively gone bankrupt as a result of German unification, economic restructuring, and decades of severe mismanagement and corruption.

"POOR, BUT SEXY"

"Berlin is poor, but sexy" is a much-quoted slogan coined by Klaus Wowereit, the city's mayor, and he has linked the city's special appeal directly to its alleged cosmopolitan qualities of world-openness, tolerance, diversity, and cultural creativity. Reinstated as the national capital since the Wall came down in 1989, the city's representatives are also eager to boost Berlin's image as a cosmopolitan world city, acknowledging that it has to compete with metropolitan centers on a worldwide scale. It is of little consequence in this context whether the role of cities in the global system has indeed changed to the extent that some analysts imagine (Smart and Smart 2003). More important is that the idea of the fundamental importance of global interconnectedness and competition has become a taken-for-granted fact upon which city planners and marketing experts can base their official branding efforts. This acceptance is closely connected to Berlin's recent history of economic decline. Having lost most of its industrial production base in the postunification economic restructuring processes of the 1990s, hopes of an economic revival have been heavily invested in the cultural industries sector. As is true for many European cities with ailing economies, culture is a key factor in Berlin's efforts to reposition itself successfully in national, regional, and global arenas (Krätke 2004). The cultural-industries sector is recognized as one of the few areas of economic growth that the city has seen since unification, and this is complemented by high levels of public funding for its cultural establishments such as theatres, opera houses, and museums. Despite the city's virtual bankruptcy, public spending for culture has continued and been justified by different city government coalitions, which have pointed to the pivotal role of culture and the arts for any future economic revival.

Berlin's immigrant population, still dominated numerically by former labor migrants from Turkey and refugees from the former Yugoslavia, has been particularly hard hit by the city's economic downturn in the years following reunification. Given the effects of rising unemployment and poverty, combined with new public concerns over immigrant extremism and youth violence, it has become increasingly rare for official branding efforts to include positive references to Berlin's ethnocultural diversity. Poor yes, but sexy? The city's cultural establishment shows little admiration for the cultural potential of Berlin's immigrant minorities and any contribution they might make to its cosmopolitan worldliness, as will be shown below. Yet, cultural activists and artists with migrant backgrounds have fought, with varying degrees of success, to claim a stake in the city's cultural life and beyond it. Urban-branding efforts have contributed to a number of different, sometimes competing, cultural events and projects that migrant artists have initiated. The grounds for such efforts have changed drastically, however, with the demise in the late 1990s of the multicultural city as a dominant form of urban branding.

THE MULTICULTURAL CITY

In Germany, where the term *Ausländer* (foreigners) was a common label for immigrants up until the mid-1990s, even in antixenophobic and promigrant public discourses that insisted that both the fact of belonging and the right to belong used to be essential dimensions of migrant activism and political art. The symbolic exclusion of certain immigrant groups from the imagined national community was challenged not so much on the grounds of wanting to be recognized as "truly" German, but in terms of having an intimate and inalienable relationship with spatial environments that are territorially located within Germany. Immigrants' "belonging" was asserted in the face of the extreme right's calls of *"Ausländer raus"* (foreigners out), and they sought to strengthen their rightful connection with places, rather than to transform the symbolic construction of German nationhood. The paradigms of multiculturalism that became influential in the late 1980s in German cities such as Berlin and Frankfurt integrated ethnic minorities into their representations of urban communities and highlighted the bond between the city and its diverse population groups. Paradigmatic was the "We are Berlin" statement of an antiracism poster campaign of the early 1990s initiated by the city's Deputy for Foreigner Affairs (see Figure 3.1). A mix of facial portraits intended to signal ethnocultural diversity was grouped around the statement, emulating the mosaic of multiple-culture groups deemed to form part of the city.

Figure 3.1 'Wir sind Berlin' [We are Berlin] poster, courtesy of the Commissioner for Integration and Migration of the Senate of Berlin.

The main intention of this multicultural branding effort was to include immigrants and those targeted by the "foreigner" label in the symbolic construction of an urban community. No particular claims were made regarding the relationship between distinct ethnic groups; the orderly grid of neatly spaced portraits represented the idea that intercultural harmony could best be achieved by giving everyone equal space and place in the multicultural city.

IMMIGRANT PAROCHIALISMS AND RAP MUSIC

The political demands for symbolic belonging were given a different twist by young musicians with migrant backgrounds in the 1990s. The rise of hip hop music in Germany is closely connected to a new political imaginary of second- and third-generation immigrants that began to be articulated in the field of popular culture. Taking to a genre that was closely associated with African Americans and Latinos in the United States, young descendants of immigrants in Germany used it to assert their claims to belong—both in Germany as a whole and in specific inner-city neighborhoods. The band credited with the first German-language rap release, Advanced Chemistry, turned it into a flaming critique of racism and symbolic exclusion:

> Gehst du mal später zurück in deine Heimat?
> Wohin? nach Heidelberg? wo ich ein Heim hab?

Nein, du weisst was ich mein . . .
Komm lass es sein, ich kenn diese Fragen seit dem ich klein bin.

[Will you go back home some day?
Go where? To Heidelberg? Where I've got a home?
No, you know what I mean . . .
Come on, stop it, I've known these questions since my childhood.][2]

The insistence on local belonging challenged the prevailing *Ausländer* discourse in Germany, a discourse that used racialized criteria to differentiate between Germans and those who, due to their phenotypical appearance, necessarily had to belong elsewhere, regardless of their citizenship status. However, the emphasis on ties to particular city spaces and neighborhoods in hip hop also imagined and remapped particular urban territories as places of belonging and exclusive membership.

Spatial awareness and the competitive defense of local ties have always been central elements of hip hop culture, despite its diasporic dimensions (Forman 2000). Practices of graffiti and tagging, breakdancing and rap music with powerful claims to represent "hoods" spread quickly among immigrant youth in the mid-1990s. In Berlin, this spread was actively supported and channeled by an array of state institutions that regarded hip hop as a "comprehensive solution to the 'problem' of youth violence" (Soysal 2004: 69). Youth centers, state-sponsored music competitions, and social workers encouraged immigrant youth to rap as a peaceful means of voicing protest and competing over urban territory, deeming hip hop their appropriate medium of cultural articulation (Çağlar 1998: 46).

However, hip hop was not only the "pedagogical tool of choice," it also contributed to the rebranding of inner-city neighborhoods. After unification, Kreuzberg became "the ceremonial ghetto for the metropolis" (Soysal 2004: 67), one that was not so much noted for its high levels of crime and poverty, but rather marketed in state-sponsored travel guides as home to a multicultural mix of people with an alternative culture scene that was both vibrant and affordable. Young people with migrant backgrounds were not just part of this mix, they were central to it and, unlike any other group, could claim to represent Berlin's urban cool. Diversity entered into brandings of Berlin in the shape of local transformations of the urban fabric to which immigrant youth could substantially contribute in cultural terms. Berlin's hip hop was hip in the mid- to late-1990s, and city officials noted with pride that the urban transformations that it signaled could hold their own in comparison with similar developments in other European cities (Çağlar 1998: 46). In their descriptions of rough street life and celebrations of locally specific hoods, immigrant youths helped to put Berlin on the map with marketable global youth-culture developments. The "realness" that allowed migrant hip hop artists to represent this particular brand of Berlin urbanism was grounded in assumptions concerning their organic link to inner-city neighborhoods.

A strong attachment to place has been a hallmark of American hip hop ever since its early beginnings in New York City neighborhoods (Forman 2000). Linked to the territoriality of gang-related conflicts, affirming ties to one's local turf and base of support has been a growing element of rap-music representations in the United States since the early 1990s. The grounding in particular urban localities is central to artists' stamp of authenticity: the connection to a home base secures the claim both to represent a certain urban life experience and to be socially embedded and represent a localized community or posse in the wider hip hop world. Rap music can thus be understood as a form of urban branding that involves claims to urban territory quite different from those of city-marketing departments, but one which the countercultural potential is far from guaranteed.

Grounding one's experience and representational claims in the spatial and communal parameters of urban neighborhoods is also an important element of tracks and representations of rap artists with migrant backgrounds in Germany. Whether this similarity is a sign of the often claimed derivative character of hip hop music outside the United States is not the issue here (see Hutnyk 2005). Neither is it important to analyze whether such spatial representations succeed in strengthening positive affiliations and support networks among marginalized youth. What is relevant to note in the German context is that the insistence on positive affiliations with local places was successful in terms of a new cultural politics of belonging: young people with labor migrant backgrounds no longer seemed to be without "roots," as the German political debate stipulated during the 1980s (Mandel 1995). Instead, hip hop artists could proclaim a new parochialism that drew upon their experience of living in deprived but potentially hip urban neighborhoods in Germany, such as Berlin's inner-city district of Kreuzberg. Berlin's notorious rap act, Islamic Force, heavily mobilized the Kreuzberg image to authenticate their music, singing: "Bu bir 'Orijinal Rap' çünkü Kreusberg baby Kreusberg" (This is an "original rap" because Kreuzberg baby Kreuzberg).[3] The band's only surviving active member, Killa Hakan, continued to draw upon it almost ten years later, releasing an album in 2006 with the title, *Kreuzberg City*. The local pride that was articulated alongside representations of struggle and hardship was based on the ability to navigate and leave one's mark upon difficult urban territories, and on the tightness of one's local social network. The parochialisms articulated in Berlin's rap music grounded young people with migrant backgrounds firmly in the symbolic urban fabric of the city. As these musical developments showed, parochialisms cannot necessarily be assumed to be relics of the past or living traditions that are rooted in the past. Instead, they can very well be new, contemporary developments through which urban space is branded as locally specific, bounded, and potentially exclusive.

Yet, migrant hip hop parochialisms were not so narrow as to exclude cosmopolitan and universalist orientations: "The whole world is my country" Islamic Force proclaimed on the same *Mesaj* album, and Berlin's hip hop artists were acutely aware of musical and stylistic trends that characterize contemporary hip hop as a global youth-culture formation (Soysal 1999). The migrant parochialisms developed in Berlin's hip hop scene were simultaneously connected to diasporic cultural flows and transatlantic articulations of minority experience and empowerment, in the same way that they were fed into urban-image campaigns and national music markets. Yet, while participating in this global youth-culture formation, immigrant youth in Berlin were still resolutely localized when it came to the mass appeal of hip hop: as potent signs of urban cool in the late 1990s, they signified the captivating qualities of "ghettoes" and "hoods" as both inescapable fate and special appeal. Reporting on the new wave of Turkish hip hop artists in the late 1990s, the German media continuously emphasized their local rootedness. Islamic Force, Aziza-A, Erci E., and Cool Savaş were true Berliners and could represent the city's new cultural trajectory. Their references to urban life in Berlin's inner-city neighborhoods became part of "tertiary communication" processes (Kavaratzis 2004) that branded the city as a vibrant place of diversity and cultural development rooted in distinct urban territories. It fitted with the vision of Berlin as a multicultural city, home to a wide array of different immigrant groups, whose children had become the true locals. Only by being rooted in local urban territories could they come to represent and market Berlin's cultural hipness and participation in global youth-culture formations. However, only a few years later, the appeal of this variant of city branding began to fade.

OFFICIAL BRANDING EFFORTS AND
CULTURAL DIVERSITY

It is, of course, important to note that the rap variety of city branding was neither exclusive nor dominant in coining marketable images of Berlin in the course of the 1990s (Cochrane and Jonas 1999). The ruling coalition in the city council was busy "re-invent[ing] Berlin as a post-industrial service metropolis" (Häussermann and Colomb 201), with the help of public–private partnerships that staged and promoted large-scale cultural and architectural events to a wide range of target groups. The "New Berlin" was staged by focusing on major urban-development projects such as Potsdamer Platz and turning them into exhibition sites. "Construction-site tourism" was a big success in the late 1990s, and the idea was expanded at the turn of the millennium to include the entire city: projects offered tours of selected buildings and routes through the city and turned different sites into stages for cultural events, generally centering on aspects of architecture, consumption, and design in areas that faced intensive urban renewal. Häussermann and Colomb described the official choice of cultural and historical references in Berlin marketing campaigns as a method of "social sorting" (212). Aimed at attracting tourists, investment, highly qualified professionals, and corporations, official branding strategies have promoted urban images and experiences that correspond to the consumption habits and lifestyles of high-income groups.

Ethnic diversity has figured in official branding strategies mainly where it has promised a diversity of consumption experiences, such as ethnic cuisine. City planners and officials have shown markedly less interest in marketing those neighborhoods that were the factual or symbolic home of young artists with migrant backgrounds: Berlin's quarters with the highest percentage of welfare recipients and unemployment. Economic recession and the neoliberal restructuring of the labor market hit these neighborhoods particularly hard, creating new spatialized economic and social divides in the city (Krätke 2004). In light of their high rates of school dropouts, and unemployment figures twice as high as among their nonmigrant peers, young people with labor migrant or refugee backgrounds in urban centers in Germany have fewer chances than ever, statistically speaking, of successfully entering the job market.

The consequences of rising poverty, youth unemployment, and steadily shrinking welfare-state provisions are making headlines in primarily culturalist terms: violent behavior and youth delinquency are discussed as signs of a failed multiculturalism. Talk of a failure of multiculturalism has become commonplace in German political debates and mainstream media representations, particularly since the specter of Islamist violence has been linked to Muslim minorities in Europe. Violence in Berlin schools, urban riots in France, terrorist attacks in London, and the murder of Theo Van Gogh in Amsterdam have all been interpreted as signs of a failure to properly integrate immigrant populations culturally, with multicultural *laissez-faire* policies accused of fostering so-called parallel societies and segregation among ethnic minorities.

As a consequence, the ethnocultural diversity to which young people with labor migrant and refugee backgrounds contribute has become more difficult than ever to integrate into marketable images of Berlin. Despite the fact that city officials aim to brand it as a cosmopolitan world city, and thus have to present ethnocultural diversity as an asset, the actual composition of Berlin's immigrant population is much more difficult to exploit for marketing purposes than that of cities such as Frankfurt, for example, with its large numbers of highly qualified expatriates working in the banking sector.

MULTICULTURALISM AND COSMOPOLITANISM

What is the purchase that cultural institutions, commercial-interest coalitions, and city representatives hope to gain from promoting Berlin as a cosmopolitan city? And what is its relationship to other concepts that have guided and fuelled different forms of urban diversity management and its cultural representation, most notably that of multiculturalism?

Like cosmopolitanism, multiculturalism in its various guises as intellectual discourse, normative ideal and political project has been centrally concerned with respect for cultural diversity and tolerance towards cultural (usually meaning ethnic or "racial") others (Taylor 1992; Kymlicka 1995). In terms of ethics, interests, and orientations, both cosmopolitanism and multiculturalism exhibit a certain openness, eagerness, and ability to engage with different cultural traditions and orientations that are strange in their origin. Cosmopolitanism shares with multiculturalism the rejection of exclusively parochial or national cultural attachments, as well as the political aim of reconciling the principle of equality with the recognition of positively valued difference. Contemporary interest in both concepts is related to the perception of a shrinking world in which human beings are confronted with others and cultural otherness in unprecedented ways. Yet, while cosmopolitanism considers the world to be its appropriate referent and scale of interest, multiculturalism tends to be more "inward looking" and concerned with territorially limited spaces such as nation–states, cities, or even local neighborhoods. Various critiques of multiculturalism have criticized its' culturally essentialist underpinnings (Beck 2002; Bhabha 1996; Werbner and Modood 1997). In contemporary discussions across the social and cultural sciences, multiculturalism appears as not only theoretically and politically problematic in its treatment of difference, but also somehow outdated, as talk of transnational connections and the global has increasingly taken center stage (Tsing 2000).

In line with its "inward-looking" orientation, multiculturalist urban policies and discourses treat the city as a local space and communally defined territory that needs to integrate its residential ethnic minority populations, seemingly regardless of their transnational affiliations and mobilities. Dominant invocations of urban cosmopolitanism, however, regard the city not as a local space that contains diversity but as a node in a global cultural network, open to a diversity of cultural flows. This is different from the multicultural city that focuses on the coexistence of cultures related to immigration, without the added sense of navigating different cultural repertoires and connectedness to the world. Multiculturalism seeks to ensure equal rights and recognition for minority cultures that cohabit as a result of migration, whereas cosmopolitanism looks outward towards the world, acknowledging otherness as a universal condition and challenge. The multicultural city is conceptualized as the endpoint of migratory movements that produce cultural mosaics, while the cosmopolitan city appears as a node in global cultural flows, ideally structuring their intermingling in a harmonious way and benefiting from them as sources of innovation.

Despite these differences, cosmopolitanism and multiculturalism can easily coexist and complement each other as different strategies and emblems of managing cultural diversities in concrete fields of urban policy making and cultural production. If "[c]ities have historically been the privileged, if not necessarily exclusive, sites for the emergence of the form of life that we call the cosmopolitan" (Abbas 772), they have also been privileged sites for the development and implementation of multiculturalist policies that have in turn influenced national debates. In Berlin, both cosmopolitanism and multiculturalism figure prominently in efforts to transform, govern, and successfully market the city. The division of labor that exists between them allows for existing contradictions and potential conflicts to remain submerged and subdued, operating along a "fuzzy logic" of ideology that is decidedly pragmatist in its orientation.

Berlin's urban cosmopolitanism presents the city as a node that intensifies and consolidates cultural flows for the ultimate purpose of relentless business innovation. Opening the city to investors, tourists, and creative classes, its cultural diversity is presented as both consumer item and evidence of a tolerant and world-open habitat in which creatives can thrive. Berlin's multiculturalism, on the other hand, conceives the city as a spatially fixed mosaic of bounded ethnic groups, in which both cultures and places are in need of protection and integration. The urban image of the latter has disappeared from official city-branding strategies, but not from the policy discourses and practices through which ethnocultural diversity is effectively managed in Berlin.

MULTICULTURALISM AND CULTURE FUNDING

The aim to incorporate migrants symbolically into the city was, and continues to be, an explicit goal of public-funding strategies for migrant artists and art projects. In Berlin, such funding is overwhelmingly tied to sociopolitical objectives of integration. While the bulk of public funding for Berlin's art establishments and projects seeks to promote their reputation nationally and internationally, the meager amounts that are dedicated to the support of migrant artists inevitably go to local and localizing projects deemed to enhance intercultural dialogue, tolerance, or the maintenance of "cultural identity" among ethnic minority groups. Such funding orientations do not imply, in and of themselves that migrant artists have to remain excluded from the mainstream public funding for culture that operates with different criteria and objectives. However, as I have described in detail elsewhere (Kosnick 2007), the current set-up functions to effectively marginalize artists with migrant backgrounds who have not yet made their reputation abroad. They tend to remain caught in sociocultural funding circuits where art serves either as a tool for dealing with urban problems, for example, hip hop music to combat the alleged alienation of migrant youth (Çağlar 1998) or as a colorful demonstration of Berlin's cultural diversity.

An example of the latter is the annual Carnival of Cultures, which draws over a million visitors each year, designed as a platform on which to exhibit the cultural riches of the city's immigrant groups and local cultural organizations (Frei 2003; Knecht and Soysal 2005). As a place-branding activity, it has been judged an extremely successful effort to capitalize on the multiethnic composition of the city and to adapt an imported cultural form to the repertoire of representational devices that help to promote Berlin as a (multi)culturally rich metropolitan center.[4] Nevertheless, the carnival and the cultural institution responsible for its organization receive funds not from the city budget reserved for the support of culture, but from the office of the Commissioner for Integration and Migration of the Berlin Senate. Most of the funding for the carnival is obtained through commercial sponsors.

The cultural flagship institutions that receive public funding in order to promote Berlin's image as a city in tune with global cultural flows and developments in the inter- and transnational art world, on the other hand, consider the city's largest immigrant groups as neither artistic contributors nor target audiences for their offerings.[5] The House of World Cultures, a gift of the U.S. government and sponsored by the federal government because of its perceived importance as a showcase cultural institution for Germany's capital, has for half a century had the task of presenting non-European cultural developments in the fine arts, literature, film, theatre, and music, and engaging them "in a public discourse with European cultures."[6] The imagined audience consists of Berlin residents to whom non-European cultural influences are foreign, external imports, not of an urban population that itself incorporates such influences in daily life and personal histories (Kosnick 2007). Immigrant artists who are connected to the city's labor migrant and refugee populations rarely feature in the lineup of events at its prestigious high-cultural institutions. Berlin's aim to compete with other metropolitan centers in and outside of Europe in terms of its cultural offerings is based on a strategy of attracting artists, artworks, and performances from elsewhere. The culturally curious cosmopolitan urbanite who is invited to sample vocabularies and discourses from a variety of non-European cultural repertoires emerges as implicitly European and affluent. In the practices and discourses of urban high-cultural institutions the cosmopolitan city is one that offers its cultural riches to the sampling connoisseur of global trends. These are not to be confused with the city's ethnic minorities, carriers of a cultural diversity that are mostly dealt with in terms of multicultural policies and agendas.

Yet, as with the hip hop musicians who managed to leave their mark upon city brandings outside the planned image campaigns and projects of city officials and public-private marketing partnerships, young artists with migrant backgrounds continue to shape new images of Berlin and of their relationship to the city in different institutional and noninstitutional contexts of cultural production. While their goal is not to market the city as such, their branding practices still aim for representations that give immigrant minorities a stake in Berlin's present and future. The insistence on local belonging and claims to represent particular neighborhoods no longer offer the politically progressive returns they did in the 1990s. Instead, given the broad political consensus that has diagnosed multiculturalism as a failure, the idea of turning migrants into locals seems now tainted with a much more aggressive integrationist agenda that is driven by security concerns, rather than by ideas of inclusive cultural citizenship and civic participation.

AUTOPUT AVRUPA

The dominant shift from multicultural to cosmopolitan imaginings of the city has meant that mobility has become an increasingly central dimension of cultural capital related to urban diversity. Recent productions by artists and cultural activists with labor migrant backgrounds have begun to respond to these shifts. The Beyond Belonging Festival produced by independent producer and cultural activist Shermin Langhoff offers an example of young migrant artists challenging both urban policy makers and a Berlin arts establishment that afford them no place in their cosmopolitan branding efforts.

Figure 3.2 Image taken from program for Beyond Belonging festival, 2007, Berlin, courtesy of the festival organizers.

The 2007 slogan "Autoput Avrupa: von Istanbul bis Berlin" (from Istanbul to Berlin) identifies the transit route that used to be the main passageway for the thousands of labor migrants who would pack their cars and embark on the long journey "home" during the summer holidays, a route that would take them through Austria, the former Yugoslavia and Bulgaria on their way to Turkey. During the 1970s and 1980s, the Autoput developed not simply into the most important transit route in Europe, but into a "contact zone," with local business ventures catering for a variety of migrant needs along the notoriously congested and accident-prone roads. When the Balkan War erupted in 1991, motorized migrants found a new, more cumbersome passage through Hungary and Rumania, before cheap air travel began to thin out the road traffic.

By choosing Autoput Avrupa as the Festival's motto, Langhoff and her fellow organizers sought to draw attention to the history of labor migrants' cosmopolitan experiences in Europe. The artwork shown at the Festival included contributions such as Angela Melitopoulos' video installation, *Corridor X*, which addresses the issue of migrants' active participation in constructing a shared "transcultural memory space" along the Autoput transit route. Labor migrants emerge as the true pioneers of cosmopolitan dispositions and life experiences—people not in search of belonging, but people who actively construct and transform European space by means of their travel practices. The Autoput thus allows for a contextualization of Berlin and other European cities as nodes in transnational flows of people, flows that involve forms of mobility, and cultural imaginings that rarely surface in dominant cosmopolitan branding efforts with their linking of mobility with different forms of economic and social privilege (Lash and Urry 1994; Turner 2007). The Festival program brochure states:

> The question of a shared perspective on the transformation of urban realities and the emergence of new cultural practices in a changing Europe require a perspective and exchange beyond the national frame. Berlin in particular is connected to other places, languages, histories, and patterns of perception in a variety of ways that point beyond territorial identities.[7]

"Beyond Belonging" signals a newly emergent political emphasis from migrant activists and artists that supersedes former political efforts to insist on local rootedness in the country and city of residence. Their attempts to show how Berlin is tied to other places and histories, a node in transnational cultural flows, fits well with the new tenets of urban cosmopolitanism. Yet, their vision of flows, identities, and cultural transformation are quite different from those that are developed in the consumer- and investor-oriented cosmopolitan image campaigns of Berlin city officials and marketing departments. The stories they tell—of mobility, encounter, improvisation, and conflict—are not the ones that lend themselves to profitability. Yet, they resonate with their audiences, both in terms of the experiences that they draw upon and the imagery and vocabulary they employ. Cosmopolitan cities are marked by more than multicultural diversity; they also need to foster "transcultural exchanges" (Evans and Foord 72). Cosmopolitanism in this sense requires an active engagement with different cultural perspectives and values, and a positive attitude towards change. It is transcultural rather than multicultural, Evans and Foord argued because it aims to break down, rather than protect, barriers "between cultures" (81). Immigrants, they realized, can act as "pioneers of cosmopolitanism" through their transnational affiliations and potential to "hybridize" cultural practices and identifications. The question that is left open, however, is whether the switch from multicultural to cosmopolitan paradigms of imagining cities and their diversity can in itself be taken as a sign of progress. The examples of migrant artists' strategies to engage with and contest dominant versions of urban branding in Berlin suggest that official cosmopolitan branding efforts can not only coexist with multicultural paradigms of managing urban cultural diversity, but may also present even greater challenges to counterforms of symbolic exclusion from the city.

NOTES

1. See Sheila Pulham's analysis at guardian.co.uk, "Inflammatory Language," Tuesday, November 8, 2005, to be found online at: http://www.guardian. co.uk/news/blog/2005/nov/08/inflammatoryla, last visited on 6 September 2008.
2. Lyrics of "Fremd im eigenen Land" [Foreigner in my own country], by Advanced Chemistry (1992), available at <http://www.completealbumlyrics. com/lyric/84381/Advanced+Chemistry+-+Fremd+im> (accessed March 8, 2008).
3. On the group's 1997 LP, entitled *Mesaj*; lyrics by Boe B., Killa Hakan, and Nellie.
4. City planners in Frankfurt have made similar attempts to get a carnival event off the ground. Yet, while Frankfurt is actually more "diverse" than Berlin, in terms of the high percentage of foreign nationals that live there, the expatriate communities in the banking and finance sectors seem to prefer Frankfurt's "high cultural" establishments such as the opera and museums to the folklore-driven populism of the carnival.
5. A notable exception was the 2002 project of Simon Rattle, conductor of the Berlin Philharmonic, which was intended to bring classical music and dance to young people in deprived city neighborhoods. It resulted in a highly acclaimed dance performance of Stravinsky's *Rite of Spring*, which involved almost 250 children and teenagers. However, the project did little to challenge the general exclusion of Berlin's largest immigrant groups from the city's high-cultural institutions and their targeted audiences.
6. Quoted in the House's online mission statement <http://www.hkw.de/en/ hkw/selbstdarstellung/anfang.php> (accessed December 12, 2007).
7. Translated from the original German by the author; see <http://www.hebbel-theater.de/media/610_Beyond_Belonging_Booklet.pdf> (accessed March 8, 2008).

Part I

Branding the City

Selling Contradiction for Global Advantage

4 London's Chinatown
Branded Place or Community Space?

Rosemary Sales, Alessio d'Angelo,
Xiujing Liang, and Nicola Montagna

INTRODUCTION

London's Chinatown, at the heart of the city, has been a powerful element in the representation of London as a multicultural city. It was celebrated prominently in London's successful Olympic bid in 2005 and has become a crucial factor in strategies for expanding political and economic ties with China. With its arches, pagoda, and dual-language street signs, Chinatown has become a tourist destination for visitors from across the world, both Chinese and non-Chinese. In 2006, Lord Mayor John Stuttard launched what has become an annual "China in London" festival. This includes the Chinese New Year celebrations that have been based in Chinatown for some years, but now have expanded into a major public event in London's major open-air meeting space, Trafalgar Square.

Chinatown thus represents a successful branding of urban space, where Chinese culture can be consumed as part of a "global ethnic supermarket" (Sepulveda, Syreh, and Lyon, 2008). Chinatown, however, is not merely a branded space. It plays a significant role in the lives of Chinese people, from new migrants to those born in London and is an important resource for the community. It is a meeting place, a place to eat and shop, a source of employment, the home of community organizations, and a place where Chinese people may seek a familiar "Chinese" environment, a refuge from "permanent racial visibility" (Ang 1998). An essential element in Chinatown's success is, however, the exploitation of other members of the community through low wages and poor working conditions (Chinese Community Centre 2005).

This chapter discusses these contrasting images and meanings of Chinatown. We explore the ways in which Chinatown is experienced and used by Chinese people in London and what it means in symbolic (or "spiritual," *jing shen shang*) terms. It thus presents a grounded understanding of the complex relationship between these different roles and representations. We draw on preliminary results from two research projects currently being undertaken: "Cityscapes of Diaspora: Images and Realities of London's Chinatown" and "The Changing Chinese Community in London: New Migration, New Needs."[1] The projects use mainly qualitative methods, including interviews with individual migrants from varying backgrounds and migratory histories and with key informants from community organizations and service providers. The identities of the migrant informants, respondents, and interviewees, as they are variously called in the following pages, have been concealed, though one or two are occasionally referred to by their first names. The Chinatown project also involved systematic observation of activities in Chinatown at various times and a detailed survey of land use in selected streets.

We begin by discussing how perceptions of Chinatowns have changed as relations between Chinese communities and "host" societies have been transformed, paying more detailed attention to London's Chinatown. The next section explores the role of Chinatown in the lives of individuals. We conclude by suggesting that there is no simple dichotomy between Chinatown's role as community space or branded place. These can be both complementary and conflicting, the product of a range of different interests and groups, and these relations have been shaped by the changing economic and political context.

CHINATOWNS: CONTENDING VIEWS AND REALITIES

The Chinese diaspora has long had a specific relation to space through Chinatowns. Initially a clustering of residence and business, often a response to discrimination and exclusion, they have developed other functions and meanings as communities have become established. Paradoxically, the recent visibility of Chinatowns has generally coincided with the increased invisibility of Chinese communities, as economic success feeds the perception that Chinese people are able to take care of themselves (Campani, Carchedi and Tassinari 1994) and do not make demands on the state (C. Chan et al. 2004: 1).

External representations of Chinatowns have been ambivalent and shifting. Those dating back to the nineteenth and early twentieth centuries were generally seen as both dangerous and exotic, the centre of risky and often illegal activities such as drug taking and gambling. These stereotypes have persisted. As one key informant put it, "I always feel that the West has a psychological problem about China . . .of being the 'Fu Manchu,' of being the 'Yellow Peril." The term *Chinatown* has been used more generally to describe areas perceived as threatening. The Raval area of Barcelona became known as *Barrio Chino* (Chinatown) during the 1920s, although at the time it had no Chinese population. A contemporary journalist described it as "the city's ulcer [. . .] the refuge of bad people" the "underworld [. . .] a forbidden zone" (Ealham 375). As Chinese migration to Spain has developed, the term *Barrio Chino* remains ambiguous, used both to describe specifically Chinese areas and those deemed dangerous and in need of control.

In Southeast Asia and North America, Chinatowns arose from discriminatory laws imposing ethnic segregation. The Chinese Exclusion Act of 1882 barred Chinese people from entering the United States for a period of ten years. The construction of Chinatown in nineteenth-century San Francisco involved the "simultaneous pathologization of the community as a place and the bodies residing within it" (Craddock 364). The legal basis for ethnic segregation no longer exists, but some Chinatowns remained, developing viable economic structures as "ethnic enclaves." Chinatowns came to be viewed, by both insiders and outsiders, as sources of solidarity fostering hard work and economic success. Kwong (1997), however, warns against seeing Chinatowns "through the prism of the establishment, perceiving only close kinship ties, ethnic solidarity and shared prosperity" (384), ignoring exploitation that is exacerbated by insecure legal status or poor knowledge of the local language.

As communities prospered, some Chinatowns became institutionalized by both Chinese organizations and city authorities and began to feature on cities' tourist maps. According to Rath (2007),

> Once a ghetto of deprivileged outsiders and a place to avoid, Chinatown nowadays stirs the imagination of mainstream people and attracts local and international visitors. [...] The image and appeal of these Chinatowns are so strong that they have become export products. Chinatowns are emerging or re-emerging in various European cities. (2)

Anderson (1991) argues that these new branded Chinatowns represent Western cultural domination and a means of managing ethnic relations. W. Chan (2005) suggests that official versions of multiculturalism embody an understanding of ethnicity in which particular developments become associated with certain ethnic groups. Describing the city of Birmingham's recent acquisition of a pagoda, a gift from a prominent local Chinese businessman, he suggests that multiculturalism becomes a means for regeneration of specific areas of the city (15). On the other hand, Chinatowns continue to be seen as community resources, which need defending against encroachments (on Boston, e.g., see Brugge and Tai 2002).

Economic and political reforms in China from 1978 brought a new emigration regime (International Organization for Migration 1995; Pieke 2005). Flows of highly skilled migrants, including professionals, entrepreneurs, and government officers, accelerated (M. Lee et al. 2002; Pieke 2005), while China is the largest source of overseas students globally (Lin 2007). China's uneven economic expansion also created the conditions for less privileged migration flows and the commercialization of emigration. Dependence on gang masters leaves many in undocumented work in exploitative conditions. The deaths of twenty Chinese cockle pickers at Morecambe Bay in the north of England in 2004 revealed the less visible face of this new migration (Song 138).

New migration breathed new life into old Chinatowns (Pieke 2005: 27). New York's Chinatown expanded with new arrivals from Fuzhou (D. Wilson 2005), while other cities established Chinatowns to do business with China and to facilitate cultural exchange. In continental Europe, where Chinese migration developed relatively late, Chinatowns provide a structure for business, social, cultural, political, and economic activities (Farina et al. 1997; Christiansen 2003). In others cities, however, for example Rome and Madrid, their development has been a source of major controversy, as Chinese business continues to be perceived as tainted with illegality and danger.

Many new Chinese migrants find work in and through Chinatown. For the unskilled, Chinatown is a considerable pull factor, as they are "willing to accept often gruelling work and living conditions," providing a new cheap labor force for established business while middle class migrants unable to get recognition of their qualifications may also turn to "the employment opportunities and institutional support network in Chinatown" (Pieke 2005: 22).

This new migration disrupts the established character of Chinatowns as most newcomers come from other regions that are linguistically and culturally distinct from existing communities. New migrants, particularly the undocumented and asylum seekers, "may taint the carefully built image of Chinese in the receiving society and jeopardize the political goodwill and influence that the Chinese have in the receiving society" (Pieke 2005: 27) and face marginalization by established Chinese groups. New migration thus both sustains Chinatowns and carries associations of danger and illegality.

LONDON'S CHINATOWN

London's first Chinatown was in Limehouse, close to the docks where sailors, the earliest Chinese migrants, settled in the second half of the nineteenth century. By 1914, there were some thirty Chinese-owned businesses in the area, including restaurants and laundries (Lau 2002: 5). They faced both popular hostility and official discrimination through the Aliens Act, 1905 (Holmes 1988: 80). Contemporary accounts of Chinese "frequently referred to their exotic or potentially provocative habits such as opium taking, gambling and sexual relations with 'white women' and girls" (May 1978: 111).

With the decline of shipping and the laundry business and the destruction of Limehouse in the Blitz, Chinese people moved to what is now Chinatown, the Gerrard Street area in Soho. Soho was then run down and sleazy, notorious as a center for sex clubs. Low rents made it viable to live and establish businesses there. With the end of the war and colonial restructuring, new migrants flowed in from Hong Kong and the new territories. These new entrants were predominantly male, generally spoke little English, and had limited employment opportunities outside ethnic business. They thus provided a cheap supply of labor for Chinatown's businesses. During the 1950s and 1960s Chinatown remained a dangerous area. According to one key informant, illegal gambling dens proliferated in basements of buildings along Gerrard Street, often operating in dangerous conditions. Their existence was revealed when a fire, which killed several people led to a police clampdown.

By the 1980s, as business prospered, Chinatown began to lose its dangerous image. Its possibilities as a commercial and tourist center were recognized and it became central to Westminster Council's regeneration program for the area. Chinatown was officially recognized in 1985 with the installation of Chinese gates, a pagoda and bilingual road signs and the area was pedestrianized. The celebrations to mark the event were addressed by the Mayor of Westminster, the ambassador of the People's Republic of China, and the Hong Kong Commissioner, who stated:

> This is an important milestone in the development of London's Chinese community. It signifies the official establishment in this great capital city of Chinatown: a commercial, cultural and gourmet centre created by the world-renowned enterprise, resilience and industry of the Chinese people. (London Chinatown Chinese Association 3)

The area grew in prosperity, attracting large financial institutions to set up branches there. One informant described local Chinese people as the goose that laid the "golden egg" for developers, who raised rents, forcing many out of business. The area became increasingly focused on restaurants and financial services. These had sufficient turnover to afford the higher rents, squeezing out the more individual shops and services. It thus became an increasingly commercial rather than residential space. As workers gained some financial security, they brought their families over and moved out of Chinatown, many of them setting up restaurants and takeaways in other parts of London and outside.

London's Chinese population has increased and diversified significantly in the past twenty years. According to the 2001 Census, 80,206 people of Chinese origin lived in London, over half were born in Britain (ONS, 2008). Estimates for 2004 suggest that the Chinese population in England had risen by 11%, a figure that is likely to be larger in London. These numbers include refugees from Vietnam during the 1970s and 1980s, many of them Chinese (Lam and Martin 1997), while the transfer of sovereignty in Hong Kong in 1997 brought further migration, although less than predicted. Chinese people also arrived from Malaysia, Singapore, and other states. The most recent migrants, predominantly from mainland China, have little previous migratory link with Britain or the colonial system, which gave migrants from Hong Kong some familiarity with Britain. While they include the most privileged, large numbers have insecure immigration status, as overstayers or "illegal" entrants. Some claim political asylum: a total of 1,945 asylum applications from China were received in 2006, down from a peak of 4,000 in 2000 (Home Office 2007). According to an informant who gives legal advice to new migrants, the majority of asylum applications from Chinese people were granted in the early 1990s. As relations with China have changed and asylum policy has become more restrictive, most are now refused.

The response of established communities to this new influx has been mixed, including both welcome and rejection. The new migration has coincided with increasing political and commercial links with China in which Chinatown has played a central symbolic and material role. Hostility, especially to asylum seekers, may reflect unwillingness to acknowledge that China is a refugee-producing country and thus involved in human rights abuses, an acknowledgement that might jeopardize these links. One informant who provides health advice for migrants explained, "We don't call them refugees," suggesting that many Chinese refugees avoid identifying themselves as asylum seekers for fear of being alienated from the mainstream community. This reluctance is also shaped by "fear, suspicion and hostility aroused by the public discourse and government policies on immigration" (Pieke 2005: 27). On the other hand, some organizations have struggled to respond to the needs of new migrants. One local service provider described how they turn a blind eye to legal status, giving advice and support, which is not available from traditional community organizations.

While they may seek to distance themselves from the undocumented status, businesses also welcome the labor of this new vulnerable group. As John, an older migrant, recalled,

> When I see them, I remember the situation when we were just arrived. But we had the right to stay and they don't. [. . .] Of course, they [the bosses who use their labor] are afraid of being caught, but everyone wants to take the risk because you have no choice, you can't find workers.

The generation that arrived in the 1950s and 1960s were reaching retirement age during the 1990s. As an informant from a community organization explained, their children often do not want to go into the business; they "want a better life, not a twelve-hour working day and no social life." Businesses are therefore sold to newcomers, providing their former owners with a pension. This change of ownership also changes the nature of business. Before 2000, only one Hong Kong-based newspaper was available in Chinatown, but now several published in mainland China are available there. Restaurants have also changed,

> Seven or ten years ago, the business owners were mainly Hong Kong people or Malaysian . . .The owners have changed to mainland Chinese. . . . Therefore the eating style has changed as well. (William)

As the population becomes more diverse and scattered, Chinese restaurants, supermarkets, and other services are widely available across London other concentrations have developed. Some have been seen as alternative Chinatowns, such as Queensway in West London. Oriental City in North London, though projecting a more general Asian image, was predominantly Chinese. The importance of Chinatown to the community may therefore appear to be in decline, leaving it as a space for tourists rather than for Chinese people themselves. Nevertheless, as many respondents suggested, Chinatown's location provides it with a unique advantage that other places cannot match. As one interviewee, Mary said, "Chinatown is in central London, Chinese people from everywhere can come to the central part, it's convenient." Far from contracting, Chinatown is expanding, with shops and restaurants in neighboring streets being taken over by Chinese owners as they become vacant.

CHINATOWN ORGANIZATIONS

Different interests have been reflected in the development of organizations based in and around Chinatown.[2] Several represent businesses either nationally or locally. The Chinese Chamber of Commerce, United Kingdom, established in 1958, was the first to organize Chinese New Year celebrations. The Chinese Takeaway Association in the United Kingdom is also based in Chinatown. The London Chinatown Chinese Association (LCCA) was established in 1978, representing local business. Other organizations have catered for the more vulnerable. The first Chinese community center opened in 1961, with the patronage of the Hong Kong Government Office (Benton 2005), but local organizations, led by LCCA, established their own community center in 1980, the Chinatown Chinese Community Centre (CCCC), which provided services to more marginalized groups to, as one informant described them, "old people, waiters, waitresses, some quite old who had nowhere to go." In its first year, according to its chair, the CCCC was used by approximately a thousand people and it has expanded, serving both new migrants and older people who have not participated in the prosperity and need support due to language barriers.

The area has attracted a range of other organizations, which provide services for Chinese people. A Chinese-speaking adviser has been based in the local law center for twenty-six years. Its location attracts Chinese clients, as he explained, "We are near to Chinatown, so it's very convenient for them. . . . The Chinese community meets there and socializes and looks for jobs and all sorts of things. And so people come to us."

The local public library has a Chinese section that has approximately 1,000 customers daily, 70% of them Chinese. As the librarian explained, "We are really providing the books that the community wants. We are not serving highly professional people, but those who work in the restaurants: after work [they] have nothing to do."

Chinatown has also been the base for more radical movements. One group provided translation of information on immigration and housing and established weekly advice sessions in a neighborhood center. Another organization, Min Quan, developed out of a Campaign to defend the "Diamond 5," five Chinese waiters at the New Diamond Restaurant who had been arrested after they had been attacked by a group of eight drunken white customers in December 1999.

Chinatown thus represents many interests that may conflict as well as complement one another. These differences were reflected in the response to the Chinatown Gateway project spearheaded by private developers with the support of Westminster Council. While CCCC supported the development, the Save Chinatown Campaign, established by Min Quan, claimed that it threatened Chinatown's "specific cultural character" (Save Chinatown Campaign 2005) and campaigned against the developers. The LCCA also opposed it, since local businesses were threatened with losing their leases or having to pay higher rents. The development company, Rosewheel, bought the lease of a building from the Council in order to develop it into a shopping center, but since it was judged that appropriate consultation had not been undertaken, Rosewheel was required by the courts to compensate the traders who were forced to move out. Planning permission was delayed and the development has not been a success. With many retail units remaining vacant, those businesses that have been established appear to attract few customers and, in contrast to the bustle of Chinatown, the area feels empty and depressing.

The issue exposed rivalries between the LCCA and CCCC. The two groups have worked together on many issues, seeing themselves as complementary, but recent differences appear to reflect both personal rivalry and different interests and expectations regarding the development of Chinatown. While LCCA represents the interests of local Chinese business, the CCCC supported the developments and is keen to promote the wider regeneration agenda. The CCCC's accommodation problem also gave it a more direct interest in development. The lease on its current home in Gerrard Street runs out soon, and the CCCC has made a deal with the developer who bought the old Hippodrome Theatre with the intention of turning it into a casino, agreeing to support the planning application in return for rent free premises in the complex. The application, however, was turned down in 2007. The rivalry developed further, as the CCCC set up a stakeholders group of businesses, landlords, the police, and others. The LCCA, however, which claims to represent the interests of Chinatown as a whole, has boycotted the organization, and the stakeholders have not met for several months.

CHINATOWN IN THE LIVES OF CHINESE PEOPLE

Besides Chinatown there is no other place I can go. (James)

I go there every three days . . .To take the newspaper, to see the changes, and developments in China, to meet friends, to eat, and to do the shopping. (Ken)

These comments from two respondents illustrate the importance of Chinatown in the lives of diverse Chinese people. James works in catering and has limited social contacts or involvement with Chinese organizations. Ken, on the other hand, has been in London many years, speaks English, and is a British citizen. Their comments suggest that Chinatown remains important to both new and old migrants. It provides both material resources— food, restaurants, information, and support—and a social space. For Ken, this involves keeping in touch both with friends based in London and with the wider Chinese community. For many respondents, Chinatown was the place they go to in order to meet friends. For example, Michael, a student, said "We go there mainly because we want to join up together and have a Chinese meal."

The pagoda in the square adjoining Gerrard Street has become an established meeting point. Throughout a half-hour observation session on a cold afternoon, the area was busy, both with people passing through and hanging about or waiting for friends. We asked some of them why they were there, and their answers illustrated the variety of users. They included a group of Chinese tourists from Beijing who had heard about Chinatown from the internet; a student from China who, although based at Nottingham University, comes to London twice a month to meet friends in Chinatown; a young man who spoke little English and works as a waiter and who shops in Chinatown twice a week; two young women studying in London who come to Chinatown because of the variety of food and restaurants; and a Dutch tourist on her third visit.

For more vulnerable migrants, Chinatown may be the only place where they can go to seek support. Many of our respondents described going there when they first arrived. Jane had heard about Chinatown before she traveled and it provided vital support when she arrived in London alone:

When I first came I went to Chinatown . . .I was so helpless. No one seemed to take any notice of me. . . . Then I saw a group of Chinese coming out from what I guess was a gambling house. I went to ask them and one of them did speak some Mandarin. I said I wanted to find a room and he said he could try to see if his friend had a room. He called his friend and eventually I found this temporary place to stay.

Chinatown offers a range of Chinese businesses that cater specifically for that market, including financial services, barbers, and traditional medicines.

If you want to book an air ticket for example, there are many travel agents. (Susan)

I go to [Chinatown] get the [free] newspapers at least once a week. . . . I go to [Charing Cross Library] there to surf the net. (David)

It provides access to information for those excluded from other sources by either a lack of English or of resources:

Wherever Chinese people come from, if they want to find some Chinese information, going to Chinatown is the quickest way. . . . Because some Chinese don't know English, or don't know how to access internet, and can't read the Chinese newspaper, they get less information, get it slowly, or only get information from Chinese friends. . . . So Chinatown plays a very important role. (Peter)

Information may be provided by the community organizations centered there, such as the law center, the Chinese Library, or the Chinese Healthy Living Association. These organizations also provide a social space for the isolated. The CCCC runs a daily lunch club, which serves an elderly population, mainly women, who speak little English. As one woman, originally from Hong Kong said,

You can talk with others and laugh together, otherwise what can I do? . . . When I go out, I come here. Here looks like my home. (Monica)

While for most participants Chinatown was an important part of their daily lives, their feelings about it, and what it represented about Chinese culture were very mixed. For some the emotional ties linked to Chinatown were more important than the material. As one student put it:

Chinatown is probably more important in terms of meeting emotional needs rather than material needs. In daily life it could provide some services. . . . I think Chinatown is even more important in terms of culture. (Nick)

Chinatown provides a Chinese space, which can make people feel at home: As Henry, a student from mainland China, said, "In Chinatown because you can see many Chinese people you will feel a bit the Chinese feeling." This feeling was echoed by Charles, a banker from mainland China: "I feel this Chinatown gives me a Chinese feeling, a Chinese atmosphere." Ken spoke of the importance of the place for helping people to live their lives in London. Although few Chinese people now live in Chinatown, it is still possible to live within a Chinese world:

London has a Chinese atmosphere, so Chinese are able to adapt to life in London, while in other cities Chinese people are rare, there is less Chinese food, so it feels like abroad. Because there are many Chinese people in London, you don't need to be able to speak English.

Its importance may change as stay is prolonged, as was the case for Lily:

> When I had just arrived, of course, I was homesick, so wanted to come to Chinatown. Coming here, [I] felt happy and intimate, even if it wasn't busy and there were less Chinese compared to now, when you came to Chinatown, you could see a Chinese face, you can feel happy. But now [I] have got used to it.

For Marion, a writer from Taiwan, Chinatown was important, but she did not feel emotional ties: "It is just a communication place: eating, gathering with friends. It is not because that place gives me any affectionate feeling. No, it is just because my network of friends is there." George, a student from mainland China, complained that "[i]t is quite noisy, and the sanitation is poor, furthermore, the business atmosphere is too strong. I don't have the feeling of being at home, it isn't that feeling. I go to Chinatown just for eating."

Tensions between different groups were evident in some responses. Sarah from Hong Kong, who works in a Chinatown bookshop, suggested that there are too many new migrants: "Now there are too many Chinese people, the people from China, too many, and less Hong Kong people." For Paul from Singapore, on the other hand, the problem was that there were too many Hong Kong people: "It looks like a Hong Kong Chinatown. I feel it is like that, because they all speak Cantonese. If everyone speaks Mandarin, the feeling would be different."

Others spoke of Chinatown's importance in representing Chinese culture to outsiders. As Joe put it,

> Foreigners like to visit, have a look, so there's contact, such as eating Chinese dim sum or things, that is a sort of communication with foreigners. I think it plays a positive role to show everybody how Chinese culture looks, how China looks, what Chinese food looks like.

Some were concerned that this presented a narrow view of Chinese culture. Ken said, "Chinese culture is not just eating. . . . The British think that all the Chinese can do is cook." Others were critical of the images projected by Chinatown. Jill, a student, said that it looked like "China used to look a hundred years ago." Ken said that the houses were "not in the Chinese architectural style. If it is Chinatown, you must represent the art of Chinese architecture."

CONFLICTING AGENDAS?

Chinatown was important in the daily lives of the majority of our respondents. The complex functions and interests involved in Chinatown can coexist and even sustain one another. Chinatown's importance to London has brought funding that maintains the area as a showcase for Chinese culture and also provides support for services which help the vulnerable. As these key informants explained,

> Westminster is proud of the Chinese community, for example the role of Chinatown as a tourist attraction and all the restaurants so they are happy to fund these kind of services.

> Chinatown is a tremendous asset to the Council and to Westminster. Because it's the Jewel in the Crown, everybody comes to Chinatown. Chinatown gets more and more influential, because of the functions, because of the Chinese New Year celebrations.

Its prominence has given Chinatown an international celebrity, publicized on websites across the world and a first port of call for new migrants seeking help as well as for tourists. On the other hand, its prominence and institutionalization have opened up the space to outsiders. The people who throng into Chinatown for the New Year celebrations are predominantly non-Chinese. This is in sharp contrast to "Oriental City" in Brent, North London, which despite being a significant commercial and social space for Chinese people, did not become a "branded" space. In 2007, developers were given planning permission to rebuild the site as a general shopping center, despite opposition from the local community, who argued that Oriental City would lose its specific Chinese character, which had taken nearly a decade to develop.

There are also more pressing contradictions between the economic imperatives of profit making and the preservation of a Chinese space. Chinatown's presence within the area has not always been secure: its occupation of a prime site makes it vulnerable to the economic interests that threaten the character of the area with high rents. These squeeze out residents and noncommercial activities, narrowing the range of services, for example, leading to a decline in the number of bookshops. Community organizations struggle to maintain a base there in the face of competition for space as the problem CCCC is experiencing demonstrates. Economic success has been won on the basis of hard work and family enterprise, a theme reiterated by several key informants. However, it also depends on the use of cheap labor from, among others, new migrants who are often without proper papers and so in the power of gang masters. This dependence contradicts the respectable image which Chinatown business has sought to develop.

These contradictions were raised in the highly public Home Office raids on several Chinatown restaurants in November 2007, when over forty undocumented workers were arrested. This incident illustrated the contrasting imperatives in the government's managed migration policy. The vigorous pursuit of controls on unwanted migration risked provoking tensions with the established Chinese community. It also risked damaging relations with the Chinese government, exposing the realities of involuntary emigration from China. Despite the invasion of Chinese space, however, the incident did not ignite a major confrontation with the Chinese population or wider protests around the issues of immigration control or exploitative working. The Home Office no doubt calculated on the Chinese population remaining "compliant" (Chinese in Britain Forum 2007) and not protesting too vociferously. Established businesses sought to defend Chinatown as their space, at the same time distancing themselves from illegal activities, while potential targets of the raid were in too vulnerable a position to speak out. A small protest march in Chinatown was followed by a public meeting in which all sides agreed to work together to outlaw illegal working. Chinese business reasserted some control over the space with promises that they would be consulted on such activities in future. A visit from Prince Charles the following month reaffirmed Chinatown's established role in London.

CONCLUSION

Our exploration of the way Chinatown is experienced in the everyday lives of our participants reveals the variety of roles which Chinatown performs. It is increasingly a branded space, but remains important in the daily lives of diverse groups of Chinese people. It suggests that we need to go beyond the binaries of "Chinese" versus "non-Chinese," or "branded" versus "ordinary" space (Hatziprokopiou 2007), to examine the complexity of what is produced and reproduced in Chinatown. There is both tension and accommodation between these agendas. Chinatown's location in the center of the city both has made it vulnerable to rising costs and developers and at the same time allowed it to play a strong role in representing the multicultural city. Its promotion as a tourist attraction has provided funding for other activities, and ensured that it remains a magnet for new migrants. With the growing economic and political links with Mainland China, Chinatown has become a base—both material and symbolic—for developing these relations, but its increasingly homogenized identity also potentially places limits on how Chinese may be expressed.

Chinatown has many faces, with complex layers of visibility and invisibility. The most visible aspects, the thriving restaurants, the gates, and pagoda, the Chinese signs and streets busy with Chinese people, may be all that tourists and casual observers see. Most would not want to penetrate beneath this surface. For Chinese people living in London, it also provides a space where they can buy goods and find services in their own language, where they can feel at home in a Chinese environment. For some, like Jane, it may provide a lifeline, a place where they can seek help in a hostile environment. There are other activities which are more difficult for outsiders to see: the workers whose undocumented status means they are underpaid and overworked, spending their lives in the kitchens of the affluent restaurants and often sleeping in upper rooms; the gambling den from which Jane's helpers emerged. Chinatown's often garish exterior also hides community organizations that provide a social space for the forgotten group of elderly Chinese people and for newer migrants.

Chinatown presents an image of success, a model community representing successful integration, whose hard work has been rewarded by official recognition. However, the raids on Chinatown, in search of the unwanted Chinese people who are vital to that success, threatened this image. It raised again the specter of Chinatown as a dangerous place, representing illegality and uncontrolled activity, brutally demonstrating the conditionality of that recognition.

NOTES

1. The first is funded by the Arts and Humanities Research Council (Rosemary Sales, Panos Hatziprokopiou, Xiujing Liang, Nicola Montagna, Xia Lin, Alessio D'Angelo from Middlesex University and Fleming Christiansen from Leeds University), and the latter by the Big Lottery Fund (Tom Lam and Rosemary Sales, Alessio D'Angelo, Nicola Montagna, and Xia Lin [Middlesex University]). Fieldwork for both projects took place in 2007.
2. See, for example, <http://www.chinatownchinese.co.uk> (accessed Mar. 10, 2008).

5 Living and Making the Branded City and Its Contradictions

Skilled EU Migrants in Manchester

Paul Kennedy

Like that of many other cities, Manchester's industrial base has dwindled, especially with the two recessions of the early 1980s and 1990s, and as many companies have moved to cheap labor havens. Furthermore, a service or knowledge economy has arisen and has partly replaced the former industrial one. It is this, probably more than any other single factor, which has played a key role both in attracting skilled migrants to the microregion and in creating a growing demand for them (Sassen 2000; Lavenex 2006). Manchester also has had to come to terms with intensifying globalization processes and the need to carve out a niche for itself in the hierarchy of world cities.

In seeking to re-invent, but also rebrand, itself at the end of the second and the beginning of the third millennium, it seems that those city agents who have taken the lead in this project have played on three linked themes. First, they have relied strongly on the claim that the city played the pioneering role in spearheading global industrialization. It was Manchester and not London that was the world's first industrial city, and this was how it was perceived during much of the nineteenth century. Second, the agents[1] who have worked to construct this image also insist that the same innovatory spirit that enabled it to become the first truly industrial city has continued to survive and over time to bubble up in new guises. Thus, while Manchester is projected as "the original industrial city" with a unique history based precisely on its continuing modernizing pedigree since the early nineteenth century, at the same time its protagonists suggest that its recent transformation is just the latest phase of regeneration—one in which it has successfully struggled to become the first postindustrial city. Finally, in a global age it has followed a route similar to that taken by other cities and projected itself as cosmopolitan and global with a strong desire to nurture earlier, and to welcome new, diverse world cultures within its embrace.

In this chapter I draw on a small study which I conducted in 2005 in order to explore and test how one group of foreign nationals perceived and experienced these three dimensions of Manchester's self-styled project of regeneration: its industrial past, and its claims to creativity and cosmopolitanism in a global context (Kennedy, 2007). At the same time the discussion also evaluates the contributions that they themselves have made to this project. In doing so I suggest that several contradictions are evident, contradictions that partly call into question the claims being made by the city's agents of regeneration.

The individuals included in the study consisted of sixty-one, EU-skilled migrants working in the city. They came from thirteen EU member, or associated member, countries. Their average length of stay was six years, but with considerable variation around this mean. Thirty-four women and twenty-seven men were interviewed. A majority, 54%, were aged between twenty-seven and thirty-four years, while 23% were aged between twenty-two and twenty-six years old and a similar percentage were aged thirty-five years or older. All but two were postgraduates and all were working, usually full-time, in a range of economic sectors, as professionals in private business, universities, medicine, nursing, dentistry, and veterinary services; in third-sector enterprises and the creative industries; or in restaurants and shops. The study is an exploratory one and makes no claims for wider validity, though there is no reason to suppose that the participants were especially different from other skilled, young EU migrants, except that they spoke reasonable English and had often stayed for some time.[2]

Although most came from comfortable middle class backgrounds and were postgraduates, they were far from being members of a highly privileged, denationalized and socially exclusive transnational capitalist class. Moreover, they formed a distinctive group of skilled migrants in that they had mostly gone abroad alone, not attached to or recruited by a corporation or other organization. Consequently, they were not members of existing work teams, nor were they accompanied by families (Bozkurt 2006; Yeoh and Willis 2005). Instead, and like certain other kinds of professionals, such as architects (Kennedy 2004), they had to construct a new social life largely from scratch and as lone agents. Similarly, they brought an individualistic, free-wheeling and culturally experimental style to the sociocultural and economic exchanges they encountered overseas (King and Ruiz-Gelices 2003; Favell 2006; Recchi 2006). Even if they possessed a few friends and contacts overseas, this was markedly different from the multiplex bonds that normally encapsulate the economic migrant from poorer world regions, whose paucity of resources and experience of discrimination is likely to push them to forge "highly particularistic attachments" (Waldinger and Fitzgerald 1178). These replicate in the host society the primordial sentiments and obligations they knew at home.

THE PROS AND CONS OF MANCHESTER'S INDUSTRIAL PAST

While this chapter was being written, a number of locally based organizations were busy hosting what was billed as the Manchester International

Festival (June 28 to July 15, 2007). Moreover, a review in the national newspaper, the *Observer* (Sawyer 2007), quoted the festival's director as stating quite explicitly that he regarded Manchester as the first industrial city that had always possessed an innate energy and dynamism. The current event was merely its most recent expression. Continuing with this theme, we first consider how the respondents assessed Manchester's industrial heritage and how they had experienced the resulting configuration of nineteenth-century buildings, physical layout, and the unique atmosphere and image all these had conjured up, but we also examine how they viewed the possible long-term social consequences of being the birthplace of industrial capitalism.

Considered overall, the respondents' positive attitudes considerably outweighed their negative ones. The most common response—made in slightly different ways by just over one-third of the sample—was that, while Manchester might not be a beautiful city in the same way as, say, Florence or Vienna, its indisputable Victorian industrial legacy gave it a distinctive and beguiling aura. Some respondents who enjoyed the old buildings and/or the industrial feel also commented on the interesting mix of old and new buildings, though several of them also had certain reservations about this. A second group (nine individuals) who were positive about the city's architecture were especially impressed with the regeneration program. For example, one commented that many of the newer buildings were exciting, and another praised the conversion of some old buildings into flats, which had helped to revive an inner-city community of permanent residents. A third group (ten respondents) thought that, although parts of it had a rather ugly appearance and the city as a whole did not really compare well with many European cities, nevertheless there were strong compensations. These included the fact that Manchester was such a lively place, that most facilities were easily affordable and accessible, and that there were a number of interesting buildings. However, a few respondents were clearly disenchanted with the city's architecture precisely because there had been too much reconstruction and this had led to the eradication of some older buildings.

The following quotes often indicate mixed feelings concerning the city's atmosphere and architecture. However, they also point to the way in which Manchester's Victorian industrial legacy is clearly enjoyed by some respondents and the fact that this went a long way towards canceling out the effects of other architectural features with which some were less enamored.

> Manchester has character rather than beauty—it seems like walking through a Dickens novel. It's nice to clean up the old buildings but a shame to lose the old ones—I like the old-fashioned ones.

> I like the old city centre, old buildings and links to the industrial revolution—railway arches—I like the kind of industrial thing . . . . They

could make more of Ancoats [a run-down location just to the east of the main city-regeneration project].

Some of the city centre is dreadful and some is nice. Manchester should market itself more on its industrial history—people's and women's movements. . . . Some exciting new buildings—Urbis and the Lowry—there's chemistry here.

A huge improvement since 1996—countryside on our doorstep and some beautiful buildings—a different kind of architecture, combining Victorian heritage and new modern ones. France is still wedded to classic buildings, but Manchester has been transformed.

Running alongside this ambivalent, but generally positive, assessment of Manchester as the first industrial city, and its corresponding architectural legacy, ran a parallel perception that its history had also generated certain long term and undesirable social consequences and that these scarred the city's contemporary daily life. More than two-thirds of the sample (forty-four respondents) alluded to at least one, and often more, of the following social "problems": the frequency with which violence and insecurity, including street fighting and "student-bashing," were evident; the incidence of binge drinking and its tendency to be associated with unpleasant behavior; the threatening atmosphere caused by local "scallies" or "hoodies" (supposedly working class youngsters with behavioral problems); and personal experiences of criminality. More specifically, several respondents argued that Manchester possessed two quite separate cultures and that these were clearly constructed around social class differences. Similarly, it was suggested that the deep divisions underlying Manchester (and probably British) society existed to a degree that was neither present nor possible in their home countries. Many respondents also believed that these social divisions were caused by multiple deprivations linked to starkly different lifestyles, educational levels, and expectations. These partly explained the sometimes violent tensions and disruptive antisocial behavior evident at times among some young working class individuals. This general anxiety and the respondents' perceptions of the differences between the situation in Britain and that of other European societies are exemplified in the following.[3]

There's an underground culture here—no-one talks much about it—people living on benefits. . . . I know this from people I see in my work, as patients—lots who don't go to work . . . going on for generations. . . . It's all ages, not just the young . . . a culture going on in families all around for a long time. . . . As a foreigner I find it shocking—and I find other foreigners agree with me. Immigrants then copy this . . . . You can't find this reluctance to work in Spanish culture. But people are not ashamed here.

The class system runs deep. I've had friends from all classes . . . but you have totally different discussions with them . . . and there's no connection between the different classes.

Here, social class hinders communication—in Finland it's quite socially even—you don't have such class differences—there's a more even standard of education.

I feel intimidated by the scallies—different clothes and an anti-student culture. This is unlike other European cities such as Barcelona— where everyone can get along. . . . Manchester's got very strong central groups—and they won't associate with people like me who are associated with students.

It appears that the attempt to create an attractive and distinctive world brand for Manchester by emphasizing its leading role in world industrialization is a two-edged sword. While it does command the attention of strangers and resonates well with their own perceptions of the architecture and everyday feel of the city, it also leads them to wonder whether recent attempts to push Manchester rapidly into the new millennium by promoting a vast number of new buildings—linked to the project of creating a postindustrial city—risks canceling out this very claim by overpowering the old architecture. Moreover, when confronted personally and through social contacts with the evidence of unpleasant and sometimes threatening social behavior, the strong emphasis on the city's world historical role in leading industrialization can raise questions concerning the possible causal connection between these two conditions, thereby somewhat tarnishing the significance of the historical claim.

LOCAL SOURCES OF THE CREATIVE CITY

In this section we explore some of the evidence from the Manchester study that largely validates the city's claim to be highly creative. Then the discussion identifies several additional or even alternative possible explanations for, and sources of, this alleged creativity.

In 2003, the London think tank, Demos, adapted Florida's (2002) creativity index and applied it to a number of U.K. cities. The thinking behind this index was that the success of contemporary cities depends on the presence of a "creative class." In order to identify the presence of such a class and to establish which cities were most likely to produce one, the Demos index adopted three criteria: the degree of ethnic diversity; the extent to which cities created conditions conducive to the blossoming of a gay culture; and the number of patent applications per head of population. This last criterion is clearly linked to the concentration of university activities and high-tech companies in a given location. More interesting, Demos then ranked Manchester as the most creative city in Britain, followed by Leicester and London. The comments provided by many respondents in the Manchester study appear to bear out the Demos appraisal. Thus, they were asked to list the three things they appreciated most about living in the city. Here, one of the highest scoring attributes mentioned by more than one-third of the respondents (36%) was, indeed, Manchester's atmosphere of vibrancy, creativity, and personal freedom. The following quotes explore different aspects of this.

Sonia was Spanish, aged 24, and worked as a dental nurse after completing her degree at a local university. Despite its industrial past Manchester felt, she said, "like a young city—in rapid transformation . . . . I find it very exciting."

Fabrizio, aged 31, an Italian who ran his own small company importing foodstuffs from across the EU, observed that "Manchester is like a village." Yet it also has an: "enterprising culture . . . I value its amazing transformation" in recent years. He went on to comment on the help he had received for his business from several Manchester-based economic agencies.

Pierre was a French lawyer in his late thirties who had lived in Manchester for ten years. In his view Manchester was "dynamic, busy, entrepreneurial, forward-looking. People are positive. There's loads of work . . . It gives you a very positive feeling. And I like the people. I think the city has done extremely well during the last ten years, you know . . . . This is the perfect place to be for me."

Marta, aged 24, a former student at one of the city universities, who combined teaching Spanish with part-time restaurant work, claimed that "the Manchester environment makes me feel happy. In Manchester you can do anything you want to."

Finally, Sandrine's observations paint an especially vivid picture of how moving to Manchester created an opening for her to undergo a self-transformation, but how this became entangled with the urgency and excitement generated by Manchester's own push for regeneration following the IRA bombing. She was French and was working as an accountant for an international company that had based some of its specialized European service activities in a Manchester affiliate. She observed,

> When I arrived in Manchester, it was a few months after the IRA bomb and the city centre was pretty devastated, with scaffolding everywhere, and I couldn't see the city and I was in the same state of mind in my own head. . . .And I had to reconstruct myself and the city had to reconstruct itself at the same time. . . . It was the realization that I have choices in life.

According to the respondents, one very definite aspect of Manchester's creativity and dynamism from which they had benefited—though it also applied to Britain generally—was the job, career, and educational opportunities it had provided. Most respondents cited several reasons why they had come to Manchester in the first place, including the desire to travel or escape from their home town or family (67%). Nevertheless, the most frequent explanations were utilitarian ones (87%): to find work, enhance career prospects, pursue better educational opportunities than could be found at home, or improve English-language skills as a route to future employment. Moreover, fifty respondents who gave views on the U.K. and Manchester economies alluded specifically to the highly favorable opportunities available in Britain compared to those found in other cities and countries. However, they claimed that jobs were not the only economic advantages they had enjoyed. For example, British employers were said to be less fixated on specific qualifications and often prepared to be adaptable, since their key concern was the employee's ability to do the job properly. Work arrangements tended to be more open and equitable compared to those encountered in other EU countries. Part-time work was much more readily available and it was easier for women to take maternity leave or reduce their work hours without risking their job or company position. Work cultures and practices were less hierarchical or likely to require deference to superiors. There was greater scope for changing career direction once you had proved yourself to be a talented and committed employee. Finally, employers were often more willing than their EU counterparts to prioritize ability and future promise over employee nationality when allocating work and granting promotion. Although these are highly impressionistic accounts, they perhaps point towards further research.

A number of respondents also described certain contradictory cultural and social practices associated with the British mentality that they believed generated creative openings, allowing foreigners to carve out a socioeconomic life space in the United Kingdom. Thus, on the one hand, British people were described as probably much more tolerant than continental Europeans towards foreigners. Coupled to this was the reality that, generally speaking, British social life was less conservative, far less grounded in an all-encompassing expectation that family commitments must come before friendships and other social loyalties. Partly this was revealed by the willingness to permit young people to leave home and become independent at a much earlier age than in most other countries. On the other hand, many respondents noted that hand in glove with this greater tolerance went a kind of indifference, occasionally bordering on contempt, towards non-British people, and a kind of national self-absorption with the qualities supposedly intrinsic to the British psyche. Accordingly, foreigners were not necessarily ignored, but they were regarded as having little to offer that was likely to capture the serious interest of most British people. The following quotes are not untypical in spelling out these contradictions. They also hint at the greater room for personal maneuver which these circumstances provide and that might have been available, had they remained at home.

Sonia commented as follows: "One thing I like about British people is that they are very open-minded, compared to [people in] Spain." Yet there can be a social distance between the locals and foreigners. "But I think they are friendly, if you speak English. If they realize that you are not English, maybe there is a conflict. . . . You speak to someone and you say that you don't understand and maybe they will be offended. . . .Maybe they get cross with you."

Antonio was in his late twenties and from Turin. After completing his doctorate he worked as a university researcher. Talking about the friendships he made through his university work he said,

> The university is very mixed, as you know, although I befriend more easily with people who are not English . . . I think the British are open to foreigners, but there are enormous barriers to sharing insights into one's private life. . . . I believe it's some sort of respect for people's privacy. On the other hand, there may be an element of, perhaps, [their not being] that used to dealing with people with very different habits, because among the countries I have been to I think this is the one where people have the most different habits to our own in Europe. . . .I felt I had a better understanding of people's behavior in France or Germany—virtually anywhere else than here.

While, at times, these contrasting experiences of toleration and permissiveness alongside a kind of benign indifference might irritate foreigners and push them into a situation of relative social isolation from British social life, they also created a social space for self-development and experimentation, which was often valued.

THE CREATIVITY OF THE "OTHER(S)": FOREIGNERS MAKING MANCHESTER.

Many respondents came to Britain intending to remain for a short time, perhaps to complete a university course, while others had longer-term aspirations, yet did not anticipate remaining for many years. However, in eventually deciding to stay, they themselves became crucial ingredients in the creative mix of resources the city claimed it was offering as part of its attractiveness to overseas investors, tourists, and others. Thus, when asked which three aspects of life in the city they appreciated most, the highest scoring attribute was the abundance and variety of activities available (48%), while in third place was the multicultural diversity (41%) to be found everywhere in the locality. The second most cited attribute, the compactness of Manchester and its easy accessibility (43%), helped to intensify the possibility of enjoying its many leisure opportunities and cultural diversity at first hand.

Focusing upon the respondents' references to preferred and enjoyable experiences, in addition to the city's historical legacy, it was evident that much of this revolved around the contribution of foreigners and the many cultural, business, and social activities in which they were engaged. Included here were the following: the art-house cinema (the Cornerhouse), which specializes in exhibitions of world films; various European food and arts festivals; the variety of music on offer in addition to pop-rock (jazz, Latin American, and world music—the city's mostly foreign-supported tango club, for example, as well as opera and classical music); the impact of food and other influences, stemming from the embeddedness into the local economy of several ethnic groups from Asia, Africa, and the Caribbean; and the range of national groups contributing to city life, partly associated with Manchester's large overseas student population,[4] or with the presence of many businesses employing non-British people. The following quotes indicate the range of these comments.

Thomas was a Spaniard who came to Manchester in 1997. He was a university language teacher in his early thirties. Manchester, he said, "is growing culturally . . . . Many new things every year, festivals, cultural mixes—the Cornerhouse, the galleries, the Commonwealth Games. . . .You are always exposed to cultural events."

Alex was Greek and he first came to study in Manchester in 2002. He was working as a dental nurse. "Manchester is not too big. . . .It has everything you want, a nice commercial centre, a busy night life . . . many different kinds of nationalities. It's also culturally good—not just theatre and operas, but festivals in summer and winter, for example the German and European markets."

Pieter from Switzerland and working here on his own business, aged 29, made the following assertion: "Manchester has everything London has, but without the hassle—bands will always come if they are in the UK—huge music possibilities and atmosphere. . . . My visitors can't believe the curry mile and the many different kinds of feelings available in various parts of the city."

Similarly, Manuel, Spaniard in his early 40s and working in the local cultural industries, observed:

I'm becoming more aware of different people living in Manchester—people from across Europe . . . my friends agree on this. And the North of the UK has become more diverse compared to the 1970s. [It] has kept its traditions, but also become more cosmopolitan . . . world foods, many things to do. Also it's more open to European as well as Third-World or Commonwealth cultures.

Later he praised the recent rise of something approaching a continental cafe-culture in the city:

Back in 1981 . . . nine o'clock in the morning nothing was open . . . for a proper croissant or coffee . . . nothing. Not in Manchester . . . but it's

a very good change because . . . now you've got many places, and sometimes with my friends from Manchester we get together for breakfast.

Space does not permit a detailed analysis of all the ways in which the
respondents' own activities were contributing to Manchester's cultural
diversity, nor to all the additional influences which, according to them,
other foreign groups were importing into the city's creative life. However,
this section finishes with a brief outline of two additional sources of cultural change.

One of these concerns the respondents' role as avid consumers of the
city's leisure and cultural facilities. I suggest that they probably participate
in a wider range of cultural activities than their middle class British counterparts and that their consumption is proportionately large in relation to
their actual numbers in the general population. For example, whereas ten
respondents cited the popular-music scene as one of the three things they
liked best about Manchester, and three included the local football culture,
twenty-nine respondents (48%) pointed to the abundance and variety of
cultural activities and things to do across a wide spectrum—many of them
made possible, in whole or part, through non-British agency. In their capacity as consumers of a wide range of cultural products, the respondents were
key witnesses to the city's attempt to brand itself as cosmopolitan and
global, and especially since many enjoyed those very same "high brow"
cultural products that the city was trying to enhance in the arts as a central
plank in its bid to attain global ranking.

Second, five respondents were proud of their roles in third-sector enterprises that were contributing to Manchester's rejuvenation as a mainly
service-based economy. Carlina and Henri were members of this subgroup.
Their observations provide an indication of the ability of many skilled
migrants to provide major inputs into the city's regeneration, but also the
extent to which they personally had derived key advantages from this participation.

Carlina, aged 32, was Italian and worked as a business consultant in
a third-sector agency. She had lived in Manchester since 1997. She commented,

> What now I find still good about Manchester, I mean I feel at home
> here now, I mean my friends are all here . . .and I have seen it develop-
> ing. I don't know, there is something about Manchester. . . .One can
> feel pride in being part of something that is happening, because [of]
> how things have changed and how the city has been regenerated and
> everything.

Henri, aged 29, managed a charity and first came to Manchester in 1999.
He claimed that he had "always been welcomed here, made to feel special
and listened too. There is a creativity here, nurtured by past hardships . . .a

sense of possibilities . . . I want to be part of this urban social regeneration that you find in Manchester."

FORMING TRANSSOCIAL RELATIONSHIPS: THE SOCIAL COSMOPOLITANISM OF SKILLED EU MIGRANTS

The city's leading agents aspired to project Manchester not only as a continuously creative city with a long industrial history, but also as a global and cosmopolitan one, increasingly linked by business, sporting, and cultural connections to other world cities. There is little doubt that much has been achieved in recent years. But what is less often understood is the abundance of informal, yet increasingly vibrant, networks of transsocial relationships generated by the many kinds of migrants living in the city. These both spread across territorial borders, as individuals maintain constant communication with family and friends back home or to other foreign sites where they have lived, and are grounded within the Manchester locale by means of the intercultural relationships many forge as part of their everyday city life. Such cultural border-crossings require and engender "critical mutual evaluation" (Turner 2006: 142), equal recognition and a kind of "ethical hermeneutics" (145), where both parties seek to respect, explore, and interpret each other's cultural differences.

*In addition, and like many other European and world cities where migrants congregate, Manchester functions as a giant "switching board" (Zhou and Tseng 131), akin to a vast railway junction, international airport, or motorway interchange. Here, travelers from many locations arrive with their own personal baggage of cultural and social capital and personal dreams of self-realization. Consequently, innumerable routes converge and a range of primordial cultures become available to be selected in whole or part for building a new social life. Consequently, Manchester's cosmopolitanism owes as much (or perhaps more) to the interpersonal interactions of its incoming migrants as (than) to the policies, management decisions, and business ventures sought by powerful macro-agents.

Turning to the evidence from the study pertaining to these underlying transsocial interactions, the respondents were asked about their three or four closest friends in Manchester and/or the United Kingdom outside work relationships, and any additional friends or acquaintances to whom they were less close, but who were nevertheless important to them. In reality, the situation was complex with everyone reporting different combinations of best friends. Most friends were living in Manchester, but respondents who had lived elsewhere in Britain might count individuals from these locations. Here I concentrate on the nationality of their best friends, irrespective of how they first met, in order to gain a picture of the degree to which they have formed transnational relationships. Thus, nearly one third (31%) had evolved very close friendships that did not involve any expatriates at all—though these might figure to some degree in their wider network. More important, over half of the sample (52%) moved in a circle of close friendships based, at least partly and sometime mainly, on other foreign nationals. In addition, more than three quarters (79%) of the respondents named at least some British people as being among their closest friends. Of course, most respondents also belonged to trans- or postnational networks that were spread considerably wider than those constructed around their closest friends. Sometimes these were other individuals living in Manchester, but they might also be people in other regions or cities of Britain or, indeed, friends originally met in another country, who were either locals or foreigners.

On the question of their romantic partnerships and/or marriages, nearly a quarter of the respondents (23%) had become involved in the United Kingdom with a long-term partner who was neither British nor an expatriate. However, if we include those who had previously had several romantic relationships of shorter duration with both foreigners and British partners, then this figure increases to 35%. More interesting, a further six respondents (10%) formed a long-term partnership with a British person while living in a third country such as Hungary, and so in a sense they too entered these relationships with people who were foreigners at that time. A quarter of the respondents (25%) had established long-term relationships with British partners during their time living in the United Kingdom. If we add the 12% of the respondents who were previously involved in temporary relationships with local people (and foreigners), we find that altogether nearly half the respondents had been or were in romantic partnerships involving British people. In total, almost 70% of the sample had formed romantic partnerships with individuals of a different nationality from their own.

Forming these transsocial relationships was by no means the only evidence that living abroad had changed their lives, or that it had pushed them in a more cosmopolitan direction (see Kennedy 2007). Thus, overall, more than four-fifths of the respondents (83%) indicated that living abroad had induced them to experience at least one—and, in many cases, two or more—of the following changes.[5]

First, through meeting others, living abroad had exposed them to such a variety of alternative life ways that they had become much more knowledgeable about, interested in and tolerant towards difference (58%). For example, Angela's parents were Italian and British, though she had lived mostly in Italy. Although part of her heightened self-reflexivity can be linked to the tensions of a binational family life, coming to study and teach in Manchester had heightened her sense of being exposed to different cultural experiences:

> Definitely, mixing cultures is a really good thing . . . because I think that's the only way to really get over some of the big problems that there are in the world, you know, when people suddenly realize that we're all part of the same thing and it's not me and the other, but we're

closer connected. And the only way to do that is to go out there and see places and bring people together.

Second, more than a quarter (27%) observed that they now looked at their own national culture with considerable objectivity and realized that there were many alternative ways of living and dealing with life's problems, and that most of these were not only equally valid, but perhaps were also available. Sandrine, whose views were quoted earlier, had this to say when asked whether living in Britain had changed her:

> Because I have met all sorts of people from different walks of life . . . and it takes a lot to surprise me now . . . when I go home now I look around and I think that things are not very sophisticated . . . It makes me a lot more blasé.

Equally, she suggested that she had become much more confident about juggling her identity and dealing with different people and situations:

> It makes my contact with people easier . . . I use my French-ness to get away with murder. . . . Yes, you can play with this indefinitely. With Londoners, when they start to look at me . . . when I talk, I have a Manchester accent . . . I play the Manchester card.

Similarly, Frank, a Finnish business consultant married to a British wife and working in a small IT company, talked about his increased confidence and ability to live in the wider world:

> I think living abroad is a really big part of my identity. I am still Finnish, but, yeah, it is a very important part to adapt and it has been changing me as a person. It makes it easier to adapt to certain situations when you deal with different cultures, it makes it easier when you relocate to Prague or Sydney or to Manchester for example.

Finally, 36% of the respondents claimed that they now possessed a much more international perspective; that is, they were better informed about and interested in aspects of world affairs, and were more open to the latter and capable of forming their own picture of the world. Elvira's case illustrates this point well. She was Norwegian and worked part-time for a clinic offering physiotherapy. She spent the last two years of her schooling at a large French state school, boarding with girls from sixteen different nations including several from Africa. She made the following comment about herself and her fellow students in France:

> They are so adaptable that I think they feel less threatened by globalization than people who are very stuck in their own country, because

that's where you get prejudice . . . where people are scared of other cultures and haven't been out exploring them. . . . I feel I belong to a set of international people. I've lived in many places.

Later, she explained why she had eventually chosen to follow a development studies course in Manchester:

> But the reasons I do development studies is that there's got to be some sort of socially conscious way of globalizing so that you don't divide the world into rich and poor. . . .It's possible to go about it in a less exploitative way. . . . When I first came to Manchester, I did international business studies, and after half a year I realized I can't be doing this, this is not what I want at all. . . . Because I'm interested so much in learning about regions I don't know anything about . . . I became so interested in regions because I went abroad.

Beatriz was Spanish and worked in a vegetarian restaurant. She lived with a British partner. Asked whether, and if so how, living abroad had changed her, she said,

> I think because I have met people from different kinds of environment. I have a friend from Malawi and I think how difficult it must be for her and how it is over there in her country. Because, one thing is what you read in newspapers and the other thing is what you really know through people and their experiences, you get the truth. You can put yourself in the skin of other people.

CONCLUSIONS

Viewed through the lived experiences of a group of EU migrants, this discussion has explored the contradictions or paradoxes that seem to exist in the context of Manchester's recent attempt to rebrand itself for a global audience. Here, it has projected itself as the world's first industrial city with a long and continuing record of creativity and has coupled this to a determined bid to become a contemporary cosmopolitan global city. With respect to the first of these claims, the uniqueness of the city's Victorian industrial history was certainly noticed and admired by most respondents. Yet, equally, they were often highly critical of its attempt to encourage a mass of new building work. Moreover, some were disenchanted by what they saw as its cumulative, long-term legacy of deep social divisions, working class cultural impoverishment and its underlying potential for violence and public disorder. Thus, what had made the city unique also threatened to undermine and perhaps nullify the entire project.

Similarly, the claim that Manchester continues to be a highly creative city, constantly responding to changing national and world scenarios, seemed convincing to most respondents. Indeed, they themselves had been beneficiaries of the city's vibrant but also flexible economy, and many had found its multicultural diversity empowering and exciting. Yet, at the same time, close questioning of the respondents' experiences and local activities revealed that a considerable input into the everyday cultural and social life which they enjoyed was being provided by other foreigners including non-Europeans, rather than by the local agents of change and/or the native inhabitants. Moreover, their own direct contributions to city life over a range of activities were impressive. They had evidently played a considerable role in enriching the cultural ingredients flowing through Manchester's life world. But they were also helping to legitimize its claims to be a creative city, successfully engaged in becoming a world-class knowledge economy and endowed with a range of cultural assets.

Finally, investigation of the respondents' social affiliations revealed that, in common with many other European and world cities, Manchester is indeed a key site in the transnational space of flows. Yet it is also a place in its own right with its own cosmopolitan, global dynamics, and reach. But much of this is being generated not simply by powerful macro-agents, but also through the interpersonal relationships constructed by many of its skilled migrant sojourners and settlers—and, no doubt, other foreigners too. Moreover, these social affiliations increasingly involve crossing primordial cultural frontiers in situ and negotiating transsocial meanings and reciprocities. Thus, again, much of Manchester's claim to be a keen global player is built on the unacknowledged role played by many of its migrant members who are engaged in building cross-national social interactions that operate within the city, but also circulate far beyond its boundaries to many other locations.

NOTES

1. Attempts to counter a decline began in the late 1970s. However, it was the IRA bombing in 1996 that galvanized these and other agents into pursuing a more focused program. The project involved an alliance between Manchester City Council, the ten boroughs of Greater Manchester and Manchester Airport, but has also been served by third-sector organizations. The airport is regarded as crucial to regional re-regeneration. These players see themselves as ahead of other U.K. cities.
2. The research used in-depth, semi-structured interviews as its main source of material. Reliable databases indicating nationality, gender, age, and occupation were not available. EU nationals are not required to register with their consulates, while employers do not compile lists including such information. Moreover, the U.K. Data Protection Act (UK Govt. 1998) prohibits the supply of information and contact details. Accordingly, the respondents were

obtained by sending out emails to likely organizations, approaching groups and associations that might offer useful leads and visiting likely venues. Initial contacts were then followed up through snowballing.

3. These are highly subjective speculations. In themselves, they do not constitute evidence for the substantive existence of two often hostile cultures.

4. In 2006, Manchester University had around 8,000 EU and non-EU foreign students (O'Malley 2006), while Manchester Metropolitan University claimed another 3,000. These figures, however, include a minority of short-term exchange students.

5. The central role that meeting other people and forming relationships had played in their personal development abroad was specifically noted by three-quarters of the respondents.

6 Understanding Cultural Quarters in Branded Cities[1]

Simon Roodhouse

This chapter is a practical explanation of the principles and practice employed in considering, developing, and establishing *Cultural Quarters* in cities, as these spatial phenomena are becoming increasingly noticeable in city branding. Many of the concepts and arguments involved have been critically analyzed over the last fifteen years or so, and are usefully summarized in *City of Quarters, Urban Villages in the Contemporary City* (Bell and Jayne 2004). In addition, there has been considerable interest in the creative cities concept, which has been thoroughly examined by Charles Landry's *Creative Cities* (2000) and Justin O'Connor's *The Creative City* (1999). There is no attempt to cover this ground again here, or to theorize the Cultural Quarter phenomenon in terms of branding. Instead, I provide an explanation of what Cultural Quarters are, how they have come about, and what they mean for the city. I emphasize case studies from the north of England where there is a recognized need to regenerate the nineteenth-century Industrial Revolution primary manufacturing towns in order to avert continuing social and economic decline. These are, in part, rebranding and reprofiling projects that involve the development of Cultural Quarters.

The Cultural Quarter has become a fashionable concept in the United Kingdom and increasingly so elsewhere in the world, particularly with city authorities, as a preferred solution to urban regeneration. This chapter focuses on the how and what of Cultural Quarters and is largely drawn from a cultural perspective. I begin by discussing the definitions employed by relevant urban regenerators and explore the associated history.

CONCEPTUAL CONFUSION: ARTS INDUSTRY, HERITAGE INDUSTRY, CREATIVE INDUSTRIES, OR CULTURAL INDUSTRIES—A VERY BRITISH PROBLEM?

Successive U.K. national governments and their agencies have defined and redrawn boundaries, resulting in continuous public cultural policy and practice turbulence since 1945. This commenced after the Second World War with the establishment of the Arts Council of Great Britain, which was based on the Council for the Encouragement of Music and the Arts (CEMA), which had begun in 1940 (Pick and Anderton 1999). The majority of Council funding was directed to organizations with which John Maynard Keynes, the chairman, had close ties. These were restricted to Central London and included the Royal Opera House. The pragmatic determination of these boundaries, which are definitions with no obvious rationale for inclusion or exclusion, lends itself to an interpretation of a public-sector domain engaged in restrictive practice. This ensures that the boundaries are constrained enough to match the level of available resources at any given time. It is then, more to do with the government administrative machinery responding to national policy by providing a manageable and controllable framework for the allocation of public funds, rather than a rational, empirically informed inclusive system, measurable, thus conforming to the requirements of evidence-based policy (Solesbury 2001). Urban regeneration (Roodhouse and Roodhouse 1997) and the introduction of creative industries (Roodhouse 2003) by the New Labour administration are examples of this practice.

The impact of this continuous boundary redefinition through national government machinery works against cohesion, interaction, and connectivity; although much is said by politicians about joined-up policy and action. As Bogdanor (2005) explains,

> Joined-up government is a key theme of modern government. The Labour government, first elected in 1997, decided that intractable problems such as social exclusion, drug addiction and crime could not be resolved by any single department of government. Instead, such problems had to be made the object of a concerted attack using all the arms of government—central and local government and public agencies, as well as the private and voluntary sectors. (1)

In particular, shifting boundaries encourage isolationism between national, regional, and local government agencies by relying on departmentalization and compartmentalization as the organizational means of delivery. As an illustration, culture that resides within the Department for Culture, Media, and Sport (DCMS), is also found in the Foreign and Commonwealth Office, which funds the British Council (British Council Creative Industries Unit 1998, 2004); the Ministry of Defence, which resources a substantial number of museums, galleries, and musical bands; the Department of Trade and Industry, which supports creative industries through the Small Business Service (including the export effort of these businesses); the Department for Education and Skills (DfES; Shaw and Allen 2001) and the Higher Education Funding Council for England (HEFCE), which provides entry to work and workforce development in the cultural field (North West Universities Association 2004). Incidentally, this excludes all the devolved cultural arrangements for Scotland, Northern Ireland, and Wales, which is another area of chaos.

This chaotic organizational pattern is replicated, at regional level, with DCMS-sponsored Cultural Consortia, the Arts Council, the Museums Libraries, and Archives Council (MLA), the Sports Council, the Tourist Boards, Sector Skills Councils (SSCs), and local authorities, along with the Regional Development Agencies (RDAs), Small Business Service, including Business Link, not to mention the plethora of subregional intermediaries funded from the public purse, all pursuing differing cultural agendas and definitional frameworks (Hamilton and Scullion 2002). Although attempts are made at overarching regional strategies, there is not as yet a shared understanding of a definitional framework that would operate and evaluate the effectiveness of these strategies. This complexity and the fractured nature of public cultural structure, provision and practice, combined with the definitional fluidity found at national level, is a major contributor to the lack of both policy cohesion in the field and integrated delivery on the ground.

In practice, there is little cohesion between these organizations or their initiatives such as cultural and museum hubs with the development of Cultural Quarters in similar urban locations, sometimes resulting in duplicated effort, which leads to additional public resources being spent on coordinating the inevitable chaos. This could be more effectively utilized in direct intervention to assist the growth of cultural businesses by establishing Cultural Quarters (Roodhouse 2004).

A useful point of departure for addressing this is the conventional view of culture, succinctly encapsulated in the Raymond Williams' (1981) definition, "a description of a particular way of life which expresses certain meanings and values not only in art and learning, but also in institutions and ordinary behaviour." He interprets culture in the widest sense, as an inclusive attitude consisting of structured and patterned ways of learning, and explains the artistic component of culture thus: "Individuals in groups—characteristically respond to and make meaningful the circumstances in which they are placed by virtue of their positions in society and in history" (12).

This definitional framework leads us into a wider understanding of our society; so, for example, Williams would recognize Britain's most popular tourist attraction, Blackpool Pleasure Beach, visited by over seven million people in 1998 and with more hotel beds than in all of Greece and its islands combined, as a cultural centre (Northwest Development Agency 1999). However, this cultural center would not be welcomed into the approved cultural family of the Arts Council of England or the MLA, although it would be, and is, seen as a significant component of the tourism industry.

Similarly, popular television programs such as *EastEnders* and *Coronation Street* are instantly recognized by social scientists, media academics, and others as a significant component of the cultural life of the United Kingdom. Notably, the Arts Council and the Film Council do not fund these activities or formally recognize them as a cultural component of equal status to the Royal Opera, not least because they are largely private-sector activities and "inartistic."

Manchester United Football Club with its fan culture is a United Kingdom and international cultural phenomenon that comfortably falls within Williams's definition. Manchester United is also a business quoted on the stock exchange, which does not receive public subsidy and is able to attract capacity audiences—a successful private-sector cultural organization.

In addition, Williams refers to values as an integral component of culture, and in this particular case he is referring to social values such as equality, individual, and religious freedom. However, little is said, for example, about the role of religion in cultural life, except when policy makers and administrators give consideration to equal opportunities and ethnicity. The arts, religion, and culture have been inextricably linked over centuries—during the Renaissance, to take an obvious example, and similarly in Muslim art and design traditions. The arts and heritage form an important component of this cultural definition.

However, it seems that debates over the last decade regarding expenditure of public funds in support of cultural activity and development have lacked coherence and ignored convergence, preferring departmentalization, with each discipline fighting for its particular corner, often based on a self-defining view of the cultural world. For example, the Museums Association in the United Kingdom has defined a *museum* as "an institution that collects, documents, preserves exhibits and interprets material evidence and associated information for the public benefit" (Museums Association *Bulletin*, 1996: 352). While this definition includes galleries, it excludes environmental heritage activity, botanical gardens, and aquaria.

What is interesting about these debates is the focused attention on particular arts and heritage constituencies at the expense of others, with little demonstrable interest in responding to and encouraging emerging and different traditions. Furthermore, increasingly over this period these arguments have not been concerned with either the intrinsic nature of the arts or those whom they benefit, as much as how they relate to the contemporary government policy of the time. So we find, for example, that in the United Kingdom during the 1940s and 1950s arts development was entirely devoted to the creation of arts centers in new towns, with the assumption that every town should have one (Roodhouse and Roodhouse 1997). It was also associated with the representation of Britain after the war and a celebration of the future.

Since the 1970s there has been little or no debate by administrators and policy makers about the purpose, value, and nature of the arts, but rather a focus of attention on how arts and heritage can meet national and local government policy in the areas of the economy, urban regeneration, regionalism, social cohesion, and community development, to name a few.

While this is laudable, we should be considering the importance of culture as a defining mechanism for communities such as Wolverhampton, Sheffield, and Bolton. In other words, I argue for coherence and convergence, the arts and heritage in culture, and culture as a manifestation of society; the "richness in diversity" concept. By taking this stance it is possible to incorporate the wider issues that concern society, such as the environment, employment, urban regeneration, social cohesion, safety, and community development, all of which directly influence a Cultural Quarter concept.

The other issue that complicates these debates—and again one that is rarely discussed in public—is how society decides what art is, including a shared view of aesthetics. In other words, many of the public agencies such as the Arts Councils are charged with promoting the arts as excellence, making excellent art accessible, and educating society in the excellence of the arts. While this may be admirable, it poses problems—such as, what constitutes excellence in the arts and heritage fields, who determines it, and using whose criteria? In other words, we have established a number of national and regional agencies that have implicitly been given by their remit the task of determining our corporate sense of aesthetic. It is within this context that questions of city regeneration, community, sustainability, the environment, and finance should be investigated. However, we need to commence by being clear about what it is we are sustaining and why.

The approach adopted here is to focus on the concept of the inherent creativity of the individual and cultural activity as business, leaving the determination of any corporate aesthetic to market interactions or public cultural agencies. Cultural Quarters then become the physical crucible for creative production and consumption.

This approach leads us to consider the emerging global interest in the creative and cultural industries as a significant economic development phenomenon, particularly for cities. It enables us not only to recognize the creative individual, but also to view cultural activity without the constraints of traditional frameworks, notions of excellence, and long standing, largely Victorian ideas of aesthetics (Florida 2002). The concept of cultural activity as business was derived from an interest in the knowledge economy and the definition employed is largely pragmatic: "Those activities which have their origin in individual creativity, skill and talent, and which have a potential for wealth and job creation through the generation and exploitation of intellectual property." The sectors that have been identified within this definitional framework are "advertising, architecture, the art and antiques market, crafts, design, designer fashion, film, interactive leisure software, music, the performing arts, publishing, software, television and radio" (Creative Industries Task Force 1998).[2]

It was the Labour-controlled Greater London Council (GLC) that instigated a significant challenge to the definitional status quo in the early 1980s, at a time of high unemployment, significant industrial decline, and diminishing public funds for the arts. These circumstances gave rise to a re-appraisal of the role and function of the "traditional" arts in economic terms and in relation to the introduction of new technologies such as instant printing, cassette recording, and video making (O'Connor 1999).

The concept of culture as an industry in a public policy context was introduced in this period. The arts, described by the GLC as the "traditional arts," were subsumed into a broader definitional framework which included "the electronic forms of cultural production and distribution— radio, television, records and video—and the diverse range of popular cultures which exist in London" (GLC Industry and Employment Branch 1985: 11). The eventual successor body, the London Assembly, and the executive Mayor of London, have picked up the theme again (London Development Agency 2003), with a focus on intervention in the creative industries' networks and linkages.

If consideration is then given to activities including the arts and heritage as businesses (the cultural industries) with products, services, and markets, then, for example, access questions are immediately answered. The judgment of excellence is simple (fitness for purpose) and funding becomes conventionally based on business planning models. So, the issue for public-sector policy and funding agencies responsible for implementation is more to do with how to support the establishment and growth of cultural businesses, as opposed to making aesthetic peer-group decisions about the quality of the individual's creative output (which is a subjective procedure).

Such an alternative perspective allows us to consider a more sustainable future for the arts and heritage as cultural businesses. Funding becomes based on a business model and, as a consequence, the cultural public-sector agency role changes to provide business support in developing this sector just like any other industrial economic activity. It leads to the suggestion that large businesses and the education sector take over the responsibility for research and development. In this way, government ensures that cultural risk and innovation are nurtured. No special pleading is required, and the art for art's sake argument (Jowell 2004) is avoided. A wider range of funding agencies with interests in social and economic development can become involved in supporting and developing the businesses.

We can then place our understanding of the creative industries in a wider definition of culture to encourage cohesion, access, participation, and ownership for the community. Culture as an all-embracing framework gives us a mechanism for making sense of our activities at a community, regional, and national level. A good example of this is the development of a cultural strategy in Rotherham, an old steel community in South Yorkshire, which defined culture as having a material dimension:

- The performing arts—music, drama, dance
- The visual arts—craft, sculpture, fashion
- Media, film, television, video, language
- Museums, artifacts, archives, design

- Libraries, literature, publishing, writing
- Combined arts and festivals
- The built heritage—architecture, landscape, urban parks

And a value dimension:

- Relationships and shared identity
- Shared memories and experiences
- Standards
- What we consider valuable to pass on to future generations. (Rother-ham Metropolitan Borough Council 2000)

It is obvious that a cultural definitional framework, encompassing far more than the traditional arts and heritages, facilitates engagement and interaction with many of the components such as the built environment, beliefs, play, and shared memories. A museum, as a focal point for reflection and interpretation of past cultural activities, becomes a sustainable project where public funding is clearly justified and is often the focal point in Cultural Quarter development. However, this should not prevent us from seeing that the combination of the arts and heritage as an integral component of the culture of a community, region, or nation, with the notion of culture as an industry, provides the most effective and powerful future strategy for all those engaged in such activities.

CULTURE AS A CREATIVE INDUSTRY OR CREATIVE INDUSTRY AS CULTURE?

Culture as an industry challenges the traditional large institutions that absorb the largest share of public funds. While they have an important role to play, such funding issues can be resolved by establishing these institutions as businesses, with public-sector money targeted at what is needed to "grow" the business. This approach, becoming more popular with the introduction of trusts and Public Private Partnerships (PPPs), can encourage the private sector (such as Blackpool Leisure Beach) to become involved in public-sector activity. In Sheffield, for example, in the late 1990s the council was having difficulty affording the operating costs of its museums, galleries, and libraries. This was largely due to a deficit created as a result of hosting the World Student Games, and it led to redundancies and reduced opening hours. The city placed the department in trust in 1998, retaining ownership of the estate, collections, and other assets, but with an independent management contracted to run the services for six years in return for a guaranteed grant income. Acting commercially to a business plan, the trust allowed the private-sector flexibility to operate the institutions as a business with the assurance of public-sector support.

Institutions such as these can be seen as creative businesses engaging with customers, developing markets and providing services and products that contribute to the development of local, national, and regional culture. This may require a re-examination of the role of local authorities or Arts Councils towards acting as contract and risk managers with a wider understanding of business development. However, such developments will not only limit public expenditure, but also provide more flexibility for the managers. Many local authorities see a long-term future for the cultural services and arts in contributing to regeneration, quality of life, social cohesion, and economic development.

If administrators and policy makers continue the static debate on public subsidies dedicated to the arts, the condition of our institutions will never improve. We now need to ensure that activities encompassed in a cultural framework such as Quarters are derived from the needs of communities and what they are prepared to pay for. Only by means of this approach can we address the issue of sustainability once and for all. Instead of asking how a particular institution or exhibition can be supported and seeking funding as required, it is possible to approach the issue from the opposite direction; we are an integral part of the culture in which we live and therefore it should be an everyday part of our personal or professional lives that we are engaged in environmental, social, or economic matters that reflect the cultural life of our town or city. Attracting funding therefore becomes less of an issue. This approach relies fundamentally on ensuring that the relationship between organizations and individuals in communities is strong and that the organizations reflect the needs, aspirations, and creative potential of the people of the town or region. The most effective way of delivering this organizational and individual interaction is to consider cultural activity as creative businesses, in fact as Cultural Quarters, which in order to survive have to identify and deliver products and services to markets and customers.

It is possible to place this emerging pattern of activity, the creative industries, in an even broader and more inclusive definitional framework than that referred to earlier, that of culture, to encourage cohesion, access, participation, and ownership. If we use culture as defined by Williams and subsequently built on by Pierre Bourdieu as the all-embracing framework for our activities, then we have a rational, strategic mechanism for making sense of our activities at community, regional, and national levels.

DEFINING CULTURAL QUARTERS AND
CULTURAL INDUSTRY QUARTERS

A useful definitional framework is informed by Montgomery (2003) and Bell and Jayne (2004). A Cultural Quarter is a geographical area of a large town or city that acts as a focus for cultural and artistic activities through the presence of a group of buildings devoted to housing a range of such activities and purpose designed or adapted spaces to create a sense of identity, providing an environment to facilitate and encourage the provision of cultural and artistic services and activities. However, a distinction can and should be made between a Cultural Quarter and a Cultural Industry Quarter. The latter is dedicated to cultural business development, for example, the Sheffield Cultural Industry Quarter, while the other serves to identify a geographical area in which cultural activity is encouraged to locate—a physically defined focal point for cultural activity, such as Wolverhampton Cultural Quarter.

A Cultural Quarter represents the coherence and convergence of the arts and heritage in culture, and culture as a manifestation of community. Cultural Quarters provide a context for planning and development powers to preserve and encourage cultural production and consumption as well as to physically regenerate a location. Up to the present time, Cultural Quarters have invariably developed from an existing embryonic cultural presence, as a result of a public-sector initiative. Cultural Quarters are often part of a larger strategy, integrating cultural and economic development, and usually linked to the regeneration of a selected urban area. A Cultural Quarter is a complex cluster of activities—networks embedded in a particular place.

A distinction needs to be made at this point between Cultural Quarters, Cultural Industry Quarters, and cultural iconographic regeneration, which include examples such as the new Royal Armouries in Leeds, the Tate Modern Cornwall, or the Baltic Contemporary Visual Arts Centre, Newcastle upon Tyne. Although these singular projects often provide a focus for regenerative activity, the distinctions lies in designation, a spatial area for a particular form of development.

The success of a Cultural or Cultural Industry Quarter can be measured in three dimensions: the activity (economic, cultural, and social), the form (the relationship between buildings and spaces) and the meaning (the sense of place, historical, and cultural), on which Montgomery (2003) elaborates.

Brooks and Kushner (4) share a similar definitional framework when quantifying Cultural Districts, the North American version of Cultural Quarters. They adopt a classificatory approach to Cultural District strategies to facilitate analysis, which involves:

- Administration (*delivery structure*): How does the institutional landscape change as a result of creating a Cultural District?
- Degree of public involvement (*funding and regulatory structures*): How is the government involved in the District?
- Degree of change in the cultural district (*spatial relationships refurbishment and new build*): How much physical change is evident in the District as a result of cultural designation?
- Programming (*cultural activity*): What is the content, centralized, or decentralized, programming of cultural activity?

If we use this framework as our main point of reference, it is apparent that the ingredients for a successful Quarter in Britain are similar to those in North America: spatial, planning, and construction issues, cultural activity, and delivery structures and identity. However, little reference is made in this model to the meaning of a Quarter, that is, a sense of place, the people's history and culture.

CRITICISMS OF CULTURAL QUARTERS

Critics of the Cultural Quarter approach to regeneration focus on the artificial planning and building development-led approach, suggesting that this has little to do with communities, their needs, or creative activity. The debate is often typified as a top-down versus bottom-up approach, or a directed versus collaborative approach. The collaborative approach engages communities to discover their needs and uses creative activity as a bottom-up means of developing Cultural Quarters, rather than the building-centered, directed, profit-oriented mechanism.

The Sheffield Creative Industries Quarter regeneration model commenced with creative individuals taking over a redundant building associated with the old cutlery industry in a derelict city-center area near the railway station and university, to provide a venue for popular music. As this became more successful, recording studios were established and more people moved into the area, including artists. For those involved in the early stages, the primary motivation was to meet their needs for a lively and cheap venue, somewhere convivial in which to play their kind of music. As has happened, in Sheffield and in many other cases, including the Manchester Cultural Quarter development, local authorities and other public agencies have progressively taken control, with the result that gentrification has crept in and creative individuals have moved out, often to another "poor" area because they cannot afford the rents or purchase price of accommodation. Sometimes, it is also concerned with a generation or cohort of creatives who enjoy being associated with one another, who want to locate and interact with one another, who eventually begin to fragment and follow their own personal and professional interests. This expulsion of the creative core is cited as a weakness of the structured approach to Cultural Quarter development.

The Custard Factory in Birmingham is a regeneration project that relied less on individual artists and more on a creative entrepreneur with vision and determination to succeed despite the odds to provide high quality facilities at competitive prices for creative businesses. The individual entrepreneur model does not fit comfortably into a planned public sector-led system with the associated regulatory requirements, procedures, and collective decision-making processes.

Finding cheap places to live and work provided the driver for the artist-led Newcastle studio development, and triggered in the 1970s and 80s artist-owned studio cooperatives such as SPACE and ACME. A London-based charity established in 1972, ACME is the largest artist-support agency in the United Kingdom, with over 380 studios, 25 units of living accommodation, and 4,000 artists involved. Yorkshire Arts Space Society, part of the Sheffield Creative Industries Quarter, performs a similar function.

THE INGREDIENTS FOR A SUCCESSFUL CULTURAL QUARTER

John Montgomery (2003) points out that Cultural Quarters are not new, and cites the examples of the Left Bank in Paris, the Lower East Side in New York, and Soho in London. Similarly, Brown, O'Connor and Cohen (2000) suggest that the models we consider are derived from the North American experience of the urban village and the British industrial district model, based on pre-Fordist economies of small and medium-sized enterprises clustering around complementary skills and services, both competing and collaborating at the same time. Science and business parks are a typical example of this approach and proved popular in the 1980s. It is suggested that

> [q]uarters are complex clusters of activities—they are networks embedded in a particular place . . . The complex networks of activity and exchange are given the context—they take place. This place acquired is a series of associations which can be iconic, but are also spatially embedded social networks. . . . (Brown, O'Connor, Cohen, 2000: 446).

Montgomery (2003) describes Cultural Quarters from an urban-planning perspective as "[t]he use of planning and development powers to both preserve and encourage both cultural production and consumption. [. . .] Cultural Quarters tend to combine strategies for greater consumption of the arts and culture with cultural production and urban place making" (3). Canter provides a useful description of the necessary characteristics of all successful urban places as "activity"—economic, cultural, and social; "form"—the relationship between buildings and spaces; and "meaning"—sense of place, historical, and cultural (130). There is a suggestion that it is possible within this framework to establish indicators that can be used to assess the relative success of Cultural Quarters—place characteristics. These are

Activity:

- diversity of primary and secondary uses;
- extent and variety of cultural venues and events;
- presence of an evening economy, including cafe culture;

- strength of small-firm economy, including creative businesses; and
- access to education providers.

Form:

- fine-grain urban morphology,
- variety and adaptability of building stock,
- permeability of streetscape,
- legibility,
- amount and quality of public space, and
- active frontages.

Meaning:

- important meeting and gathering spaces,
- sense of history and progress,
- area identity and imagery,
- knowledge ability, and
- design appreciation and style.

Cultural or Cultural Industry Quarters are emerging internationally as a democratic and effective sustainable model that is less dependent upon the conventional and traditional public cultural agency structure and more on the local, social, economic, and cultural community need—identity. It is less about determining what is "good art" and more about creative business in the community—a recognized and identified marketplace.

Bell and Jayne have helpfully echoed the principles and realities of Cultural Quarters by suggesting that

> these encompass aesthetic improvements of soft infrastructure, ranging from the building of squares, the provision of benches and fountains to the greening of streets and improved public spaces, the establishment of late-night shopping and 'happy hours', and cultural events and festivals. Augmenting this has been the support and promotion of creative and cultural industries. [. . .] With buildings and facilities such as museums, art galleries and arts centres, theatres, convention and exhibition centres, as well as a supporting cast of restaurants, café bars, delicatessens, fashion boutiques and other cultural facilities the buzz of 'creativity, innovation and entrepreneurialism' brought about by the clustering of these activities in certain areas of the city centre is seen as crucial to contributing to the competitiveness of cities (3).

However, this approach to cultural regeneration and development tends to focus attention on one physical area at the expense of others and ultimately drives rents up and creative businesses out. There is a continual danger of gentrification and a subsequent loss of the creative nucleus or life of the Quarter. Sometimes, the Quarter development fails to act as hub for other cultural or related activities, as Sheffield illustrates, or attracts the "wrong culture," such as the stag- and hen nights in Temple Bar, Dublin.

CRITICAL SUCCESS FACTORS

General critical success factors have been derived from studies of Cultural Quarters. The principles to be applied to the design and delivery of these models can act as a general guide for those planning to engage in establishing a Quarter, and provide a useful set of initial performance criteria. These include generation of jobs and graduate retention; variable rental levels to meet differing needs; the strengthening of small-firm economy, including creative business and infrastructure; and old and contemporary architectural juxtaposition and an environmentally responsive approach.

The key success factor is consultation with stakeholders. This is essential when local authorities are involved and provides a means of encouraging genuine ownership of the project. The alternative is the cultural entrepreneur model, when an individual provides vision, energy, and drive to establish the project. Inevitably, there are risks in all cases, and these need to be understood and addressed in any attempt at developing a Quarter.

Cultural Quarter principles have been practiced and risks addressed using a spectrum of management vehicles, all of which require a differing public and private-funding package mix, from the almost entirely state model of Vienna MuseumsQuartier to Dublin's private-sector influenced Temple Bar project. The concept is now an integral component of regeneration strategies in the United Kingdom and internationally, increasingly contributing to the emerging global knowledge economy, including the creative industries. However, in any venture focused on culture, at the end of the day success comes down to creative people being given a chance to make a sustained social and economic contribution to their communities.

"Creative people, in turn, don't just cluster where the jobs are. They cluster in places that are centres of creativity and also where they [can afford and] like to live" (Florida 2002: 232). Perhaps this is the most important issue in city Cultural Quarter branding, and so the point of discussion on which to conclude. There is evidence that creative people do indeed cluster in centers of creativity and often initiate the cluster, particularly where rental levels are low and open working space is available. A good example of this is the early stages of development in East London around the Docklands area, when artists' cooperatives such as Space and ACME took over disused warehouses and converted them into studios. However, developments like this do not last long; as was pointed out earlier, with greater visibility comes gentrification. Creative people cannot afford the rental levels and move out to other peripheral areas, professional people and private-sector operators fill the vacuum. It should also be remembered that, quite often, Cultural Quarters are not "greenfield sites"; rather, businesses such as shops, small cafés, hairdressers, repair businesses, and automobile sales and repairs are already located in the specified and branded area. It is often the creatives who are the initial outsiders and, by their actions, that the nature of the place is changed, often to the detriment of these earlier inhabitants. These "outsiders" are often graduates, who wish to stay together in the locality. As a result, the local university not only acts as a catalyst for the physical development of the Cultural Quarter in the city, but also supplies the creatives, its graduates. The mix of existing inhabitants and their businesses, young creatives, history, geography, architecture, design, and the ethnic mix of the place (activity, form, and meaning) provide the uniqueness that makes for a successful branded city space, a Cultural Quarter.

NOTES

1. Sections of this chapter were first presented as "Creating Sustainable Cultures" at the culture@com.unit: the arts and cultural domain in New South Wales Conference, Oct. 5–6, 2001.
2. See <http://www.culture.gov.uk/creative.industries> (accessed Mar. 18, 2008).

Part II

Idea of the City

Cinematic Futures and the Grounds of the Present

7 London Undead

Screening/Branding the Empty City[1]

Christoph Lindner

> The true identity of London is in its absence. As a city, it no longer exists. In this alone it is truly modern. London was the first metropolis to disappear.
>
> —Patrick Keiller (writer and director, *London*, 1994)

> A particularly favourable condition for awakening uncanny feelings is created when there is intellectual uncertainty whether an object is alive or not, and when an inanimate object becomes too much like an animate one.
>
> —Sigmund Freud ("The 'Uncanny,'" 1919/1997)

DESERTED CITIES

This chapter considers the representation of empty urban space in contemporary British cinema. Focusing on London, I am interested in the way Danny Boyle's zombie-horror film, *28 Days Later* (2002), employs postapocalyptic panoramas of deserted cityscapes that reinforce an iconic image of the city. My argument is that, despite its deeply uncanny properties, the film's vision of an undead metropolis nonetheless plays to the aesthetic and commercial needs of the tourist and city-branding industries. To develop this line of thought, I want to begin by placing the motif of the empty city in the broader context of cinema culture, before addressing how *28 Days Later* extends in innovative ways the sort of urban emptiness envisioned by lavish Hollywood productions such as *Vanilla Sky* (Cameron Crowe, 2001). Seeking to show how such re-imaginings of the city have been an enduring cultural fantasy since the rise of capitalist urbanization, the discussion then draws on Michel de Certeau's thinking on the erotics of high-rise voyeurism to explore resonances between Boyle's cinematic cityscape and two very different, yet interconnected, urban texts. The first is William Wordsworth's London sonnet "Composed upon Westminster Bridge" (1807), one of the first great cityscape poems of urban modernity. The second is the revolving spectacle of the London Eye, the massive Ferris wheel installed on the South Bank of the Thames and initially conceived as a temporary riverside amusement for the capital's millennial celebrations.

URBAN UNCANNY

Images of empty—or deserted—cityscapes have been a recurring motif of the urban uncanny in film from the silent era onwards. Most notably, *Metropolis* (Fritz Lang, 1927) contains a number of slow panning shots of a dehumanized, mechanical city virtually devoid of motion and life. In this dystopian, futuristic cityscape, partly conceived as a warning against the geometric tyranny of modernist urban design, the human population is reduced to invisibility and insignificance in the face of the autonomous urban machine. Lang's vision of a monstrous city of the future was partly inspired, or so the publicity myth goes, by his first encounter in 1924 with the sky-scraping architecture of Manhattan (Elsaesser 9). It is interesting that, in his fantastical cinematic re-imagining of the skyscraper city, Lang relied on the distancing, depopulating perspective of the high-rise view to gain a visual purchase on the modern metropolis, since the same observational technique was also used by many documentary and avant-garde filmmakers of the 1920s concerned with recording the sprawl and spectacle of vertical New York.

Among New York films produced in this period, *Manhatta* (Charles Sheeler and Paul Strand, 1920), which derives its inspiration and structure from Walt Whitman's *Leaves of Grass* (1855), stands out for its vision of an unhomely city, polarized between majestic, vertiginous heights and gloomy, subhuman depths. Crucially, as it goes about chronicling a day in the life of New York, Sheeler and Strand's six-minute experimental reel repeatedly employs static views of deserted cityscapes in order to capture what they saw as the inherently photographic nature of this paradigmatically modern city. Here, in what quickly becomes a repeated pattern in urban cinema, the motif of the empty city is used to immobilize the urban frenzy and scrutinize it in stasis.

As such aesthetic indulgences suggest images of empty city space have long been a source of visual fascination in films concerned with interpreting the unhomeliness of the city. From *Manhatta* to *Metropolis* and beyond, these images have also had a profound and lasting impact on the "urban imaginary"—what is best understood in Edward Soja's (2000) terms as "the mental or cognitive mappings of urban reality and the interpretive grids through which we think about, experience, evaluate, and decide to act in the places, spaces, and communities in which we live" (324).

A particularly striking example of how this impact on the urban imaginary registers in contemporary film can be found in *Vanilla Sky*, an urban nightmare narrative that prefigures *28 Days Later* in important ways. An American remake of the Spanish film *Abre los Ojos* (Alejandro

Amenàbar 1997), *Vanilla Sky* follows the psychological breakdown of multimillionaire David Aames (Tom Cruise), who becomes lost in a computer-generated dreamworld that allows him to escape the ugliness of his reality. The film opens with a key scene in which Aames drives his vintage black Ferrari into New York's Times Square during what should be the morning rush hour. Strangely, impossibly, Times Square is completely empty: no people, no traffic, no life. Aames then exits his car and proceeds to run—panicked yet elated—down the middle of the street, finally stopping in the center of Times Square to raise his arms towards the sky and release a wordless scream at the surrounding neon lights and advertising billboards. At this point in the film, there is no explanation for the emptiness, although the experience is later revealed to be a dream within a dream.

The opening of *Vanilla Sky* is significant for several reasons, and all of them relate to the scene's uncanny properties—to the way that it defamiliarizes Times Square. First, from a production point of view, the scene is remarkable because it does not use computer-generated imagery to create the visual effect of emptiness. Cameron Crowe's production team managed to secure permission from the Mayor's Office of Film, Theater, and Broadcasting to close Times Square at four o'clock on a Sunday morning in order to shoot the scene, something that had never been done before on such a large scale. This means that what we see in the opening of *Vanilla Sky* are real images of deserted city space. Yet at the same time, since these images are impossible to experience in any conventional reality, the scene still looks and feels deeply unreal.

The reason for this sense of unreality is, of course, that an integral part of what defines Times Square is conspicuously missing from this scene: the never-ending chaos of crowds and traffic is inexplicably absent. At the same time, however, the visual pandemonium of the enormous electronic screens and neon advertising billboards—which is another defining element of Times Square—remains present, offering the only busyness and movement in the scene apart from Aames' frantic running. The implication is that the automated consumer spectacle is not only the most important feature of this urban space, but has also acquired a strange, autonomous life of its own, operating and thriving independently of the city's human involvement.

Vanilla Sky enacts a particular urban fantasy that derives from Times Square's status not only as a global icon of tourism, but also as one of the most commercialized and hypermediated public spaces in the world today. It is, above all, a fantasy of escape and release: escape from the urban crowd and release from the spatial confinements of everyday urban life. In other words, what Aames experiences is the freedom to move alone and unobstructed through the ultimate site of urban congestion and consumer spectacle. The effect is a double sense of exhilaration and anxiety produced by the impossible, disorienting experience of consuming Times Square—and being consumed by Times Square—in total solitude.

UNDEAD CITIES

In his 1919 essay on the uncanny, Freud finds that the *unheimlich* (literally, the unhomely) is "in reality nothing new or alien, but something which is familiar and old-established in the mind and which has become alienated" (Freud 217). He further suggests that one of the most powerful sources of the uncanny is uncertainty about whether something is alive or dead, so that things which occupy the indeterminate space between life and death possess tremendous power to unnerve. For Freud, this is why "many people experience [the uncanny] in the highest degree in relation to death and dead bodies, to the return of the dead, and to spirits and ghosts" (218). The images of empty city space in *Vanilla Sky* occupy precisely this liminal space of the undead. Through their manipulation of a deeply familiar view of the cosmopolitan city, they become caught ambiguously between absence and presence, between motion and stasis, and between the spectral and the spectacular. This, of course, is the entire point of the scene. Crowe uses images of empty city space in order to create a disorienting encounter with the familiar rendered strange and alien. It is an experience of wonder and unease that prepares the spectator for the unhinged nature of reality within the world of the film.

These representational strategies are what link New York and *Vanilla Sky* to London and *28 Days Later*, in which images of empty city space are similarly used not simply to defamiliarize and unnerve, but, in the process, to establish the crisis of reality underpinning the premise of the film. An important difference between the two films, however, is that *28 Days Later* takes the idea of an undead metropolis to conceptual and visual extremes. Moreover, as a zombie film, it is concerned quite literally with the undead.

Written by Alex Garland and directed by Boyle, who formerly collaborated on the screen adaptation of Garland's novel *The Beach* (1997), *28 Days Later* is the product of a creative partnership between two prominent countercultural British voices. Retaining something of the nihilism of Boyle's *Trainspotting* (1996) and the social cynicism of *The Beach*, the film's re-interpretation of the zombie-horror genre, which builds on earlier classics like *Omega Man* (Boris Sagal 1971) and *Rabid* (David Cronenberg 1977), uses the trope of the living dead in order to comment on the self-destructive potential of a society consumed by rage and paranoia. In so doing, *28 Days Later* takes obvious pleasure in imagining and presenting its postapocalyptic fantasy.

The film's savoring of the aesthetics of urban disaster is most pronounced in the opening scenes, beginning when the character of Jim (Cillian Murphy) wakes up in a deserted London hospital after spending twenty-eight days in a coma. He leaves the hospital and soon discovers that all the surrounding streets and buildings have been abandoned as well. The explanation, which he only learns later in the film, is that a lethal virus released from a research facility has swept across the country while he was comatose, turning most of the human population into enraged, homicidal zombies who have either killed or infected almost everybody. Only a handful of survivors remain. The opening scenes of the film track Jim's wanderings through the empty city, effectively creating a montage of deserted London landmarks that begins with a panoramic shot of Westminster Bridge (Figure 7.1) and ends with a close-up of Piccadilly Circus. Throughout, London remains completely empty.

As with Crowe's treatment of Times Square, my interest in Boyle's cinematic vision of the city derives from its uncanniness—from what Nicholas Royle (2003), adapting Freud, describes in terms of "a peculiar commingling of the familiar and the unfamiliar" resulting in "a sense of homeliness uprooted" (1). First, it is worth noting that, from a production point of view, the empty London scene from *28 Days Later* is even more remarkable than the empty Times Square scene in *Vanilla Sky*, since here as well no computer-generated images were used to create the visual effect of emptiness. And yet, the scene covers a significantly larger geographic area of the city. Shot throughout central London during the early morning hours,

Figure 7.1 Westminster Bridge, from *28 Days Later* (Danny Boyle, United Kingdom, 2002), © 20th Century Fox/Photofest.

what the viewer sees are real images of empty city space. Collected into one continuous sequence in the film, however, those images clearly belong to the realm of the impossible.

Significant here is that, unlike Crowe in *Vanilla Sky*, Boyle uses far more than just one isolated space to envision a fantasy of urban emptiness. Roaming throughout London, he shows a series of deserted city spaces, ranging from Westminster Bridge, the Houses of Parliament, and Downing Street, to Whitehall, Horse Guards Parade, and Piccadilly Circus (London's Victorian precursor of Times Square). Moreover, the images of these urban landmarks are interspersed with sweeping panoramas of a completely depopulated, motionless city in which even more London icons are showcased, including St Paul's Cathedral, Oxford Street, and—most notably—the London Eye, whose incongruous circular form reappears in the background of several shots. There is also a brief intertextual moment in which the camera shoots the area around the Bank of England from the elevated point of view of a roof-top figurine, subtly evoking the bird's-eye Berlin of the angel voyeur in *Wings of Desire* (Wim Wender 1987).

The full effect of Boyle's treatment of London is that the sense of dislocation and unreality encountered in *Vanilla Sky* is even more pronounced in this extended vision of the deserted city. It is a vision, in other words, that occupies in an even more ambivalent way the indeterminate space of the uncanny. After all, the purpose of the empty London sequence in *28 Days Later* is to create uncertainty as to whether the city is alive or dead, and in the process to locate it somewhere between these two conditions. The deadness of London is suggested by the absence of people and traffic, elements that normally animate the space of cities. Its deadness is also suggested by the residual signs of abandonment and violence: trash and tourist trinkets littered through the streets, looted shops and businesses, luxury cars deserted in the middle of intersections, paper money scattered on the pavement. Perhaps the most poignant image of abandonment and violence comes in the form of an overturned, smashed-up London bus. In the wake of the 2005 London Transport bombings, this film image has acquired a new, heightened significance, particularly in the disturbing way that it both prefigures and resembles the real images of the bus wreckage in Tavistock Square, which were broadcast and printed in news media around the world.

Despite the overwhelming sense of death and stillness, Boyle's empty London also contains a few moments of movement and sound that gesture towards life. The river gently flows beneath Westminster Bridge. A car alarm suddenly activates on its own. A Benetton billboard shows the fetishized image of smiling yuppies frolicking in brightly colored clothes. And there are the slow shuffle and occasional shouts of the film's lone pedestrian, Jim, searching for other human life. But these fleeting moments of real and illusory animation only reinforce the larger sense of emptiness and stasis dominating the film's vision of London—a vision that despite the many unsettling and disorienting visual elements, nonetheless presents a serene and sublime sight for the accidental tourist.

In creating such a tension between the urban sublime and the urban uncanny, the undead metropolis of *28 Days Later* is very much in tune with the aesthetic and commercial needs of London's tourist and city-branding industries. This, moreover, is not despite the way the film produces an effect of estrangement. It is actually because of the effect of estrangement. In other words, *28 Days Later* offers another version of the voyeuristic fantasy explored in *Vanilla Sky*—a fantasy that is linked to the iconography of urban tourism, and involves the impossible pleasure of consuming the city in perfect solitude. To develop this idea further, as well as to bring it around to the topic of urban branding and the London Eye, which is the final destination of this chapter, I need to make a short detour via the urban musings of Michel de Certeau and William Wordsworth.

WESTMINSTER BRIDGE AND THE TWIN TOWERS

In *The Practice of Everyday Life*, de Certeau famously talks about his experience of visiting the observation deck of the World Trade Center in New York in the late 1970s. Looking out over Manhattan from the summit of a skyscraper, he finds himself "transfigured into a voyeur" (de Certeau 92). In his description of the "voluptuous pleasure [of] seeing the whole," the gigantic undulating parts of the city become immobilized into a unified, graspable image:

> Seeing Manhattan from the 110th floor of the World Trade Center. Beneath the haze stirred up by the winds, the urban island, a sea in the middle of the sea, lifts up the skyscrapers over Wall Street, sinks down at Greenwich, then rises again to the crests of Midtown, quietly passing over Central Park and finally undulates off into the distance of Harlem. A wave of verticals. Its agitation is momentarily arrested by vision. The gigantic mass is immobilized before the eyes. [. . .] To be lifted to the summit of the World Trade Center is to be lifted out of the city's grasp. [. . .] It transforms the bewitching world by which one was "possessed" into a text that lies before one's eyes. It allows one to read it, to be a solar Eye, looking down like a god. [. . .] The 1370-foot high tower that serves as a prow for Manhattan continues to construct the fiction that creates readers, makes the complexity of the city readable, and immobilizes its opaque mobility in a transparent text. (91–92)

De Certeau's urban panorama is marked by several distinctive features. Not least among these is the perception of the rigid geometry of New York's skyline in terms of motion and fluidity. Another distinctive feature of this aerial view is that the sense of mobility is simultaneously countered by an effect of immobilization. This frozen, long-distance image of the city is what de Certeau goes on to contrast with the chaos and confinement of the city street: the space and level of everyday life. For de Certeau, the pleasure of high-rise voyeurism lies precisely in the liberation it offers from the quasi-illegible mess of the street, a liberation made possible by the distancing, estranging perspective of the high-rise view.

It is questionable whether such an extreme spatial dichotomy between the vertical and horizontal axes of the city actually holds up under closer scrutiny. In particular, I disagree with de Certeau that the high-rise view offers anything remotely approaching a totalizing image of the city, even if that image does represent, as de Certeau is careful to stress, only an "imaginary totalization" (93). Setting aside this point of contention, however, I do want to draw on de Certeau's broader idea that the high-rise view produces a depopulated and immobilizing image of the city, frozen in a state of suspended animation, caught somewhere between the living and the dead. For what the viewer encounters in the empty London of *28 Days Later*, and in a more limited way in the empty Times Square of *Vanilla Sky,* is the visual experience of high-rise voyeurism brought down—complete with all its deadening, distancing effects—to the level and space of the city street. Here, as in de Certeau's narrative of scopic pleasure, the result is not only deeply unnerving, it is also aesthetically appealing.

The strange and borderline-morbid aesthetic draw of the empty city is something that the British Romantic poet William Wordsworth understood and exploited to artistic ends a full two-hundred years before Crowe and Boyle. In his sonnet of urban epiphany, "Composed upon Westminster Bridge, Sept. 3, 1802," Wordsworth attempts to capture the sublime and uncanny appearance of London's slumbering form in the early morning hours. To achieve this aim he relies on the panoptic perspective of the cityscape view, offering a vision of London that bears certain similarities to the deserted metropolis of *28 Days Later*.

More interesting, Wordsworth observes the city from the exact perspective that comes to dominate its pictorial representation in both high art and tourist ephemera in the centuries that follow. In what becomes a prevalent city view from the turn of the nineteenth century onwards, London is seen from Westminster Bridge looking north across the Thames towards Parliament, the City, and St Paul's. In other words, Wordsworth sees the city from almost the exact location and perspective as the opening shot of the empty London sequence in *28 Days Later*. And while the view of his poem has yet to include either the 1840s neo-gothic excess of the rebuilt Parliament buildings or the grandiose architectural folly of the London Eye—both of which feature prominently in Boyle's cinematic cityscape—it does nonetheless contain the underlying shape and structure of London's postmillennial riverside skyline:

Earth has not any thing to show more fair:
Dull would he be of soul who could pass by
A sight so touching in its majesty:
This City now doth like a garment, wear
The beauty of the morning; silent, bare,
Ships, towers, domes, theatres, and temples lie
Open unto the fields, and to the sky;
All bright and glittering in the smokeless air.
Never did sun more beautifully steep
In his first splendour, valley, rock, or hill;
Ne'er saw I, never felt, a calm so deep!
The river glideth at his own sweet will:
Dear God! the very houses seem asleep;
And all that mighty heart is lying still!
(W. Wordsworth, 1807, 118)

Wordsworth may be writing about the proto-modern London of 1802, but he could just as easily be describing Boyle's postapocalyptic London of 2002. The poem itself was inspired by a chance visual encounter with the sleeping city during an early morning stagecoach ride. Crossing Westminster Bridge on his way to Dover, Wordsworth happened to glance back at the London riverfront from the roof of the coach and was struck by the splendor of the silent city in the unusually clear air (Barker 2000: 301).

Dorothy Wordsworth (2002), who accompanied her brother on the trip, vividly recalls the scene in her journal:

> It was a beautiful morning. The City, St Paul's, with the River & a multitude of little Boats, made a most beautiful sight as we crossed Westminster Bridge. The houses were not overhung by their cloud of smoke & they were spread out endlessly, yet the sun shone so brightly with such a pure light that there was even something like the purity of one of nature's own grand Spectacles. (123)

This journal entry is important not just because it offers a prose counterpoint to her brother's poem, but also because there is evidence to suggest that he may have relied on details from her description to reconstruct the empty London of his sonnet (Reed 188). Whatever Wordsworth's artistic debt to his sister (and this would not have been the first time he depended on her keen observational eye to strengthen his writing), both the poem and the journal entry see the aesthetic marvel of the sleeping city in almost identical terms as a spectacle of nature, not of the city. Indeed, what enables the ungainly urban sprawl to be transformed into a placid natural landscape in the imagination of both observers is precisely the absence of the city's human population and, through this absence, all other signs of urban life, including the blanket of smoke normally smothering the daytime London of the early 1800s.

An even more striking parallel between Wordsworth's poem and Boyle's film, however, is that both present London explicitly in terms of undeath. In Wordsworth's writing, the city is anthropomorphized and brought to life only to stress its paradoxical look of lifelessness. Like de Certeau's vertical New York, Wordsworth's horizontal London is depopulated and immobilized by the voyeuristic urban gaze. Even the city's heart has ceased to beat, as if the whole of London were momentarily caught in a state of suspended animation. Here, as in *28 Days Later*, a tension is created by the anticipation of the deadened metropolitan body coming back to life. The point of Wordsworth's uncanny urban vision, moreover, is essentially the same: to make us see the everyday metropolis in an unusual, defamiliarized way. In this case, Wordsworth seeks to capture an aesthetic wonder available only to the solitary onlooker and visible only in that ephemeral, early morning moment just before the city wakes up and starts the working day.

As it happens, to capture the twenty-first century city looking similarly motionless and deserted, Boyle shot most of his film's empty London sequence (including the Westminster Bridge scene) during the same short interval between dawn and the start of the morning commute—that other source of the urban uncanny famously described by T. S. Eliot in *The Waste Land* (1922/1961) as a spectacle of the undead: "A crowd flowed over London Bridge, so many / I had not thought death had undone so many" (43). Undead cities may be a recurring aesthetic concern in modern and contemporary film but, as Wordsworth's lifeless metropolis and Eliot's zombie commuterscape suggest, it is a concern that also preoccupies cultural production in other fields, and that belongs to a long line of critique aimed at addressing the nature of urban life and extending back well beyond the relatively short-lived moment of modernism to the rise of capitalist urbanization in the late eighteenth and early nineteenth centuries.

LONDON EYES

To bring my discussion more fully into dialogue with this book's overarching concern with urban branding, I want to consider next how the undead London of Wordsworth's poetry and, in a more indirect way, the undead London of Boyle's film have recently been co-opted by the city's tourist industry, contributing to the emergence of a particular branded image of London. The site of this urban branding is the London Eye, one of the city's newest and most popular tourist attractions, and arguably an iconic centerpiece of the capital's postmillennial skyline. In fact, the prominence of the Millennium Wheel (as it is also known) in London's contemporary urban imaginary is graphically registered in *28 Days Later*, where its ghostly silhouette haunts the background of almost every panoramic shot, as if to suggest that the entire city is subject to the prying gaze of this giant revolving eye.

For instance, the film contains a long still shot of Horse Guards Parade, in which the London Eye ominously overtowers the squat government buildings, creating the impression that the oversized observation wheel, the largest in the world at the time of its construction, has placed the capital under aerial surveillance. The Eye later reappears in a wide-angle shot of Tottenham Court Road, effectively highlighting its seeming omnipresence within the city. Finally, of course, the Eye dominates the film's riverfront panoramas, where its towering vertical mass, facing out towards the North Bank, overshadows the seat of British government. The care Boyle takes to include the London Eye in so many different shots of the city comments on more than the hypervisibility of this distinctive urban landmark. It also evokes the Eye's visual perspective on the city, implicitly connecting the high-rise experience produced by the wheel to the film's undead rendering of the city.

One of the most intriguing aspects of the London Eye experience, however, is not the aerial view itself but, rather, the way visitors are ideologically primed for this view by being ushered past the text of Wordsworth's cityscape poem, which has been monumentalized in large stainless steel letters near the entrance to the wheel (Figure 7.2). The idea is not just to give the Eye added significance by linking it to London's cultural heritage and the creative product of a treasured national icon. The poem also invites visitors to see the city from the Eye in precisely Wordsworth's undead terms—as the sort of strangely empty, still, and silent metropolis also envisioned by Boyle in *28 Days Later*.

In this respect, the London Eye actively promotes a similar fantasy of urban voyeurism and escape in which the individual is unhinged from the everyday space and experience of the city. As with the Twin Towers in de Certeau's thinking, the wheel offers an overview through which spectators, sealed within their air-conditioned observation capsules, become temporarily empowered with a panoptic aerial gaze. Seen from 135 meters above the ground, the sprawling mass of London is immobilized, distanced, and defamiliarized.

The Eye's press office describes the effect as "a new and exciting perspective on the city" that also introduces "a new [. . .] sense of calm into the chaos of the city" (London Eye Press Pack 3). Presumably attempting to illustrate this strange dynamic between stimulation and pacification, the Eye's 2007 press pack includes a series of panoramic photographs of London, showing daytime views from the top of the wheel in all four compass-point directions. More interesting, the serial presentation and letter-box shape of these photographs are strongly reminiscent of film stills, almost as if to suggest that they represent the proto-cinematic flickerings of a screened event. In turn, the images themselves, showing vast, depopulated

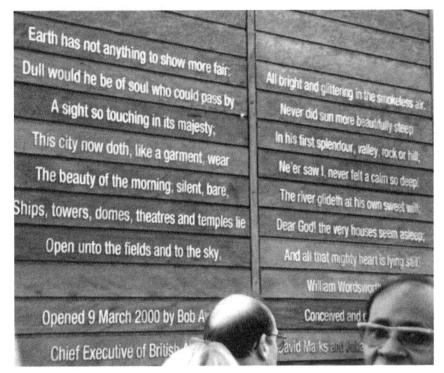

Figure 7.2 Wordsworth inscription at the London Eye, 2005, courtesy Sheldon Wood.

urban vistas of central London, could easily be inserted directly into Boyle's empty-city montage in *28 Days Later* without looking out of place.

These resonances between the city views of *28 Days Later* and the London Eye are not entirely coincidental. After all, as we have seen, Boyle repeatedly evokes the Eye's visual perspective on the city in the framing and composition of his deserted cityscapes. In other words, he clearly has the view from the Eye in mind while filming London. This makes sense if we consider that, as in the opening of Boyle's film, the main objective of the London Eye is to engineer a visual encounter with the urban uncanny—with the everyday city made newly strange. When it comes to high-rise voyeurism, however, the Eye is hardly exceptional in this respect. In fact, as Mark Dorrian (2006) has argued, generating such forms of sensory disorientation and exhilaration has been the guiding principal of all the "iconic ascensional apparatuses of modernity," including the original Ferris wheel inaugurated at the World's Columbian Exposition in Chicago in 1893 (19). What is perhaps less conventional about the Eye is that, by placing Wordsworth's poem at the entrance to the ride, the operators are publicly asserting in a self-conscious and intertextual way that, despite its uncanny properties, the empty city produced by the wheel's orbital experience should be seen and savored as an aesthetic marvel: "a sight so touching in its majesty [that] Earth has not anything to show more fair" (W. Wordsworth 118).

The way in which the London Eye composes and disseminates its over-view of the city becomes even more significant if we consider that the tour-ist attraction opened under the corporate sponsorship of British Airways (BA). In fact, the full, official name of the attraction is the BA London Eye. To reinforce this link between the airline and the wheel, visitors are explicitly encouraged to think of their ride as a BA flight. In the promo-tional discourse of the Eye, visitors become "passengers" who "check in" for "flights.". Further paralleling contemporary airline practices, London Eye passengers are also instructed that, in view of heightened security, a minimum of carry-on "luggage" will be allowed on board flights.

The consequence of British Airways' involvement with the Millennium Wheel is that this corporate giant of pan-global aviation has branded much more than a tourist attraction. Both the wheel's high-rise view and—more important—the way of looking at that view are branded as well. This idea is overtly articulated by the London Eye's distinctly cosmopolitan advertis-ing slogan: "The way the world sees London." It is a slogan that stresses British Airways' proprietary claim over not only the view *of* the wheel, but also the view *from* the wheel. More to the point, if the slogan is right that the London Eye represents the way the world sees London—and this is becoming increasingly true in both real and symbolic ways—then the com-mercialized panopticism of this massive mechanical wheel is in fact produc-ing the dominant globalized image of the city. Although British Airways is unlikely to see it in these terms, it is a branded image characterized by the fundamentally uncanny nature of its urban aesthetic.

In 2006, British Airways sold its shareholdings in the London Eye Com-pany to the Tussauds Group, a prominent purveyor of mass tourism in the United Kingdom, whose corporate identity is rooted in London's original waxworks museum. Although the airline still maintains its brand involve-ment and corporate sponsorship, Tussauds is now entirely responsible for day-to-day operations. Given the Eye's urban aesthetic, it is somehow quite fitting, and not a little ironic, that the tourist attraction has come under the management of a leisure and entertainment company made famous—through the uncanny likenesses of its celebrity wax doppelgangers—by staging sensational encounters with the undead.

The broader implication is that the mass appeal of the London Eye and the astonishing speed with which it has become an established urban icon suggest that an important part of what we seek in the cosmopolitan space of cities is precisely the defamiliarizing visual experience described in Word-sworth's poem and later re-imagined in Boyle's film. Whether produced through film, literature, or even the urban spectaculars of mass tourism, the voyeuristic fantasy of the empty city exerts a powerful hold over the cultural imagination. It is a fascination derived not only from the oddly compelling experience of estrangement, but also from the perception of beauty involved in that aesthetic encounter. For what is ultimately shared by the undead London of Danny Boyle, William Wordsworth, and the London Eye is a strange yet beautiful vision of the everyday metropolis caught between the living and the dead.

NOTES

1. Parts of this chapter draw on research carried out while on a British Academy grant at the New York Public Library, and I would like to thank the British Academy and the NYPL staff for their support. My thanks as well to Elizabeth Bowman for her excellent research assistance and to Sharon Baker and Mark Russell for insights into London's geography.

8 Branding the Modernist Metropolis

The Eternal City and the City of Lights in Cinema after World War II

Mark Shiel

In this essay I explore the ways in which certain practitioners of European art cinema interrogated the branding of cities by government and big business in the three decades after World War II. I focus on the representation of Rome by Roberto Rossellini in the late 1940s and of Paris by Bernardo Bertolucci in the early 1970s, with an emphasis on what I see as their shared modernist skepticism of the branding of the city as an easily consumable visual object and their rejection of its governmental or capitalist significations in favor of an exploration of its enigmatic form and texture, and its physical, social, and existential crisis.

In my view, the terms *modernist* and *branding* may be said to be emblematic of different historical epochs, different conceptions of culture, and different attitudes to the city. Historically speaking, modernism has been a term used to describe a set of questioning aesthetic values and practices, political positions and philosophical attitudes, which emerged with the Industrial Revolution and lasted until the 1960s. Branding, on the other hand, notwithstanding its gradual evolution over centuries, seems to have come into its own as a postmodern phenomenon, becoming a central feature of global capitalism with the historical shift to a neoliberal economic and cultural order that has taken place since the 1960s, greatly shaped by multinational corporations and ushered into maturity in the era of Reagan and Thatcher. Culturally speaking, modernism and branding may also be opposed: the former involves the critique of traditional codes and conventions of representation, including brands, especially in capitalist societies; the latter has to do with the creation of a commodified image of a manufactured product, place, or event for the purposes of realizing profit from it.[1] The modernist city was a place of distinctive physical and social density, dominated by industry, class struggle, alienation, and new forms of artistic and political engagement, especially by avant-gardes at the level of the street. Many of these features continue, but the city in the recent heyday of branding (in which we are still living) has also been characterized by postindustrial restructuring led by government, civic bodies, and business interests who have sought increasingly to capitalize upon the city's inherited iconic value and special social dynamism by repackaging it as a site and object of consumption. Moreover, there has also been a shift from an older arrangement in which the key external relationships of most cities were to their rural hinterland, the nation and the state, to a newer arrangement, in which cities (especially what Sassen calls "global cities") exercise an historically unprecedented degree of relative autonomy from the countryside, the nation, and the state, while competing globally on a city-against-city basis for resources, manpower, investment, and publicity (Sassen 2006: 32).

The marketing of cities as places of exceptional opportunity has a long history, the first signs of which Harvey has identified in the early "urban entrepreneurialism" of Italian city states in the Renaissance, and which Ward has explored in the promotion in the nineteenth century of burgeoning American frontier towns by local "boosters" as magnets for westward migration, and of new metropoles such as Chicago as hubs for trade and commerce (Harvey 3–17; Ward 28–82). The marketing of cities has also encompassed their self-conscious and international promotion as the venues of specific momentous events to be enjoyed by a mass public, a tendency which accelerated following the Great Exhibition at the Crystal Palace in London in 1851 and the inauguration of the modern Olympic Games in Athens in 1896.

This history of the marketing and promotion of cities was anticipated by the branding of commodities. Wilkins' history of brands traces a development from the thirteenth century, when basic commodities such as bread were stamped by bakers' guilds as a mark of quality or of government duties paid. During the eighteenth century, goods new to the West, such as rice, coffee, and tea, were marketed in terms of their country of origin, and in the late nineteenth and early twentieth centuries trademarks first became widespread and their function shifted from one of quality control to one of the marketing of "differentiated product[s]" (Wilkins 15–17). In economic terms, the rise of branding may be seen as part of capitalism's gradual historical improvement of its mechanisms for the management of production, demand, and consumption. But the rise of branding, I would suggest, may be also be seen in terms of visual representation, as a response to the increasing size and geographical complexity of the known world of Western capitalism, from its mercantile origins in medieval Europe through the "age of imperialism" and into the present era of globalization. The need for brands as recognizable and reliable icons, identifying specific producers, and places of origin, intensified in proportion to the expansion and consolidation of modern urban-industrial societies. These societies were typically characterized by a growing separation between the consumer in the city and the origin of the thing consumed, whether raw materials, foodstuffs, or manufactured goods, which tended to come from the countryside, another city, or another part of the world altogether.

In this context, branding may be seen as a relatively conservative form of representation not only because it emerged as a pillar of an emerging corporate and consumer capitalism, but because it served to rationalize a spatial disjuncture between everyday life and the origin of things. Modernism, on the other hand, emerged as a deliberate cultural engagement with, and interrogation of, that same spatial disjuncture in which various practitioners sought to give literary, visual, musical, and then cinematic form to the inherent disorientation of the modern world. This sense of modernism as a new response to a new spatial dispensation is central to many of the most convincing descriptions of it. For Berman, for example, the at once energizing and threatening experience of modernity is best encapsulated in Marx's phrase "all that is solid melts into air" (Berman 1983). For Jameson, the crisis of representation that underpinned modernism from the paintings of the Impressionists and Cubists to the films of Hans Richter and Stan Brakhage was as an inevitable consequence of the increasing unfigurability of the economic, political, and social forces governing the everyday life of the individual in the modern world (Jameson 2007: 155–230).

Of course, modernism manifested itself in different ways in different cultural forms and the degree to which it was antithetical to branding depends upon which cultural form one happens to be talking about and when. Most critical studies of modernism in literature or painting, for example, have emphasized its explicit or implicit critique of the modern world in which capitalism, and attendant processes of urbanization, technologization, and Taylorization, were an important target of censure through the second half of the nineteenth century and the first half of the twentieth. A minority of studies has focused on the relationship between modernism and the business world as such, but even these have tended to agree that the aesthetics and ethos of modernism proved quite problematic from a marketing point of view. Jensen, for example, demonstrated that while what we now know as modernism in painting was elaborated as a discourse, as a roughly grouped set of ideas promoted by art dealers, gallerists, collectors, and critics who were caught up in the buying and selling of art works in an increasingly institutionalized art market, at its origin was a body of Impressionist and then Art Nouveau paintings from France, Austria, and Germany in the late nineteenth century whose approaches to representation implied a critique of the social and cultural status quo (Jensen 1994). In literature, as Turner argued, modernists such as Gertrude Stein, F. Scott Fitzgerald and Ernest Hemingway used marketing and publishing houses in order to maximize their readership, and their publishers carefully promoted literary modernism to a broad public, but these efforts did not diminish the antipathy towards many facets of urban modernity and capitalism, which marked their literary work and the marketing of literary modernism remained "a gamble" throughout the first half of the twentieth century (Turner 2003: 17).

In cinema, and in architecture, this tension between modernism and the market was even more acute because both forms were reliant to a far greater degree on capital and technology in their production. As a result, in both forms the finished work was much more likely to be expected to perform a certain function—in the case of a film, to narrate a story in such a way as to provide popular entertainment while guaranteeing a financial return, a tendency epitomized by Hollywood cinema more than any other; and, in the case of a building, to provide a sensibly organized and useful structure in which to house the activities of residents or of workers, and within a limited budget. A significant amount of modernist experimentation disregarded these demands but, in doing so, was usually bound to be "confined" to avant-garde or underground film screenings or, in the case of buildings, to the drawing board or architect's model.

Historically speaking, the ambivalent interaction between modernism and the market, and the formal and technical correlation between cinema and architecture, have rarely been more evident than in Europe in the three decades after World War II. In this era, efforts to rebuild, and then expand, the city physically took center stage alongside efforts to reconstruct it iconographically in an affirmative way as a place in which to live, work, and do business. But simultaneously this reconstruction and expansion of cities provided one of the main points of focus for the art cinema, the popularity of which was one of the most striking features of the postwar cultural landscape, and in which new approaches to the cinematic representation of urban environments played a key stylistic, thematic, and narratological role. Images of the city as a social and physical landscape in crisis proliferated internationally in the work of a wide range of filmmakers including Vittorio De Sica, Federico Fellini, Luchino Visconti, Michelangelo Antonioni, Jean Luc Godard, François Truffaut, Louis Malle, John Schlesinger, Lindsay Anderson, Nicholas Roeg, Wim Wenders, Rainer Werner Fassbinder, and Roman Polanski.

Notwithstanding their different individual stylistic tendencies and thematic preoccupations, and the variety of European cities in which they lived and worked, and which they committed to film, the output of these filmmakers was shot through with a consistent and insistent interrogation or negation of the city as a place and as an icon. But two cities, Rome and Paris, occupied an exceptional position in postwar art cinema for a number of reasons. In them, two of the most important and productive movements in art cinema emerged, neorealism in the late 1940s and 1950s and the *nouvelle vague* in the 1960s. Hollywood cinema, with which European art cinema engaged in a constant dialogue, was especially drawn to them as the most romantic and glamorous capitals of Europe. Both cities had long and first-hand experience of imperialist and fascist regimes that gave particular priority to the aestheticization of power in the urban land-scape. Both were vigorous and antagonistic battlegrounds in the cold war between free-market capitalism on the one hand, and socialism or communism on the other.[2]

ROBERTO ROSSELLINI'S ROME AND THE CONTEST
FOR THE URBAN IMAGINARY IN POSTWAR ITALY

In Rossellini's legendary *Rome Open City* (1945), the Italian capital became one of the most recognizable cinematic cities of the postwar era, demonstrating what André Bazin (28–29) described as a "prodigiously photogenic" architectural environment, physical setting and social make-up, combined with a favorable climate, and what Siegfried Kracauer (71) recognized as Rome's rich "flow of life," its distinctive materiality of built space matched by a unique density of social interaction. Rossellini's Rome is a neorealist Rome in which location filming presents the city as a maze of alleyways, basements, courtyards, and piazzas, by turns deserted or crisscrossed by the hustle and bustle of authentic working class life in the district of Prenestino to the southeast of the Stazione Termini. While depicting the brutality of a thoroughly modern war, Rossellini's Rome is encrusted with layers of ancient, medieval, and Renaissance history that remind us always of the presence of the past—and, indeed, of Italy's relative lack of urbanization, given its peripheral position in southern Europe, at least until the 1960s. Rossellini's Rome is muted by the effects of war: the collapse of Rome's economy, including a lack of food and other basic commodities; the suffocation of the normal rhythms and routines of peacetime daily life by fascist oppression and warfare; and the physical destruction of the city itself, its buildings and infrastructure, by street fighting and bombs.

Like other neorealists such as De Sica, Visconti, and Fellini, Rossellini keeps specific buildings and their iconic power at arm's length. Virtually no landmarks readily recognizable to a non-Roman audience feature prominently in *Rome Open City*. In his film *Paisà* (1946), two Italian urban landmarks do appear: the Colosseum, very briefly, in the background of one shot, as a somewhat dejected American GI jumps aboard an army truck to leave the city and a woman with whom he has had a brief sexual encounter; and, later in that film, the Duomo and the Uffizi of Florence, but obscured by the noise and smoke of street fighting as the Allies and Italian partisans seek to liberate the city building by building from bitterly dug-in German troops and Italian fascists. In Rossellini's *Germany Year Zero* (1947), a film set in Berlin immediately after the War, Hitler's once-grandiose Reichschancellerie features prominently in the action, but only as a barely recognizable ruin whose lack of form speaks volumes. In *Rome Open City*, only the dome of St Peter's stands out, appearing on the horizon in the final shot, after the Germans' execution of the resistant priest Don Pietro. But here St Peter's, arguably the most iconic of all Italian buildings, is presented unassumingly in the frame surrounded by a patchwork of ordinary roofs and walls, empty space, and a gaggle of despondent boys. Rossellini's use of Rome is casual and modest, and as such it answers to two dominant approaches to the "branding" of the city in whose shadow neorealism's distinctive approach was formed. First, Rossellini's Rome undercuts the deliberate and bombastic ways in which the Italian capital had been mobilized and promoted by Italy's fascist regime on behalf of its programs of national self-aggrandizement and the idealization of *il duce* from 1922 to 1943. Second, it contrasts clearly with the myth of the Eternal City as a place of classical beauty and order that had been central to the imagination of Rome by outsiders since at least the eighteenth-century Grand Tour, and which would become prominent again shortly after the war, both in a resurgent tourism industry in the capital and in the projection of Rome as a city of romantic wonders and delight by Hollywood, for which Rome became "Hollywood on the Tiber" in the 1950s.[3]

In the fascist era, there had been two dominant approaches to the cinematic representation of the Italian city. One approach was typified by romantic comedies by Mario Camerini such as *Grandi magazzini* (1939), which presented the modern Italian city as a testimony to the industry, commerce, and personal ambition fostered by fascism, but these films were mostly set in Milan. Representations of Rome tended to play upon the city's ancient glory and its symbolism of national "pride, power, and discipline," as in the famous example of Carmine Gallone's historical epic *Scipio Africanus* (1937), whose recreation of the ancient city on celluloid mirrored the restoration by the fascists of parts of the real ancient city such as the Markets of Trajan. Like its archaeological works, the fascist reorganization of Rome was ambitious and, of course, highly symbolic, based on a principle of "monumental axial planning," which sought to centralize government offices around the Piazza Venezia, while clearing working class communities in the *centro storico* to make way for modern thoroughfares such as the now famous Via della Conciliazione, which stretches out in front of St Peter's Basilica (Fried 31).

Monumentality was a characteristic of many architectural movements internationally in the 1930s, including those in democracies such as Britain, France, and the United States, but the monumental architecture favored by Mussolini's regime was particularly explicit in its nationalist posturing and rhetorical flourish, usually preferring one of two approaches or some combination thereof. On the one hand, the clean functionality of Italian *razionalismo*, inspired by Walter Gropius and Le Corbusier, was the distinctive Italian manifestation of what would become known elsewhere as the International Modern style. In the work of architects such as Adalberto Libera and Mario De Renzi, for example, it was often preferred for the design of public buildings such as post offices and fascist party offices, where it could advertise the supposedly forward-looking urban industrial modernity of the nation and of the regime itself. On the other hand, a visually and texturally aggressive type of classicism was employed, which reached its apotheosis in the planning and construction of the Esposizione Universale Roma (EUR) of 1942, a project intended by the fascists to be the largest world fair in history and a testimony to Italy's "Twenty-Seven Centuries of Civilization." In *Rome Open City*, however, Rossellini undercuts the fascist symbolism of the EUR by unceremoniously displacing one of its most prominent buildings, the part-rationalist, part-classical Palazzo della Civiltà del Lavoro (1938–43), to the distant horizon, while Communist resistance fighters heroically ambush and overcome a German convoy in the foreground, rescuing, and releasing a truckload of recently arrested partisans.

In seeking to undo the fascists' work of ideological investment in the city of Rome and its built environment, Rossellini's filmmaking formed part of a wholesale reorientation of thinking about, representing, and designing Italian cities in the late 1940s and 1950s. This reorientation was evident too in other anti-iconic depictions of the city, such as De Sica's *Bicycle Thieves* (1948), Visconti's *Bellissima* (1951) and Fellini's *Nights of Cabiria* (1957), and it was central to professional discourse in urban planning and architecture, leading to a redesign and reconstruction of Italian cities that would fundamentally shape the *mise en scène* of Italian films for a generation. This was the basis of the large number of modest and understated social-housing projects produced by neorealist architects and planners under the auspices of the state-sponsored INA-CASA housing-development program and epitomized by the Quartiere Tiburtino (1949–54), designed by Ludovico Quaroni and Mario Ridolfi, which was modern and functional but built in a style that echoed the village architecture of southern Italy and, thereby, paid homage to traditional, premodern ways of life. It was also the motor behind the proliferation of a significant concentration of important urbanist journals such as *Urbanistica, Domus,* and *Casabella,* which provided Italian architects and planners with a forum in which to review the status and assess the future of their cities in a broad historical perspective and comparatively against a wide range of other cities internationally. Such publications were directed by figures of international renown, including Adriano Olivetti and Giovanni Astengo, Gio Ponti and Ernesto Rogers. Furthermore, alongside Italy's world-leading schools of architecture, including those of Milan, led by Rogers, and Rome, led by Pier Luigi Nervi, they would be central to the increasing international prominence of Italian design in the 1950s.[4]

In Italian cinema and in Italian urbanism, the fundamental issues at stake were remarkably similar. In cinema, a conflict raged between the socially responsible ethics and visually innovative aesthetics typified by Rossellini, and a commercial type of cinema that was pushed with increasing aggression by a coalition which included Italy's dominant Christian Democratic Party, the Catholic Church, the United States government, and Hollywood, and whose output was typified by the comedies of Sophia Loren and Gina Lollobrigida, or by Roman epics such as *Quo Vadis* (1951) and *Ben Hur* (1959). In architecture and urban planning, a conflict raged between neorealist and free-market models of urban development. The former, as in the projects of INA-CASA, prioritized social housing, environmental manageability, and ethical architecture. The latter—for example, in the form of the emblematic Pirelli Building (1955–58) by Ponti and Nervi—prioritized industrial rebuilding, corporate expansion, and a rapid return to economic profitability after the war, while relying upon a rejuvenation of the International Modern style in Italian architecture of the kind so recently discredited by the association of *razionalismo* with the fascist regime. This kind of architecture, relying to a great extent on corporate commissions rather than public money, also typically involved the design and promotion of buildings as extensions of a brand, a tendency especially evident in Gio Ponti's journal *Domus*, which devoted much space to highly sympathetic studies and reviews of the latest developments in New York, such as the opening of the first Olivetti store on Fifth Avenue in 1954 and the construction of the Pan Am Building on Park Avenue in 1959.[5] Postwar reconceptualizing of Rome also reached a peak at this time in the run-up to the enactment of the Rome *piano regolatore* (city plan) of 1962, the formulation and evaluation of which prompted two special issues of *Urbanistica* in 1959 (*Urbanistica* 1959a, 1959b).

By the late 1950s, however, neorealism both in cinema and in architecture and urban planning had been marginalized—the neorealist sense of the city and its people as poor but noble and humane, typified by Rossellini's *Rome Open City*, suppressed by the resurgent capitalist economy of *il boom* (the economic miracle). In films such as Pier Paolo Pasolini's *Accatone* (1961) and Antonioni's *Il deserto rosso* (1964), subsequent Italian cinema spent much of its energy critiquing this postneorealist dispensation, foregrounding the increased alienation of the individual within the modern city that it necessarily entailed. The city in Italian art cinema became not a site of ideological investment, let alone idealization, but a landscape full of private agony, dominated by persistent existential problems of displacement.

Of course, Hollywood cinema (for the most part) denied this. In films such as William Wyler's *Roman Holiday* (1953) and Jean Negulesco's *Three Coins in the Fountain* (1954), a newly confident United States, driven by a new type of corporate capitalism, centered as much on Madison Avenue as industrial Michigan, reasserted the importance of escapism and romance in films and in the city itself, a process that continued with *Seven Hills of Rome* (Roy Rowland, 1958), *Rome Adventure* (Delmer Daves 1962) and

Gidget Goes to Rome (Paul Wendkos 1963). Such Hollywood cinematic representations of Rome affected three types of branding at once. First, the films themselves were presented by the marketing departments of Hollywood studios as consumer objects, light-hearted entertainment vehicles made with the sex appeal of stars, high production values, and spectacular new technologies such as Technicolor and Cinemascope, at a time when the Hollywood film industry was struggling to compete with television, and against which Hollywood deployed an array of exotic urban terrains. Second, in their storylines and visual imagery, these films often foregrounded other consumer objects such as Fiat cars, Lambretta motor scooters, Salvatore Ferragamo shoes, and fashionable clothing by Sorelle Fontana, presenting them as desirable and, indeed, empowering in an era of economic recovery in which the memory of the material privations of wartime was still very vivid. (Indeed, in a landmark 1965 sociological study of migrant workers from Italy's rural south to its industrial northern cities, Alberoni and Baglioni drew attention to the importance in the lives of such migrants of consumer goods not only for their practical value but as signs of their participation in modern city life (Alberoni and Baglioni 1965; Alberoni 1964). Third, Hollywood's cinematic Rome was represented by means of classical conventions of *mise en scène* and cinematography that sought to foreground its architectural beauty and monumentality, and the vivacity of its people, and its street life, merging seamlessly with the packaging of the city as a destination of choice for a new era of mass tourism and affordable air travel, especially for Hollywood's mainly American spectators who could "visit" the city on the screen or visit it in the flesh.

As a function of the long wartime and postwar economic boom experienced by the United States, in tandem with its military, geopolitical, and cultural dominance of the Western hemisphere, and particular initiatives such as the European Recovery Program or Marshall Plan (1948–51), the major capitals of Europe became key and increasingly important destinations for visitors from the United States. Intercontinental links between New York and Rome became especially important (see Figure 8.1). As many of the protagonists of Hollywood's films about Americans in the Eternal City originated in the Big Apple, so the business of traveling back and forth between the two cities became an increasingly important sector of economic activity in the real world, which contributed to the forging of new connections between cities thousands of miles apart—connections which were actual, but also psychological and representational, because of their high-profile advertising in mass media on both continents. Trans-World Airways inaugurated a regular passenger air service between New York and Rome in 1951; Alitalia commenced its service in the spring of 1960; and throughout the late 1940s and '50s, transatlantic sailings by major passenger shipping lines such as Italia Società di Navigazione also played a prominent role.[6]

Solo la Pan Am serve direttamente 15 città chiave degli Stati Uniti da ben 22 centri europei

Dovunque nel mondo viaggiate
vi troverete meglio con la Pan Am
la piú esperta Compagnia aerea del mondo

(Interpellate il vostro Agente di viaggio)

Figure 8.1 Pan Am advertisement, Urbanistica, no 38, March 1963, inside front cover, © Istituto Nazionale do Urbanistica, 1963.

CAPITALIST–UTILITARIAN URBANISM, THE HIDDEN HISTORY OF THE CITY AND BERNARDO BERTOLUCCI'S *LAST TANGO IN PARIS* (1972)

Only Paris attracted more erotic spectacularization than Rome in post-war Hollywood films as a city of special cultural and historical richness, distinctive style and luxury, romance, and sexual liberty. Indeed, regular air services between it and New York commenced significantly earlier than between New York and Rome, with Pan American World Airways announcing the inauguration of its service with a full-page advertisement in the *New York Times* of 14 January 1946, followed by TWA in 1948 (Pan American World Airways 1946: 36). And representations of Paris in Hollywood cinema were even more numerous. Some of these, including *April in Paris* (David Butler 1952), *Lovely to Look At* (Mervyn LeRoy 1952), *Gentlemen Prefer Blondes* (Howard Hawks 1953), *Ma and Pa Kettle on Vacation* (Charles Lamont 1953) and *Silk Stockings* (Rouben Mamoulian 1957), were shot mainly on Hollywood studio sets simulating the City of Lights. However, most involved some (and sometimes extensive) location filming in the real Paris: *An American in Paris* (Vincente Minnelli 1951), *The Last Time I Saw Paris* (Richard Brooks 1955), *Funny Face* (Stanley Donen 1957), *The Happy Road* (Gene Kelly 1957), *Love in the Afternoon* (Billy Wilder 1957), *Paris Holiday* (Gerd Oswald 1958), *Bon Voyage!* (James Neilson 1962), *A New Kind of Love* (Melville Shavelson 1963), *In the French Style* (Robert Parrish 1963), *The Pink Panther* (Blake Edwards 1963), *Paris When It Sizzles* (Richard Quine 1964), and *What's New, Pussycat?* (Clive Donner 1965).

In Donen's *Funny Face*, one of the most successful of such films, and perhaps the most archetypal in terms of its content and form, Paris is presented largely in terms of visually intense, montage sequences that surrender geographical plausibility in favor of song-and-dance numbers, splicing together picture-postcard views of famous landmarks from the Arc de Triomphe and the Eiffel Tower to the Opéra and Notre Dame. The urban environment of Paris, which occupies the majority of the film, is traditional and picturesque, a fact highlighted by the setting of the opening sequence in New York, a city that is identified in terms of a brash and hard-edged physical environment and way of life.

This is typified by the offices of a dynamic Madison Avenue magazine, which are emblematic of the new corporate culture of 1950s Manhattan, while being somewhat more flamboyant than average, a visual amalgam which calls to mind *American Vogue*, the buildings of Mies van der Rohe, and the canvases of Barnett Newman. But American interaction with Europe in the 1950s was fraught with mixed feelings: economic and military superiority on the one hand, cultural and ideological anxiety on the other. In *Funny Face* this ambivalence is evident in Audrey Hepburn's infatuation with beatnik subculture, a phenomenon inaccurately characterized as native to Paris (originating with Sartre and the existentialists), but which threatens to spread from Saint Germain des Près to Greenwich Village. In this respect, the film is ideologically reactionary, tending to corroborate the conservative American perception of Paris in the 1950s as a source of suspect ideology, a front-line position in the cold war with Communism, while laying Paris out somewhat reassuringly as a visual feast, available for possession on screen, just as the Americans in Paris represented by the film buy the city with their abundant disposable income. The scale and richness of the *mise en scène* of the city in *Funny Face* is facilitated by VistaVision widescreen and Technicolor, but it may also be understood at a deeper level in terms of the sense of geopolitical attraction and revulsion that under-girded the appetite of American audiences for Hollywood images of Paris in an era which witnessed a new kind of economic, cultural, and military dominance by the United States.

If the late 1940s had seen the overthrow of fascism by neorealism and a revision of representations and debates about Rome, inherited images of Paris also came under attack from a variety of directions in the post-war era. The city's cultural richness and prestige had guaranteed it a privi-leged place in the international marketing of cities for generations, an early twentieth-century edition of Baedeker's *Paris and its Environs: Handbook for Travelers* declaring in inflated terms that "Paris has long enjoyed the reputation of being the most cosmopolitan city in Europe, where the art-ist, the scholar, the merchant, and the votary of pleasure alike find the most abundant scope for their pursuits" (xxv). During and after the war, the existentialism of Sartre and De Beauvoir was formulated in the midst of a rapid modernization and perceived Americanization of Paris, which contributed to a growing sense of the romantic obsolescence of much of the urban landscape. This was demonstrated, for example, in Louis Cheron-net's book of old photographs of the city's streets and buildings, *Paris tel qu'il fut* (1951), in which he declared,

> We have always spoken of Paris. And if Paris, at any moment, had to disappear, we could always talk about it. In truth, this city is already a city of legend; even dead, how could she not leave a marvelous halo in the imagination of men who would continue to dream of her? (5)

However, if the cinematic reorientation of the image of Rome was at its most intense during the neorealist heyday of the late 1940s and 1950s, the cinematic image of Paris came to the fore internationally in the 1960s in the era of the *nouvelle vague*. This was a moment of crisis for the tradition of narrative fiction film epitomized by Hollywood, challenged by the art cinema of Jean-Luc Godard, but also by the agitprop documentaries of the *Newsreel* movement in the United States, and the poetico–political studies of Third Cinema in Latin America, Africa, and elsewhere. The sixties was also a moment of crisis for the modern city and for the postwar model of what I would call "capitalist–utilitarian" urbanism. Calls for a rejection of capitalist cinema were matched by calls for a rejection of the capitalist city, which emerged from the social and political ghetto activism of the Black Panther Party, the architectural playfulness of avant-garde groups such as Archigram, and—in Paris—the so-called "unitary urbanism" proposed by the Situationist International and echoed by Guy Debord and Henri Lefeb-vre, all of whom rejected the promotion of the city as a seductive consumer landscape.[7]

The Situationist International placed the question of the city and its image at the heart of its agenda. Flourishing in Paris from 1957 to 1972, it

developed the notion of a unitary urbanism as a means of intellectual, artistic, and political engagement with a rapidly changing metropolis marked by
the building of new freeways such as the Boulevard Périphérique (1956–73)
and the Voie Express Rive Droite (1964–67); the construction of brutalist
high rises such as the Tour Montparnasse (1957–72); the gentrification of
the *arrondissements*; the removal of the working class to the *banlieues*;
and the destruction of old *quartiers* such as Beaubourg and Les Halles.
Through these and other projects, large swathes of the city were redeveloped by a new technocratic and corporate rationalism in architecture and
urban planning that was official Gaullist policy and enthusiastically supported by Georges Pompidou, first as prime minister and then as president
of France. In this context, the Situationists recognized the special meaning
of obsolescent and derelict spaces in the city, whose very presence revealed
the fragility of the dominant urban social order during the Fifth Republic
from 1958 to 1974.

Arguably the most geographically detailed unmasking of Paris in a feature film in this period is provided by Bernardo Bertolucci in *Last Tango
in Paris* (1972), a film that has long been recognized for its stylistic sophis-
tication, its profound and often sexually explicit inquiry into the nature
of human existence and human relationships, and its ideological critique
of the French bourgeoisie. Yet what I would call the "spatial surgery" that
Bertolucci performs on the city in the film has hitherto been neglected,
although it is at least as meaningful as that performed on Rome by Rossellini, for whom the younger Bertolucci has expressed the highest admiration (Bragin 39–44). Like Rossellini, Bertolucci chooses locations in such
a way as to present neither a city of tourist attractions nor a city that is
entirely modern and contemporary. This is perhaps not surprising, given
that Bertolucci praised Paris as a location for filming in an interview with
Le Monde by quoting Baudelaire for whom Paris was "'la plus sinueuses'
des vieilles capitales" ("the most sinuous" of the old capital cities; "Dernier
tango à Paris" 1972: 15). This sinuosity is evident in Bertolucci's filming in
winter in the shabby-chic residential district of Passy, where Paul (Marlon
Brando) rents an apartment for no other reason than as a place in which
to indulge in an intense but destructive sexual liaison with Jeanne (Maria
Schneider), a young woman half his age, whose attention distracts him
from the recent suicide of his wife. As a libidinally transgressive space,
the apartment stands as a rejection of bourgeois domesticity, but the film's
mapping of what Lefebvre theorized as the "colonization" of everyday life
in postwar Paris is more thoroughly developed outdoors in a number of
carefully selected exterior locations, whose use countermands the conventional iconography of the city (Lefebvre 2008: 11).

Presenting a *flâneur*'s map of Paris, cutting back and forward between
the apartment in which Jeanne and Paul play out their sexual self-absorption
and their movement on foot outdoors, the film largely ignores late twentieth-century functionalist buildings, with the brief but significant excep-

tion of a scene near what appears to an office-block building site in which Paul accosts a prostitute's client and another in which Paul and Jeanne run in distress past modern shopfronts on the Champs Elysées. In centering the drama on the neighborhood of Passy, Bertolucci presents a Paris still dominated by the *art nouveau* spaces and structures of the *fin de siècle*, a moment that the new urban planning of Haussmann made the most intense phase of modernization in Parisian history, in which the Parisian bourgeoisie consolidated its power after the Paris Commune of 1870, and in which a consumer-oriented market economy played an increasingly important social and cultural role (Williams 1982). Filmed by cinematographer Vittorio Storaro in a deliberately understated way, avoiding grand establishing shots, favoring a slowly moving camera with decentered framing and a deliberately depleted color spectrum that augments the film's sense of loss, this Paris was once modern but it now appears as a "trace" of the past, countermanding the dehistoricizing, depersonalizing, and commodifying logic of late twentieth-century urban life, which is the real subject of the film's critique (Amiel 1973: 60–63).

In the opening sequence, we see Paul screaming in anguish in a very specific place that has had a significant, multilayered, and ideologically variable role in the modern history of Paris (see Figure 8.2): the Pont de Bir-Hakeim, an official historic monument of the city, first built in 1878 as a pedestrian bridge, and known as the Passerelle de Passy, but redeveloped as a result of the 1900 Exposition Universelle with a then state-of-the-art iron and steel two-tier construction to carry both a road and the new Paris Métro overhead (Lambert 1999: 226). The tiny island in the middle of the Seine, which the bridge traverses, the Allée des Cygnes, later became a key site

Figure 8.2 Marlon Brando on the Pont du Bir-Hakeim, from Last Tango in Paris (Bernardo Bertolucci, US/France, 1972), © 1972 Metro-Goldwyn-Mayer Studios Inc. All Rights Reserved. Courtesy of MGM CLIP+STILL.

in the 1937 Exposition Internationale des Arts et des Techniques dans la Vie Moderne, housing the eleven exhibition pavilions devoted to French overseas colonies (France d'outre mer), in an exhibition that encompassed a large section of the whole city, stretching from the Trocadero to the Eiffel Tower and Champs de Mars, to Les Invalides in the south and to the Grand Palais and Petit Palais in the north. As Hobsbawm explained, the Paris Expo of 1937 remains one of the most important events in the history of the world fair. It was especially notable for the way in which the architecture and spatial arrangement of the pavilions of the fascist regimes of Mussolini and Hitler on the one hand, and of Soviet Russia on the other, expressed the gathering geopolitical tension in the late 1930s between the opposed totalitarian states and aimed "to demonstrate the glory and triumph of power itself [and] to organize [art] as public drama [. . .] with the people as audience and [. . .] as organized participants (11–12). In 1949, the Passerelle de Passy was renamed the Pont de Bir-Hakeim in commemoration of the 1942 victory of Free French forces over German troops in Libya, the bridge also featuring in Louis Malle's *Zazie dans le Métro* of 1960. But, at approximately the same time, it developed another association, when the Allée des Cygnes was identified by the Situationist International as the best site for a new SI headquarters, a kind of Antarctic research laboratory, from where they would launch psychogeographic expeditions across the city of Paris and campaigns of *détournement* against its redevelopment as a landscape of consumption and bureaucracy, a "society of the spectacle" (Sadler 1999: 122).

To which point in this multilayered ideological history of a particular place the film *Last Tango in Paris* is most sympathetic is evident in the brief shot, which Bertolucci presents of a menacing group of Police Nationale in riot gear hanging around under the bridge, a shot that reminds us of the recent events of May 1968 and the heavy police presence which was still a fact of life on the streets of Paris three years later. Bertolucci's choice of camera angle concentrates on a northward perspective of the hill of Passy and the apartment building at 1 Rue de l'Alboni, a choice which cannot have been accidental. If any other angle had been used, the camera's view would have had the very different effect of encompassing an image of the high-rise commercial and residential real-estate complex known as the Front de Seine, begun in 1967, which controversial concentration of towers was bigger than the Tour Montparnasse and more central than La Défense, and which was intended as a flagship office and residential development to put Paris firmly on the map of forward-looking, free-marketeering world cities ("Front de Seine"1968: 90).

Indeed, two other key locations used in the film signify in a similar way a romantically outmoded, if possibly more humane, past, while also prompting reflection on the evolution of the real city subsequent to the making of the film itself. At the Gare d'Orsay and at Beaubourg, crucially, the action does not revolve around the destructive relationship of Jeanne and Paul, but around Jeanne and her young boyfriend Tom (Jean Pierre Léaud)—a romance that is presented with a much greater sense of potential and hope, but whose naïveté contrasts with the poignant histories of the real locations in which they are filmed. The Gare d'Orsay, where Tom surprises Jeanne with the news that he is making a film, was inaugurated in 1900, along with the Gare des Invalides and the refurbished Gare de Lyon, to cater for the Exposition Universelle. By 1963, however, it was already designated for redevelopment, either as a luxury hotel or as the site of a giant 105 meter-high crystal tower designed by Le Corbusier, before it was saved by Valéry Giscard d'Estaing in 1974 and preserved for conversion into the museum of nineteenth-century art, now one of the present city's most visited tourist attractions. The district of the Beaubourg and the Marché des Halles, where Jeanne tries on wedding dresses, was demolished in 1971, soon after Bertolucci captured it on film. Its redevelopment caused a major public scandal and prompted intense protest activity by the Situationist International, its daily life having been fondly captured for posterity in Guy Debord's film *Sur le passage de quelques personnes à travers une assez courte unité de temps* (1959). A few years after *Last Tango in Paris*, its landscape would be reborn as the modern underground shopping mall, Le Forum des Halles (1976–80) and the nearby Centre Georges Pompidou (1977).

Whereas Rossellini's films of Rome answered back to the branding of the city in the recent past by a fascist government no longer in power, and questioned its rebranding after World War II by an alliance of Catholics and capitalists, Bertolucci's film is full of trepidation in the face of a coming rebranding of Paris by a nascent neoliberal order. Both films interrogate the long-standing iconographies of their respective urban environments, which predate the history of cinema by centuries. But, more particularly, both films shed a critical light on the self-conscious and self-serving foreground of the image of the city by political regimes at the expense of the city as a real, lived, physical, and social environment, and in a way that requires a process of historical forgetting or denial—which, for Bertolucci and Rossellini, it is one of the cinema's most important vocations to reveal. In this respect, despite the differences between the cities that they treat, and despite the stylistic distinctions that can be drawn between their work, both Rossellini and Bertolucci present a quintessentially modernist critique of the branding of the city in all of its forms not only in the past, but in a way that has arguably even greater relevance today.

NOTES

1. In this paper, I implicitly take issue with the widespread present-day characterization of brands as part of a pluralist-democratic market-oriented culture in which consumers participate like citizens in the traditional republic. This position is typified by the argument of Arvidsson that

   brands should be understood as the logic of a new form of informational capital—much like the factory embodied the logic of industrial capital. Brand management is a matter of putting to work the capacity of consumers [. . .] to produce a common social world through autonomous processes of communication and interaction. This capacity to produce a common social world is empowered and programmed to unfold in ways that create the measurable kinds of attention and affect that underpin the commercial values of brands. Like informational capital in general, brands extract value by putting to work the very basic human capacity to create a common social world. (vii)

In my view, such arguments attempt, unconvincingly, to create a sense of the relation of the subject to the brand as one of knowing cooperation and participation in a social process in a way that sidesteps questions of ideology from the outset and entirely ignores the political economy of branding—that is, the reality of the massive consolidation of corporate power, including media—in the global economy.

2. Besides Rome and Paris, of course, other cities produced seminal cinematic representations, but not to the same extent. For example, it is generally acknowledged in film history that the so-called New German Cinema, which was that country's distinctive contribution to European art cinema after World War II, did not emerge to international acclaim until the late 1960s or, arguably, the early 1970s (in the films of Wim Wenders) and, in any case, neither Berlin, the historical capital, nor Bonn, then the actual capital of West Germany, was at that time able to achieve such an iconic presence. London, on the other hand, had an internationally recognized iconic status in popular culture during its "Swinging Sixties" heyday, but its cinematic representations—in John Schlesinger's *Darling* (1965) or Lewis Gilbert's *Alfie* (1966)—were outnumbered in that era by representations of the very different northern English industrial city, for example, in Schlesinger's *A Kind of Loving* (1962) and Roy Boulting's *The Family Way* (1966), films which made regional cities at least as iconic, if not more so, than London itself, at least in cinema.

3. The term *Hollywood on the Tiber* was coined in recognition of the sheer concentration of American "offshore" filmmaking going on in Rome in the 1950s and early 1960s, both on location and in the film studios of Cinecittà. For an early example of its use, see *Time*, August 16, 1954, p. 34; on the Grand Tour, see Hornsby 2000.

4. For an encyclopedic account of the international influence of Italian design in the postwar period, see Celant 1994.

5. *Urbanistica* generally devoted much less coverage to the United States than either *Casabella* or *Domus*, and *Domus* clearly devoted the most attention and space in its pages to American developments: in the late 1940s and 1950s almost every issue contained some significant article or feature on American cities, American architecture, or Italians in America. On the Pan Am Building, see "Un nuovo grattacielo a New York,", *Domus*, 1959, pp. 1–3; on the Olivetti store, see "Italia a New York," *Domus*, 1954, pp. 3–10. On New York architecture in general, see also Ponti 1952. *Domus* was much more explicitly sympathetic to the International Modernism of 1950s New York skyscrapers than other journals. A representative example of the coverage given to American architectural developments in the journal *Casabella* is its feature on the design of the Seagram Building on Fifth Avenue (Rogers and Rossi 1959). For an example from *Urbanistica*, see Calzolari 1960.

6. A typical advertisement for Italia Società di navigazione services from Genoa to New York may be found on the inside front covers of *Domus*, no. 274, December 1952, and *Domus*, no. 296, July 1954; and for Alitalia

air services, on the inside front cover of *Domus*, no. 348, November 1958.

7. Guy Debord made many films of his own in the 1950s, 1960s, and 1970s, many of which are powerful, if often quite abstract, explorations of the city in their own right. These are important works, but, being (intentionally on Debord's part) so far from the tradition of narrative fiction film, they fall outside the scope of the present essay.

9   Nantes's Atlantic Problem

Bill Marshall

In recent years the port city of Nantes has been one of the most successful in France at reinventing itself. Indeed, the rebranding narrative that can be told is one familiar from elsewhere in the Western world. In 1989, the Parti Socialiste returned to municipal power under Jean-Marc Ayrault, who has been the mayor ever since. The city's new image was developed with the aid of the advertising firm Saatchi & Saatchi, and the narrative selections that emerged favored openness, *métissage*, qualified employment in the tertiary sector, culture, and the environment over old industry and social confrontations. (The last shipyard in Nantes closed in 1987.) These strategies have worked, as the economic growth rate enjoyed by the city in the 1990s ran at twice the national average. The mayor's editorial in the municipal journal in 1992 took up the idea of the port and thus of openness to the outside world, to adventure—the Jules Verne museum is a significant tourist attraction, though there is little on Nantes in his novels—and cosmopolitanism: "When Nantes opens wide its doors and windows, it's a city capable of anything"; the taste for adventure is inscribed in her genes, the city's motto, dating from the Restoration, is *Favet Neptunus eunti*, "Neptune favors those who set off." In Nantes, there is a "West Coast" effect, its identity is an Atlantic one, for the city "has always experienced periods of take-off when it has opened out to the world" (Ayrault 1992). (This despite the fact that Nantes' population of foreign birth is around 2%, instead of the national average of 7%, although since the French census does not ask about ethnicity, this figure can only be guessed at.) The phrase "Nantes-Atlantique" names the airport, football team, and port itself, which, taking into account the agglomeration with St. Nazaire at the mouth of the Loire (where successful shipbuilding still takes place) is the most important on Europe's Atlantic façade.

Indeed, the Atlantic has formed the basis of Nantes' positioning in European institutions, including the Conference of Atlantic Arc Cities created in 2000, whose thirty members—including Cork, Glasgow, Wigan, Vigo, and Lisbon—co-operate on a variety of projects, including urban and economic development, transportation, maritime activities, culture, and heritage. Within the latter, the Cultur*At project has as its objective the creation of a cultural management tool to promote a cultural identity for the Atlantic Area through the establishment of a research center on Atlantic culture. It also aims to set up a website to bring together the cultural and tourism resources available in the Atlantic Area, to organize training and cultural action seminars to structure an Atlantic cultural network that permits a better mutual understanding of cities' cultural policies, and to launch cultural events that would spread the Atlantic Area identity. The familiar policy language continues with the primary objectives of the project, namely the reinforcement of Atlantic cultural identity, emphasis on the artistic, historic, and cultural heritage of the "Atlantic Arc"; the stimulation of artistic and cultural creation, production and distribution; the encouragement of artist mobility, and sustainable development of professional activities and events in culture and leisure activities, and the development of a guide to Atlantic Area cultural policies and offer criteria for joint development of these policies.[1]

And yet, an enthusiastic 1999 report on the city in *Le Monde* could not resist conjuring up the eeriness of the vast *friche* (wasteland) that is the former shipbuilding area dominating the western end of the Ile Beaulieu, between the two still-existing branches of the Loire:

> Crossing this windswept, weed-covered no man's land, you reach the quai des Antilles and the island's prow, a joyously cinematic décor with its lane of ghostly plane-trees, its unlikely all-night bar, its massive sugar-tong crane, an atmosphere like the ends of the earth. (Belleret 1999: 2)

The sentence is eloquent and economical: the (nostalgic) references to the décor of poetic realist films such as Marcel Carné's *Le Quai des brumes* of 1938; the evocation of the empty vacant space that Gilles Deleuze (2005) in his cinema book would call an "espace quelconque/any-space-whatever," a space that has lost its *raison d'être*, its connections, its homogeneity, "a space of virtual conjunction, grasped as pure locus of the possible" (109). Writing in the aftermath of a March 2005 conference in Nantes on *les friches portuaires* (port brownfield sites), Pierre Gras remarked how "their future challenges the symbolic relation between 'the modern' and 'the archaic', between what is 'valorized' and 'abandoned', thought and lived, and between the real and the virtual." (Gras 2005: 37) Indeed, the metaphor of the industrial crane and the metonymy of the Quai des Antilles (so named, of course, because of colonial commerce) to be found in the article in *Le Monde* point to a virtual dimension of the present-day city that returns to question and trouble "Nantes-Atlantique," namely the slave trade on which the eighteenth- and even early nineteenth-century city built its wealth.

Part of Nantes' current self-promotion is as a cinematic city because of its association with Jacques Demy (1931–90), a native son who returned there in 1960 to make one of the key films of the French New Wave period, *Lola*. This was followed by *Une Chambre en ville* (1982), and his widow Agnès

Varda's biographical portrait of him in *Jacquot de Nantes* (1991). Indeed, *Lola* begins with a view of the Atlantic, as a returning *Nantais* in the nearby seaside resort of La Baule gazes out to sea. The film, which places its eponymous night-club singer (Anouk Aimée) in a whirling, mobile love triangle with a gloomy existentialist-type Frenchman, an American sailor, and her long-lost lover who has made his fortune abroad, has been read as a conciliatory narrative for the postwar French modernization period, as Lola ends up with the "first love," who is both French and "American" because of his wealth and accoutrements, including a Cadillac (Ross 204). *Jacquot de Nantes* is also eloquent of the influence of American culture on the young Demy, so that it combines a French republican upwardly mobile success story with an evocation of the restratifications in French society impelled by changing cultural and economic power relations between Europe and America.

However, more unstable readings of Demy are possible, as he tracks his protagonists through the city streets and their differently embedded historical strata, including the rue Kervegan on the Ile Feydeau, home to a third of the slave-trading *armateurs* of the eighteenth century, who decorated the entrances to their homes with appropriately transatlantic *mascarons* or emblems (Lelièvre 1988). That tracking takes place across contradictory mappings of Nantes in terms of home and departure, container and flow, openness and closure, embracing the Atlantic or turning its back on it, as happens in *Une Chambre en ville*, which recounts an episode in the city's militant working class history from the 1950s. But in Demy there is always a third term, that of the fantastic, the virtual alongside the real, violence beneath the enchantment. (Like that of his most famous film, *Les Parapluies de Cherbourg* (1964), the dialogue of *Une Chambre en ville* is entirely sung.) Here, a nineteenth-century arcade, the Passage Pommeraye built in 1843, becomes a key site (see Figure 9.1). A speculative attempt in the Louis-Philippe period to emulate the arcades that had sprung up in Paris, the passage was the brainchild of a solicitor, Louis Pommeraye, who had married into a wealthy Nantes commercial dynasty; he went bankrupt shortly after its creation and it was sold to Baron Le Baillardel de Lareinty, who belonged to a dynasty that owned plantations in Martinique. Unusually, the Passage Pommeraye is built on three levels, as it descends 9.4 meters from the city's Opera House (the Théâtre Graslin) and commercial district to the district of la Fosse, near the stock exchange, but traditionally an area of prostitution and lower class life ("progressive," hygienist motivations were given for the construction of the passage). Confident use of glass, stone, and ironwork, typical of the period, is accompanied by details such as in the upper gallery, where the sculptor Guillaume de Grootaërs created medallions of local celebrities, including the privateer Jacques Cassard (1679–1740) and the naval officer Couedic de Kergoualer (1740–80), above arcades decorated with stucco birds of paradise and lianas. The gallery also contains twenty allegorical statues of children sculpted by Jean de Bay, looking downwards, representing concepts such as agriculture, industry, spectacle, and, hair waving in a sea breeze, international trade.

Figure 9.1 Passage Pommeraye, Nantes, France, © Erick Martineau.

An early representation of the passage in travel writing by Gustave Flaubert is eloquent and economical on the sensory seductions of shopping, looking, and touching as well as dreaming; all the more so in that these coexist oxymoronically with the emptiness of the pure exchange value they represent as they circulate. These processes, it is clear, are bound up with the world "beyond the seas," the bringing of the world to Nantes, and to this special microcosmic space (Flaubert 51). In Demy, the phantasmagoric and virtual possibilities of the passage contain a dark side. Lola's suitor Cassard (Marc Michel) enters there a sinister hairdresser's shop, into a backroom past curling tongues and hairdryers that look like instruments of torture, and is drawn into a diamond-smuggling plot. The kids in *Jacquot de Nantes* speculate about a white slave trade going on in a lingerie shop. In *Une Chambre en ville*, unfaithful wife Edith (Dominique Sanda) twice visits at night her ogre-like husband in his lair there, a struggling television shop that produces a murky, aquatic light; he flushes her keys down the toilet before slitting his throat, she literally has to break out, or up, through a skylight.

The passage has been used by other artists, including the *bande dessinée* creator Tardieu, whose *La Véritable Histoire du soldat inconnu* (1974) has the narrator encounter there monsters from his unconscious. But the most sustained illustration of the other-worldly depths contained by the Passage Pommeraye, and, along with Demy's films, its most famous representation, is the eponymous short story by André Pieyre de Mandiargues, first published in 1946. Here a male narrator, descending from the commercial Rue

Crébillon end, is lured into the depths of the passage by a mysterious female creature, who then takes him to a place outside, where another entity transforms him on an operating table into a half-man, half-alligator creature (*l'homme-caïman*). Pieyre de Mandiargues was close to the surrealists, and the story is indebted to the Passage de l'Opéra sequence of Louis Aragon's *Le Paysan de Paris* (1926/2004), which explores in this arcade the unexpected poetry of everyday life, consistent with surrealism's emphasis on chance, the unconscious, the irrational, dreams, and magic. Nantes is, in fact, significant in the history of surrealism: it was there in 1916 that André Breton, as a young medical auxiliary, met a young proto-dadaist, Jacques Vaché, and in *Nadja* (1928) Breton wrote that, with Paris, Nantes was the only city in which something worthwhile or adventurous could happen to him. Although they were interested in the city's different embedding of historical epochs, the surrealists' take on the city, and on Nantes, needs to be historicized further. The limitations of their construction of woman as Other (de Beauvoir 1993) are well known, as is their feminization of urban sites: the Passage Pommeraye in Pieyre de Mandiargues is also a damp, castrating uterine space that leads the narrator to his doom. When we look at the relationship between surrealism and capitalism, we may recall Walter Benjamin's ambition to dissolve mythology into the space of history, for, whereas Aragon "persists within the realm of dream, here the concern is to find the constellation of awakening" (Benjamin 458). As the translators of the Arcades project put it, "The nineteenth century was the collective dream which we, its heirs, were obliged to re-enter, as patiently and minutely as possible, in order to follow out its ramifications and, finally, awaken from it" (Benjamin ix). This awakening is to crisis, to the recognition and defamiliarization of the workings of capitalism. Habitual perceptions need to be overcome, and in turn, it might be argued, the surrealists' aesthetic disposition, seeking to reinvest both the commodity and linguistic systems with poetic aura, needs to be understood in materialist terms. The encounter between art and commerce impelled by the creation of the first arcades produced unsettling effects even on the intimate life of the individual, generating realities both very material and very estranged or spectral.

It is here that we can return to the representations of the Passage Pommeraye in Pieyre de Mandiargues's short story and in *Une Chambre en ville*. For, whereas the most optimistic readings of surrealism emphasize its capacity for generating counteritineraries and especially countermemories, whereby the rediscovery of fragments of a demolished past burst through the contemporary spectacle to imply alternative futures (e.g., Crary 1989), in representations of Nantes the memory of the slave trade is at the center of processes of displacement. The (marginalized, phantasmagoric) commodity forms enumerated by the narrator of *Le Passage Pommeraye* include a whole litany about sugar (twenty-nine different kinds of sugar lump, from "Cupid's sugar" through "giant squid" and "torpedo" sugars to "devil's sugar"). Juxtaposed with the description of the crowded cattle train taking its imprisoned passengers to their doom, along the very quayside from which slave ships sailed and sugar was unloaded, the reference can easily be read metonymically as such a displacement. Similarly, the depths of the passage are associated with instruments of torture and white slave trade rumors, as we have seen, a fantasy that goes back to Aragon (151). (Significantly, the fixation on a slave trade that purportedly afflicts white women rejoins a colonial discourse which constructs a sexually threatening racial male Other.) Demy, in a response to the budgetary veto on the use of color stock, energizes the black and white photography of *Lola* by establishing incandescent moments of whiteness (as when windows are opened, for example), and polarizing blacks and whites (Cassard's dark suit and the sailors' uniforms) ostensibly to establish a series of oppositions and choices or destinies, but in fact perfectly complicit with Richard Dyer's defamiliarizing analysis of the way "[the] photographic media and, *a fortiori*, movie lighting assume, privilege and construct whiteness" (89). This could even be extended to the relationship between Lola's white skin and facial beauty spot, as well as her dark hair, and to the fixation on Snow White in *Jacquot de Nantes*.

This foregrounding of whiteness is further developed in another movie that is set in Nantes, Jean-Loup Hubert's *La Reine blanche* of 1991, the narrative of which unfolds in the year *Lola* was filmed (1960). In what is basically a liberal melodrama, Catherine Deneuve and Richard Bohringer play Liliane and Jean Ripoche, a married couple who live in Trentemoult, a suburb that is a ferry ride away from Nantes on the south side of the Loire, where they run a bathroom showroom and bring up their four children. Their lives are disrupted by the return to metropolitan France of Yvon Legualoudec (Bernard Giraudeau), along with his Guadeloupean wife Annabelle (Laure Moutoussamy) and mixed-race children. Yvon, Jean's rival for Liliane's love, had left Nantes twenty years earlier, heavily in debt and at the prompting of Liliane's parents, a few hours before Liliane appeared as the "white queen" on the family carnival float. The conciliatory narrative ends with Yvon and Annabelle's teenage daughter Mireille (Muriel Pultar) becoming, after the final overcoming of some racially inspired hesitation, the new "white queen," and Liliane leaving Nantes to find Jean and save her marriage. The nature of Jean's business is not accidental: Ross has argued that in the 1950s the new apparatuses of domestic hygiene associated with the new consumer capitalism—and *La Reine blanche* abounds with images of dirt and cleanliness, in the antics of the young Ripoche sons or Jean smeared with plaster of paris as he sculpts the float—figured not only the privatization of everyday life in France, but also echoed the monstrous Other of Algeria and its colonial war, where, for example, torture practices took place in those very spaces of kitchen and bathroom (Ross 71–122). One scene in the film is set in the Passage Pommeraye, but, with an Ophuls-like emphasis on its melodramatic space (staircases, the confrontation between two former lovers), its nineteenth-century Frenchness punctuated by Yvon using the "exoticism" of a pet monkey to try and sell peanuts.

The metonymic "displacement"' and metaphorical "condensation" are, of course, standard Freudian terms to describe the labor of the dream work, and it is not difficult to develop psychoanalytic arguments, of the hydraulic kind, in favor of a return of the repressed—the silenced history of the slave trade—in these representations of Nantes. Beyond even this, the depths of the Passage Pommeraye, most notably its figuring at the boundary of reality, whether as a transition to an alternative world, or in the border zone conjured by the toilet scene in *Une Chambre en ville*, point to a trouble at the heart of Nantes's self-representation. In Slavoj Žižek's terms—and here the juxtaposition of his analysis in *The Pervert's Guide to Cinema* (2006) of the toilet scene in Francis Ford Coppola's *The Conversation* (1975) is telling—the "real" thus hinted at is the void that makes social "normality" incomplete or inconsistent. While psychoanalysis sometimes struggles to historicize the symptoms it unveils, at the very least it is possible to argue that somewhere in the self-representation of Nantes, and beyond that the wider French society, there is a traumatic kernel that the social order is unable to symbolize or to account for, "an imbalance in social relations that prevented the community from stabilizing itself into a harmonious whole" (Žižek 217–18). The stain/s washed out by Jean Ripoche's bathroom suites, or the open wound constituted by the former river beds of the Loire and Erdre, also point to this psychic reality.

The French Atlantic slave trade itself accounted for 19.2% of the twelve to fourteen million Africans shipped during the activity's existence, the third largest after England/Britain (41.3%) and Portugal (29.3%). From 1707 to 1847, Nantes ship owners or *armateurs* conducted an average of 45.5% of all French slave trading, outstripping the activities of the next three most important ports, Bordeaux, Le Havre, and La Rochelle, at 11 to 12% each. These are average figures, and during the first half of the eighteenth century almost two-thirds of the slave trading was conducted from the city. To this must be added the rest of colonial commerce. In the eighteenth century, sugar constituted 61% of the total value of imports to Nantes, and as late as 1850 the figure was still at 50%. Everyone involved in the city's maritime commerce was implicated with the slave trade in some way. The French presence in the West Indies, at first a military and strategic one impelled by Cardinal Richelieu, had begun in 1629 with the occupation of St. Christopher, and then Guadeloupe and Martinique (1635), and, officially by the Treaty of Ryswick (1697), but in reality decades earlier (the first French governor arrived in 1655), the western third of the Spanish island of Hispaniola, Saint-Domingue. Since the native population had been exterminated by the encounter with the Spanish, *engagés* had to be recruited in France to form the first workforce on the tobacco plantations, the islands' first source of wealth; the first shipload of these volunteers left Nantes in 1636. But as the production of sugar took off in the West Indies from 1670—aided by the arrival of Dutch and Jews expelled from Brazil, where cultivation of the plant had begun—there was greater demand for

African slaves. Colbert, architect of the French colonial system granting exclusive trading rights in the colonies to French goods and French ships, attempted to organize the trade in 1664 by granting a monopoly over the slave trade to the Compagnie des Indes Occidentales, but the colonies' ever-increasing demand for labor led to the legalization of more companies and the activity of individual entrepreneurs. The first slave expedition left Nantes in 1688, and its importance soared after the signing of the Treaty of Utrecht in 1713.

Slave trading and the linked colonial commerce turned the fortunes of Nantes around, elevating it by the eighteenth century from eighth to third place in the ranking of the nation's ports, and changing it from a relatively modest centre for coastal and fluvial shipping, mainly based on the movement of salt and wine. A well-established, relatively autonomous local capitalism developed, which was responsive to economic change and the need to seek out new trading opportunities. Early eighteenth-century names of traders—and the founders of slaving dynasties—include René Montaudoin, a merchant born in Nantes of a Parisian family of mainly artisans (and whose family built a magnificent *hôtel* on what is now the place Maréchal-Foch in the cathedral quarter of the city), and the Shiell family from Ireland (Catholic Irish had settled in the city after the events of 1689–90). The Montaudoins, for example, were among the first to found textile factories and sugar refineries to supply, and to process, the trade. By the end of the eighteenth century, economic and political life was dominated by the dynasties—around twenty in all—involved in what was euphemistically called *le négoce*. The milieu of *négriers* (slave traders) constituted in the eighteenth century a microsociety ahead of its time, imposing bourgeois values locally, aspiring to be *notables*, with an immense power of attraction, wealth "trickling down" from these elites to an extensive middle class of artisans, shopkeepers, ship captains, and the like.

These *négriers* made considerable investments, a capital sometimes drawn from local subscription, but more often from familial networks, in organizing the fitting out with supplies and crew of the ship that would sail first to West Africa laden with goods such as locally produced *indiennes* (brightly colored textiles often decorated with motifs especially destined for African clientele), as well as guns, metal tools such as axes, wine and spirits, and luxury items such as porcelain. The voyage to the West African coast took three to four months, with Nantes ships sailing especially to the Slave Coast (present-day western Nigeria and Benin, where France had a permanent fort, at Ouidah), and to Angola/Cabinda. The average French slaving ship spent about five months in Africa, enough time to conduct bartering and payment arrangements with local merchants and rulers, and to procure the requisite number of slaves. The appallingly crowded conditions for the human cargo during the middle passage of two to three months are well-known. Although it was in the interests of the *négriers* to deliver their captives in intact numbers to the Caribbean, the century-long mortality rate was 13% (and, among the captors, the crew, 7%, mostly through diseases contacted on the African coast). In the Caribbean, the ship would stop first at Martinique, where slaves would either be sold, or cleaned and exercised before a further voyage to Saint-Domingue, which, because of its enormous prosperity, was receiving more than 90% of slaves traded by Nantes ships after 1760. The *négrier* then commenced the two-month Atlantic crossing to Nantes, laden with the colonial goods of sugar, coffee, and indigo. The *armateur*, his capital tied up for a year, quickly sold on these goods to local middlemen, receiving the first of several payments and returns which, within three years of the expedition, would start generating overall profits. Nantes's prosperity was also based on the direct liaisons (*droiture*) that took place with the Caribbean, but which were linked to the slave trade, as they often involved transporting the rest of the return cargo.

By 1789, Nantes's economy totally relied on the slave trade, "a specialized business which subordinated virtually all other economic activities" (Stein 1979: 130). On the eve of the Revolution, *le négoce* at Nantes, as expressed in Jean-Baptiste Mosneron Dupin's *Réformes dans l'ordre social, et particulièrement dans le commerce* of 1788, was campaigning for the dissolution of aristocratic privileges and the creation of autonomous structures for "la classe du commerce" with influence on government decision-making (qtd. in Pétré-Grenouilleau 1998: 147). But that class, in Nantes at least, where in 1790 twelve out of eighteen municipal officers were from the world of *le négoce*, soon clashed with the new revolutionary regimes on the subject of the evolving situation in Saint-Domingue. In 1789, the city's *cahier de doléance* (grievance book), a quarter of which was devoted to colonial commerce, had demanded the maintenance of the slave trade and of the incentives and fiscal advantages provided for it by the French state. An address to the National Assembly on August 28, 1790, and a petition of February 26, 1791, virulently opposed giving equal political rights to free people of color in the colonies, and then, as slave revolts and racial violence erupted in Saint-Domingue, the slave traders and other representatives of Nantes commerce lobbied for the straightforward reconquest by France of the territory. Throughout this period, the arguments were pragmatic rather than moral; or rather they sought to overcome the moral focus on the slave trade by placing the latter in a broader nexus of national economic interest.

However, as Pétré-Grenouilleau (1998) points out, the early 1790s also marked a coalescence of discourses defending slavery (violence and backwardness of Africa, unsuitability of tropical climates to white labor) that tipped into forms of racism that were to develop conceptually in the following century. Despite this lobbying—which took the form, for example, of a forty-strong delegation of *négociants*, mariners, and shipyard workers leaving Nantes for Paris in March 1792—slavery was abolished in the French colonies on February 4, 1794. During the Terror, from September 1793 to July 1794, republican Nantes was caught between the royalist Vendée revolts in the countryside, and the zeal of the proconsul Jean-Baptiste Carrier, who arrived in October 1793 and took aim at wealthy *négociants* as well as at aristocrats and other enemies of the regime. About 12,000 died at Nantes before he was recalled to Paris and guillotined in December 1794.

Abolition and war with Britain, which dominated the seas, meant that continuing the slave trade was unthinkable, and, indeed, Nantes *armateurs*, ever practical, had begun winding it down in 1792–93. For the next ten years, transatlantic trade was disrupted in the context of total war mobilization and the collapse of trade with the Caribbean islands (worth 22 million *livres* in 1790, 2.5 million in 1801). Some *négociants* left Nantes, and for a time the main activity of the *armateurs* was fitting out privateers (basically, state-sponsored pirates). The class polarizations of the 1790s also led to a general withdrawal of those slave traders ennobled before the fall of the *ancien régime*. And yet, as soon as Napoleon restored slavery in 1802 and the Treaty of Amiens provided was a glimmer of hope for a general peace with Britain that year, certain *armateurs* rushed in. Twelve slaving expeditions left Nantes in 1802–03. From the Restoration, in 1814, to the final and definitive abolition, under the Second Republic, of slavery in the French colonies (1848), Nantes continued to send out slaving expeditions—a total of 318, constituting 70% of the metropolitan French total (due to the ending of the colonial *exclusif*, expeditions were now being organized from Martinique), reaching a peak in 1825.

In the nineteenth century, the *Nantais* conducted slave trading in a very different environment from that which had prevailed in the previous century. While some slaves continued to be sold to plantations in the remaining French Caribbean possessions, the main market was now Cuba (Saint-Domingue having been irredeemably lost in 1803–04). In addition, the trade was now conducted in a context of increasing international and national illegality. The slave trade was outlawed in the British Empire in 1807, and, following a provision in the original American constitution, the United States abolished trade in slaves from Africa the same year. In France, timid laws in 1817–18 merely equated slave trading with a customs violation. The case of the *Petite-Betsy* is exemplary of this new climate. Having set sail from Nantes on February 15, 1822, after undergoing a cursory customs inspection (the cargo of gunpowder, shotguns, machetes, and textiles was noted, as was the declared destination of Sumatra), it loaded 218 slaves at Bonny in present-day Nigeria, but on April 15th it was bombarded, along with other slave ships, by the Royal Navy, and surrendered. The Africans were freed, the *Petite-Betsy* taken to Britain but returned to the French. Legal action was taken against the captain, the ship owner, and the investors.

Nantes was in the firing line of a reorganized and revivified French abolitionist movement, and very publicly so. In 1825, amid much publicity, Auguste de Staël, son of the writer Mme de Staël, went to Nantes to purchase slaving irons and manacles. He was also the brother-in-law of the duc de Broglie, who in 1822 had founded the Société de la morale chrétienne, one of whose goals was the abolition of the trade. Tighter ship inspections were enforced, and this explains the decline in Nantes slave trading after 1825 (in the following year the number of departures was only half as many as in that year). For a time Nantes *armateurs* tried to get round this either by flying foreign flags or by organizing slave trading from the Caribbean itself. By 1827, when a more repressive law was passed, most of the big players had withdrawn from the trade, but it was continued by a few into the 1830s, by which time many in the Société de la morale chrétienne now held power in Paris following the July Revolution. The third and last—and draconian—abolitionist law was passed in 1831. Some 100,000 African slaves had been transported since 1814, mostly by Nantes ships or ordered by Nantes ship owners. Nantes was the last French port to cease trading in this commodity.

In 1998, the black British photographic artist Joy Gregory created an exhibition entitled "Memory and Skin," based on images she had taken round the Atlantic shoreline, including in Nantes. For example, a low-angle shot of a townhouse in the Rue Kervegan denotes the grandeur of the edifice, while connoting much with its attention to the ironwork and especially the bars on the ground-floor window that deter contemporary burglars but connote the paraphernalia of confinement. In another photograph, a black doll sits smiling in a shop window, linking consumer desire, past, and present through the filtering of the image via the glass reflection, which offers blurry images of contemporary life (Gregory 1998: 101–13; Coombes 1998: 99–101). While the memory of the slave trade is the shadow or virtual partner of representations of modern and contemporary Nantes, and even of some its icons—the attractive blue lines of the Béghin-Say sugar refinery on the Ile Beaulieu, even the Lieu Unique cultural centre, whose former role as a factory manufacturing LU biscuits was an offshoot of the sugar trade—the city itself was slow to generate official commemorations of that past. Indeed, well into the 1950s local historiography tended to produce hagiographic portrayals and evaluations of the days of the *armateurs* (see Pétré-Grenouilleau 1998: 246–47), and politicians, in hard times especially, to invoke the golden age of prosperity that was the eighteenth century.[2] (Since then, however, thanks to the extensive records to be found in the Archives départementales de Loire-Maritime, much more has become known about the slave trade in Nantes than in any other port.) Under the Gaullist local administration of Mayor Michel Sauty, subsidies were refused to a conference organized in the city to mark the tercentenary of the Code Noir (the document regulating the treatment of slaves in the French colonies) in 1985.

However, in 1992 the new Socialist city administration supported the creation of a new association, Les Anneaux de la mémoire, under the chairmanship of city councilor Yvon Chotard, the polysemic "anneaux" suggesting the iron rings confining captured Africans, as well as the links to the past. In addition to the organization of conferences, cultural events and the creation of a journal that continues to this day, the association's main task in this early period was to organize a major exhibition on the slave trade in the city museum housed in the Château des ducs de Bretagne. This was an enormous success, attracting more than 300,000 visitors between December 1992 and May 1994. Although the enterprise was keen to be inclusive and to open the events out to a dialogue between Europe and Africa (with the creation, for example, of a partner association in Dakar), it also illustrated how historical memory is a site of contestation, and that there is a politics of commemoration. Critics of the city council's initiative included the associations Mémoire de l'outre-mer, which, led by Octave Cestor, emanated from the city's population of Caribbean origin, and Regards croisés, of African nationalist inspiration. The latter organized alternative events, promoting the idea of the slave trade as a crime against humanity that could be abolished by "justice" but not by "memory." The former, which had been active since the mid-1980s in promoting awareness of both the trade and of other racial issues, saw profound identity questions at stake (*négritude* versus *créolité*, but also an interrogation of the French republican state's capacity to integrate and get beyond that history, especially given the nature of the republican colonialism that developed in the late nineteenth century). For, indeed, in his preface to the exhibition catalogue, Jean-Marc Ayrault had written, just after (cleverly) quoting Senegalese historian Babacar Fall on certain African élites' complicity with the slave trade:

> Is it at all necessary to point fingers of blame here? In any case, this is not what we want to, for if we have the duty to face up to our history, as we have done, there is no point in lingering on it. (*Les Anneaux de la mémoire* 8)

And in a letter to UNESCO, dated January 7, 1991, (successfully) seeking the organization's backing for the Anneaux de la mémoire project:

> There's no guilt to confess for anyone today, no nostalgia, no complacency either for these times gone by. Only the desire not to hide them away, and especially the will to overcome them and to build new bridges between the lands and the peoples of the Atlantic. (qtd. in Lastrucci 1999: 145)

And in an article in *Ouest-France* on June 2, 1994, Yvon Chotard linked memory and tourism: "To sell itself as a tourist destination, a city such as Nantes must draw on its memory: Brittany, the Revolution, workers' history and of course the triangular trade" (qtd. in Guyvarc'h 1999: 138).

This is not necessarily to argue the African nationalist view, which, for example, took issue with the section of the exhibition devoted to African collaboration. Nor is it to minimize the achievement of the enterprise in its extensive examination of Nantes' role and of the process of historical amnesia that followed. What is irrefutable, however, is that the exhibition was part of an overall "branding" strategy by the city administration, an image making of a progressive, outward and forward looking, and republican city. The flip side of the dispassionate approach to history favored by Ayrault was to withdraw the slave trade and its aftermath from any meaningful economic, political and, indeed, legal challenge to the contemporary world order, especially notions of genocide or crime against humanity, which might have juridico-legal repercussions. Instead, the memory of the trade is neutralized within a now homogeneous Atlantic space (or "Arc"), in which cities co-operate or compete within an international division of labor and a global market for goods and services.

The unraveling of the consensus that had been attempted by the city authorities continued after the close of the exhibition. Mémoire de l'outre-mer lobbied for a permanent commemoration of the slave trade in Nantes, and on April 25, 1998, the 150th anniversary of the abolition of slavery in the French colonies, a provisional monument, a sculpture by Lisa Marcault-Dérouard, of the outline of a human figure lifting its arms heavenwards, its chains broken, was unveiled by the Loire. A few days later it was wrecked by vandals and is now hidden away in a corner of the refurbished city museum. Eventually, in 2002, the committee set up by the city authorities to assess alternative memorial projects decided on a commemorative garden and underground archival passageway to be created on the Quai de la Fosse by the Polish-American sculptor Krysztof Wodiczko, working with the Argentinean Julian Bonder, next to the pedestrian pont Victor Schoelcher. (Schoelcher was the abolitionist and republican under-secretary to the Colonies, who signed the historic document of April 27, 1848.) Delivery is due in 2009. In the polemic, via the letter and opinion pages of the local press, that followed this decision, it was the fate and meaning of *France* that were at stake. (Already, Jean-Marc Ayrault had stressed after the 1998 incident, "Those who attacked this statue attacked one of the symbols of values that ought to be unanimously shared and that play a role in founding the unity of a nation" [1998:7]). Some irredentists were against the whole idea: Raymond Kerverdo, of the Comité nantais de documentation historique de la marine, complained about the Maison de la mer being included in the memorial (a suggestion later withdrawn), as the expeditions that left Nantes had an interest in maintaining the good health of their captives, slaves had been sold by Africans and the French crews, more of whom had died than the slaves themselves, had not inflicted any suffering, all couched in an appeal to "healthy objectivity" (Kerverdo 2004). More serious critics such as Pierre Péron, who had designed posters for the Anneaux de la mémoire exhibition, had complained of the "communitarianism" (a scare word in contemporary French debates referring to American identity politics) implied by the proposal (Péron 2004), and Pierre Giroire rejected any reference to Pierre Nora by asserting,

His proposal is in the very trendy lineage of "compassion and meditation" which tends to invade all *lieux de mémoire* in the world and
which is to commemoration what McDonalds is to gastronomy, thus
condemning "the choice of an approach which is very foreign to our
culture rooted in rationalism." (Giroire 2004)

Faced with the gravest accusation of all in the current French climate
that of caving in to Americanness, the officials on the steering committee
defended their choice of Wodiczko, who had lost his family in the concentration camps, by referring to their impeccable French republican and
left-wing credentials. Yannick Le Marek, a history teacher and committee
member, thus wrote, "At a time when public services are threatened by
the devastating onslaughts of unbridled economic liberalism, the people of
Nantes can rejoice at having an active and ambitious cultural policy in the
public service." Replying to Péron's assertion in *Ouest-France* on March
27, 2004, that the proposal exuded a politically correct, communitarian,
Disney World view of the slave trade, Le Marek was at pains to stress that
the monument would not be about shame and guilt, nor would it be just
about Nantes: "[I]t will transmit universal values and proclaim our wish
to fight for a world without slaves" (Le Marek 2004).

Here, far from the slave trade calling into question French self-identity,
it is used to bolster it, even though it—and the anti-African racism it inaugurated—have accompanied French republicanism like a troubling, contradictory shadow ever since 1789. Rather, in the pages of the Nantes press
we get the re-assertion of a major national identity, whose relationship to
the foreign Other is just that, one of alterity. And yet, as was hinted at in
Jacques Demy's films, a much more ambiguous relationship between home
and away, Self and Other, France and America, can be imagined on the
streets of Nantes, one that captures a mobile and provisional sense of self,
and of Frenchness, even if—or is it because?—its energy is partly drawn
from the recognition of traumatic kernels within. Nantes continues to deal
with the postcolonial echoes of its contemporary appeal, and aspiration, to
cosmopolitanism and the Atlantic.

NOTES

1. <http://www.arcat.org/Francais/cvaa.html> and <www.culturatlantic.com>
   (both accessed March 12, 2008).
2. See the declaration in 1945 of the then mayor Clovis Constant, quoted in
   Guyvarc'h 1996: 81. See also Guyvarc'h 1997.

Part III

Family Histories
The Remembered City

Part III

10 Stripes and My Country

or, On Not Being at Home

Stephanie Hemelryk Donald

ON NOT BEING AT HOME

The day after the London bombings on July 7, 2005, I was due to attend a "soirée" with friends in Sydney. The gathering took place in an apartment overlooking the harbor. The apartment itself was modest but it was located in a prime position, and typified the easy luxury of those lucky enough to have a harbor view. I use the term *soirée* advisedly. All the guests (many of whom were performers or artists themselves) had been asked to bring a song, a poem, a piece of music, a work of their own, or an anecdote to share with the others across the evening. Surprisingly perhaps, everyone complied. It was a whimsical event in parts, but with moments of bravura and talent and the sweetness of unexpected, intimate performance. It worked, just that once I suspect. My own contribution was a reading of "On Westminster Bridge," Wordsworth's sonnet to the still heart of London, looking down the river in the morning quiet. I selected it that particular day as homage to a beloved city, for perhaps the same reason that it is celebrated, or deployed, in the manner of poems on the underground, or, as quoted in the new slavery museum at the Docklands: "I love this concrete jungle still,[1]/with all its sirens and its speed,/the people here united will,/create a kind of London breed" (Benjamin Zephaniah, 2007(1996)). As with Zephaniah's lyrical rap, "Composed upon Westminster Bridge" says it all. It is formally precise, with just parochial sentiment enough to grab at the nostalgic itching for London, a longing for inclusion that works on you while you are there almost as much as when you are not.

I was *not* there the morning of the London bombings. As Tony Blair made unfortunate comments from Gleneagles, and Ken Livingstone made poignant ones from the center of London, I was safe, in Sydney, under a stunning blue winter sky, which was oblivious to the carnage elsewhere. Why then was I not utterly relieved to have been somewhere else? Having scraped past the London bombing seasons of the 1980s, failing to find a taxi to get away from Bishopsgate minutes after it blew, walking to London Bridge station, confronted by Thatcher's Army, drunkenly singing "Five more glorious years," having watched a pluckily unfazed friend on the BBC news several years earlier, as she got out of Harrods (where she was working on an ice-cream counter) after that explosion—I had actually seen enough of the shock of bombs to know that they are very frightening. Nonetheless, I felt alienated by my absence from this latest, awful set of attacks. A bit of nostalgic sonnet-eering was hardly a response, but it was all that I could think of to do, as if I needed to make up for having been profoundly negligent. I should have known that for London, a city where 200,000 people (Ackroyd 2001: 189–91) used to walk into work on a weekday, and where now a quarter of the working population were born overseas, that belonging and transience collude in shaping any moment of London's demographic reality. Consequently, once you leave, you are gone, and quite irrelevant—both to the city itself and to the generations who shape her. And, arguably, the city may also become irrelevant to you. If it does not, then perhaps it has achieved a poignancy that exceeds its "brand." Perhaps, for instance, it encapsulates for the returning migrant, a (false) sense of belonging to members of the many diasporas who visit and re-visit the city as their birthright, including rural and provincial English/Dutch/Irish such as myself.

Why do I start here? Perhaps because, while I traced the city's tragedy on the international news, knowing that I was missing every local detail, I was reminded that I did not belong in this most inclusive of cities anymore. The rule of belonging and inclusivity in London is that you have to be in London. It is not "belonging" to utter acts of homage. In that sense, the city epitomizes Jeff Malpas's observations in this volume. First, if the cosmopolitan city is a branded entity, then it is also an optimal life choice as much as it may be an intrinsic home or a cosmopolitan meeting point. In this argument, the city and its people, and the memories they collectively generate, are theoretically replaceable in the global imagination by "somewhere else," which may brand itself differently or more expertly against its historical, topographical, economic, or political attractions. However, that is not to say that a population can simply re-attach itself to somewhere else should London ever return to being "uncool," but rather that the idea of particular cities at particular times may have more persuasive power than at other moments in their history. Zheng (this volume) also points to the internal parochialisms of lived cosmopolitanism. It is the detail on a dress, or the shared commentary on a major event, which makes the city cohere. Given that access to local detail is the stuff of parochial status, and given too that an engaged actor in society must be grounded in the stuff of daily interaction, culture, and gossip, the grounded cosmopolitan again seems the only one worth being, or regretting: "The city, and not the globalized 'world,' turns out to be the primary place of ethical and political engagement" (Malpas, this volume, chap. 13: 144–194).

The current cosmopolitan secret of London is that everyone can join in. When I did return to London on a research trip a few weeks after July 2005, I noticed how well the London brand was operating in this context, and how deeply its operators understood the importance of belonging to the unforgiving impermanence of London's population. As had happened in Hong Kong after SARS in 2003 (Stephanie Hemelryk Donald and Gammack 2007: 82–86) the brand "London" was actively called into service of recovery. The Mayor of "LondON" brand, which declared "WE ARE LondONErs" (see also, Nava 2007: 162–64), and, later in 2007, "seven million Londoners, one London" coupled with images of eyes, ears and a tongue—look, listen and follow your instincts to avert danger—signified the defiance of London in the face of division and attack. Now, whether one subscribes to branding as a cultural turn on a matter of principle, there it was, the brand at a moment of crisis, at once a call to belonging and, against those who were just visiting, a barrier to belonging—which in the manner of the perfect brand, promised attachment and cosmopolitan association to those who stayed on, or came back. So, my first observation is that cosmopolitanism in London is indeed intensely local, trades on the parochial need to belong, and is nonetheless fluently coupled with the pragmatism of branded visual and visceral identities.

THE FAMILY TREE: VISCERAL COSMOPOLITANISM

In the final chapter of her book on "visceral cosmopolitanism" (2007), Mica Nava discusses the cosmopolitanism of her own family to debate the nature of her own allegiance to England (not, notably, to Britain). She comes to the tentative conclusion that she feels both pride and shame in England. She takes the former to mean that she has a sense of belonging, while the latter persuades her that it is not a complete identification. In actuality, I would suggest that the shame as much as the pride indicates that she is a local, albeit a cosmopolitan local, and one who has settled for London and nowhere else in the United Kingdom. Nava's narrative encourages me to expand on my own. In order to discuss the cosmopolitan parochial, and the ways in which branding might explicate or "perform" the visceral connectivity of large cities and their inhabitants, it seems that cosmopolitanism might be teased out as a familial imperative.

In her story, Nava recalls her parents' relationship as romantic, emotionally, and politically muscular in all the right places. Her father is a Viennese Jew and her mother is Dutch, and they are portrayed as daring, generous, and ultimately very serious about the responsibilities of survival. Her parents' marriage and escape from fascism eventually takes Mica herself on the journey of her own escape from rural England to London. As Nava's family groups and regroups over the past fifty years, one is struck by a history that acts as an exemplary cosmopolitan reminder of what was under threat from fascism and state socialism, and what grew from survival. She tells us of her own husband, a Mexican—José Nava—their sons, their sons' partners, and of their activism, vision, and commitment to making London what it is, and ought to be.

Before I read Nava's book, I had drafted a meditation on the relationship between the idea of branding and the history of striped cotton. The connections between those two categories lies in the slave trade, where slaves were branded on arrival from the middle passage (between Liverpool/Bristol/Plymouth and the colonies) and then, in the plantations, required to wear annabasses, coarse striped cotton worksuits as a uniform of enslavement. I had made this link in part to explore and test the cosmopolitanism of my own family background, which has roots in the Liverpool cotton industry—after the abolition of slavery, but we were possibly involved earlier in the Dutch trade, when slavery still flourished in Holland's colonies—and to point to the parochial contradictions and indeed, cover-ups, which touch that history. My point is that cosmopolitanism is both parochial and guilty, as well as disarming in its scope. In my own Devon childhood, we used to play in Buckland Abbey, in the days before entry fees were charged and every secret passage or backstairs shortcut roped off, and we would pretend to hear the footsteps of Frances Drake, a former occupant and local hero, and slaver.[2] The meditation led me to consider the cosmopolitanism of everyday trade and commerce, where there was no necessary impulse to a benevolent global order—and so back to September 11, 2001, July 7, 2005, in a contemporary period of equivocal cosmopolitanism, competitive world visions, and vulnerable global cities. Nava's assertion of visceral and domestic cosmopolitanism encourages me to call on my relatives unannounced to exemplify the imperfections of cosmopolitan pasts. Her story also prompts me to ask how London excludes as much as it includes certain stories and trajectories of experience and more generally, how one can talk of cosmopolitan origins and impetuses, when neither are especially cool or politically admirable. In other words, what do we do with a cosmopolitanism that falls headlong into Malpas's concerns about branding practices, which support trade and commerce as an end rather than as a means to collective well-being. In their day, Bristol, Liverpool, and Plymouth were exceptionally visible on the trade routes, and in the life circumstances of those who relied on, or else were mauled by, them: traders, slaves, sailors and bankers, among many more in complex economies of the sea and land. But now they are ordinary, nonglobal cities, in less fashionable parts of the British Isles. They have been subject to place branding in recent years, and to discussions about Creative Quarters (see Roodhouse, this volume) and arguments have raged, especially in Bristol, around the appropriateness of re-establishing mercantile quarters that owed their first incarnation to the slave trade. In Plymouth, which was also implicated in slavery, although to a lesser degree, a recent (2007) exhibition set out the timelines of the practice and drew links with cities and nations in Africa that participated in the trade or else suffered from it. Meanwhile in 2007, to someone returning to the city after an absence, there appears to be little evidence of urban regeneration. There is a new shopping center, some good University buildings in the center of town; there are new routes off the motorway, and Morrisons, traditionally a northern British supermarket chain, is challenging Tescos for supremacy at Crownhill. But it is cumulatively an unexceptional rate of change. Nevertheless, if we are to probe the stitching of ordinary cosmopolitanism, the trading posts that facilitated it must still surely be counted as counterpoised urban narratives to that of cool Britannia aka London. At the very least, Plymouth reminds us that there are hierarchies of parochial aspiration beyond the GaWC global cities index, which cannot cumulatively compete without the cachet of being a capital city or the money of existing eminence in finance and trade, or the current replacement—creative industries.

Paul(us) E. J. Hemelryk, Justice of the Peace and member of the Order of the Rising Sun, was born in Leiden in 1840, and came to Liverpool to pursue a career as a cotton broker in the late 1860s. At some point he served as Consul to Japan, and this experience was clearly fundamental to his image in Liverpool. Likewise, his command of "six or seven languages" (Coop and Taylor 1908, no. 48) was both useful in his trade and a noted characteristic of his own unusual foreignness, which he valued, and made widely known. His image in a 1908 collection of cartoons of eminent cotton traders (see Figure 10.1) is singled out from the seventy-plus other images in that his is the only one so clearly "foreign," marked by the difference of Chinese characters announcing his status as "Consul to Greater Japan." He is particularly distinguished from his partner in the firm "Hornby, Hemelryk, and Co." Mr. Edgar C. Hornby is described as belonging to a "well-known Liverpool family," "educated at Winchester College [. . .] served his apprenticeship with the eminent house of Messrs Nicholson and Wrigley, on the completion of which he went to the influential firm [. . .] his father being at that time the senior partner." Edgar (see Figure 10.2) is not noted for his business or linguistic acumen, but as a "well-known cricketer, [as] member of the Formby Golf Club [. . .], the Palatine Club, and the Racquet Club [and] is popular on 'Change and in society generally" (Coop and Taylor 1908, no. 51). Paul Hemelryk's contributions are pragmatic rather than social or sporting: he is effective but is not described as hugely popular. His major inputs to the industry were twofold, and both in the realm of increasing the potential of overseas trade and communications:

Figure 10.1 P. E. J. Hemelryk cartoon from *Bulls and Bears*, Coop, J. & Taylor, S. (1908), cartoons of Liverpool cotton merchants, courtesy of the British Library.

To him is due the credit of establishing direct telegraphic communication with Havre and Hamburg, a much needed reform consummated in
1889. But of far more importance to the cotton trade was the initiation
by Mr. Hemelryk in 1883 of the settlement system in the local market,
than which no greater boon was ever bestowed upon a commercial
community, and his services in this connection alone must ever be appreciated. (Coop and Taylor 1908)

The short biographical note in the Coop and Taylor collection praises
Hemelryk's work in the Futures market,[3] which was doubtless extremely
important, ensuring as it did a price stability across good and bad seasons.
The great achievement was the extension of the telegraph, and the connections thus made to continental Europe. The innovation brings to mind similar
developments in China in the 1890s.[4] Only tradesmen and migrants understand the need to communicate at long distance. It suggests not only a sense
of what is possible through communications technology, but a determination
on the migrant-cosmopolitan's part to maintain and build the relationship
between the multiple territories of belonging, which both support his innovative tendencies, and define his foreignness at home. Indeed, even the rather dull
publications of telegraphic codes for transatlantic and cross-channel communications are rendered witty by his capacity to play with language. English is
a plaything to be explored and juggled with, rather than a solemn birthright.
The early edition of the Telegraphic Cipher Code for Cotton (Hornby and
Hemelryk 1884) uses English words like private jokes. It was important, of
course that there was nothing in the code to indicate what it meant, but there
were sleights of wit and irony, which hint at the polyglot who compiled this
manual. A few examples, randomly selected, make the point,

Shipping codes

Pregnant: we have shipped ...'s Cotton, and expect that remittances for
approximate invoice amount are on their way to us

Prelatical: Balance in your favour is $ (pounds) . . .

Personal/Travelling codes:

Ruralism: Do not travel too quickly, take it easy.

Russeting: Has ... been operating with you lately?

Spot Market reports:

Socialist: market opens flat

Societies: market opens with fair demand. (Hornby and Hemelryk 1884)

Figure 10.2 "Edgar Hornby," image taken from *Bulls and Bears*, 1908, cartoons of Liverpool cotton merchants, private collection. Courtesy of the British Library.

A later codebook compiled by Hornby and Hemelryk (1924) is figured in numbers, and the element of word gaming is lost. The attention to foreign credentials, including English, is apparent in Hemelryk's memoirs (Hemelryk 1916), and, especially, in the family tree, which he compiled in 1913. This is a complex document, tracing relatives from Leiden, Prussia, America, and England, and has been added to by subsequent amateur genealogists. The foreword carries an oblique reference to the family's change of name in the fifteenth century, but no explanation, and no suggestion that dropping the 'van' may have also been about losing Jewish connections in favor of mercantile security. The family tree is written in French, and in the foreword Paul Hemelryk is at pains to enumerate his credentials for the task of family historian. When his various parochial as well as international (the precious Order of the Rising Sun) honors are repeated in French, the absurdity of a document written in a Liverpool upper middle class house at Woolston, for an assumed cosmopolitan—which here implies European—family readership, is quite endearing. Somehow 'l'Ancien Président du Conseil Municipal du Wavertree' has a finer ring in French translation than in the original

In sum, then, Hemelryk was a cotton broker with some very clever ideas, a keen ear for languages and a good grasp of finance. He was however, in a trade which was built—in Holland and England—on the slave trade, which had only ended for English ships in 1807, and then finally been abolished empire wide in 1833 (Emmer 2006). Did this matter to him? Or what might he have thought of it, if he had been born a mere three decades earlier? To what extent did the movement of ships and cotton, and the movement of codes, financing agreements and profits relate, in a cosmopolitan man's memory, to the sins of empire?

THE WORLD OUTSIDE

> The attack on the World Trade Centre—the two jets flown into the two towers—was a dystopian perversion of this Modernist dream of free movement through cosmopolitan space. Much damage was done to the great vision of the skyscraper and to New York as the capital of this dream. (Foster 2001: 13)

The attack on the world's sense of urban security in 2001 was widely (not universally) condemned for its ruthless brutality. It has also been discussed as an inevitable implosion of U.S. capitalism (Kearney 2003), and a "media event" hardly to be imagined when Dayan and Katz coined the term in the early 1990s (1992). The visceral visual character of the events of 9/11 was conveyed worldwide by simultaneous broadcast, but was not consumed in homogeneous ways. For some, it was a feast of vicarious retribution. For others, who had never seen violence wreaked in such close up and at such close quarters, it was a sudden understanding of what it is to be in danger, to be "hated to death." The subsequent effect of the attacks on global mobility and cosmopolitan confidence was significant. It was not that people stopped moving around the world, but that they moved differently, with a different kind of self-consciousness, and with a different set of expectations of welcome and hospitality. The post-9/11 world rapidly transformed itself into pockets of us and them, paraded as offshore prison camps and military training zones, and into parallel cosmopolitanisms across the Arab and Western worlds. Whether or not these parallels had already existed and were in fact part of the causation of the attacks themselves, we cannot be certain. What however, is beyond doubt is that the splits became both more visible and more stridently articulated in the physical movements of troops and prisoners, and in the online hostage executions. Amartya Sen has argued that this foreclosure of identity and belonging was already prefigured in Huntington's 1996 book, *The Clash of Civilisations and the Remaking of the World Order*, which argues that "the thesis of a civilisational clash is conceptually parasitic on the commanding power of a unique categorization along so-called civilisational lines" (Sen 2006: 10). Sen points out that the causation of violence and inhospitality is built into such theses of separation.

In the essay cited earlier, Hal Foster suggests a further casualty in the loss of innocence in the skies is "the Modernist dream of free movement through cosmopolitan space" (13). This is a compelling thought, although, to the extent that we are free in any dream, I would suggest that free movement has not stopped, but has rather become re-spatialized by the trauma of 2001, and the numerous incidents of violence and invasion that have followed. At the same time and as a part of this retraction, versions of cosmopolitanism in global society are shifting away from an ethos of hospitality to one of pragmatics and security, which in turn redefines our expectations of both guest and host. This also affects the spatial confidence that supported the Modernist experience of free movement. However, by revisiting the pragmatics of early cosmopolitan adventure, the slave trade, we notice that the movement of peoples is contradictory and often a symptom of the banal localism and parochial ferocity of one man towards another. That kind of ferocity, or its aftermath in the years of decolonization, prompted many of the migrations described by Mica Nava. But they also created the climate in which my own family moved and tried its luck in different places: Leiden, Liverpool, Argentina.

An appropriate *visualization* of this particular "dystopian perversion" of cosmopolitanism (an allegory suggested by Bill Marshall's work on the French Atlantic, in this volume, as much as by Hal Foster's comments above) is the *stripe*. A ubiquitous visual expression of radical modernism, the stripe also has medieval and colonial histories of allocating both status and opprobrium. It has operated both as a *mark* and brand, and articulates the bounds of hospitality within societies as well as across transnational "cosmopolitan space." The stripe demonstrates the temporal and spatial loops created by the cosmopolitan and colonial "hospitalities of exclusion" (Molz and Gibson 2007 title page): "The demand for the Manchester goods, exported from Liverpool, was not confined to the British West India Islands. The French and German looms had long supplied the Spanish colonists in America with checks, stripes and osnabergs" ('Dicky Sam' 1884: 132).

In Michel Pastoureau's *The Devil's Cloth*, a short but exquisite history of the stripe, the connection is made between fashions in cotton production and sartorial meaning. Pastoureau records the stripe's contradictory trajectories, daring in a woman's stocking, radical on the coat of a Cistercian, and by degrees at first unthinkable and then fashionable in furnishings. A mattress could decently be striped, but not the sheets, at least not before the late nineteenth century. The semiotic meanings of the stripe are legion, and ring eloquently through the centuries: devilment, promiscuity, revolutionary patriotism, but also a polite English compromise of (finally) striped bedsheets and undergarments, neither colored nor plain, suggestive visual expressions of decoration, modernity, and the technical possibilities of the founding industry of the British Empire. And then, of course, not so polite, the stripes of cheap linen/cotton mixes used to make black and white ticking on mattresses, and to produce the annabasses. By the eighteenth century in the colonies, striped rough cotton was the epitome of an early, compromised, and brutal branding strategy, worn by slaves and by convicts, by madmen and raving women. Stripes were a kind of prelogo *logos* of modern aspiration, and a metonym for a workforce branded by its own product.

But where in all this is the relationship to hospitality and free movement? Slaves were taken to the Americas to grow cotton. Cotton was processed in England, France, Ireland, and The Netherlands, and then shipped back as striped rough cloth for the slaves to wear in the fields. This is a dystopian vision of the workings of imperial expansion and the beginnings of transglobal flows of capital. Kant argued that the cosmopolitan guest should be treated well, but should also expect to leave (2007/1796). But what if both host and guest are visitors, and if neither intends to, or is allowed to, contemplate leaving. It is hospitable to offer warmth and comfort to one's guests. It is a perversion of hospitality to force men and women from one side of the world to another, coerce them into labor, and then to dress them in ways, and with the very materials, that confirm their servitude. We might say that one never dresses a guest because to do so is infantilizing, and makes them excessively dependent on us. But this is not so, or may not be so, for as good hosts, we offer everything but insist on nothing, and measure nothing. A slave owner determines every detail of the sojourn, especially the extent of profit and loss in the transaction: "The slave trade was an unmitigated scene of tyranny, wretchedness, and demoralization; any sparks of virtue that might have flickered for a better growth, was soon quenched, plucked up by the roots, and forgotten" ('Dicky Sam' 1884: 45).

Foster's fear that the free movement of modernity has been conquered by recent terror is contextualized by this history of forced migration. Also, the continuing confusion over whether modernity is better signified by religious dress or by corporeal display reminds one of the hospitality of clothing slaves. Surely, whatever one wears or does not wear can only be understood in relation to the status and strength of gender power, religious freedom, social success, and so on that one experiences or has access to and the choices one makes in respect of these. Contradiction reverberates too with a version of contemporary cosmopolitan welcome to place, whereby investors, tourists, and transnational executives are enticed to a city as a branded entity, "Hong Kong!: Asia's World City" or "LondON." Thus, commercial hospitality is extended in the form of a carefully evaluated narrative of the city unmade and made again as a venue for consumption and investment. Place branding is as treacherously imperfect as history itself, however. It inadvertently reveals the contradictions between the hospitable city and the histories of violence that support the city's rise to prominence, between the soft cotton for ladies' gowns and the rough slave suits, plowing backwards and forwards on the free oceans of modernity between Europe and the Caribbean. Branding strategies claim to narrate the city through its immediate character and its contemporary specificities, but, in the reverberations of history, they always risk ambivalence.

Is this ambivalence related perhaps to the art of hospitality as described in Derrida's reading of Kant, whereby host and welcome visitor are mutually responsible for the transaction? (Derrida 2001). The host must make perpetual *welcome* and the guest must always be aware of the need to eventually *leave*? If this is so, then the branded city plays both parts. It welcomes and informs the guest of what they may look forward to, the character of their place of sojourn, the limits of what they can expect, and the roles they should play: consumer, investor, transnational brand builder: always temporary, wealthy, young enough to contribute. The finitude of the branded city's hospitality represents an abdication of modern cosmopolitanism in an age of migration. If we think now of the nation–state as a host to many visitors, some of whom may need to stay forever, then hospitality needs to be more like forgiveness, in that it has to breach the impossible and be sustained over a lifetime. Migrants who stay forever never forget their status as migrants, and neither do those who arrived a generation or many centuries earlier forget the value of coming first. Those who arrived as slaves were the key to the business plan of the modern empires of the nineteenth century, and it is impossible to forget that too. It is impossible to forgive what Derrida asks that we forgive, and impossible for hospitality to remove that remembrance, but both acts are nonetheless required for cosmopolitanism to be more than transience. How seriously then should we mourn the free movement of modernity, and can we really see any break in the (un)virtuous cycle of the cotton stripe? Is it actually more important to concentrate our modern political attentions not on movement but on the vagaries of arrival and the challenges of staying on and living together?

I am fortunate—or not, as the case may be—in that my own family is deeply implicated both in the slave trade and in the branding of a city, Liverpool, as a trading center for cotton in the eighteenth and nineteenth centuries. Indeed, its fortune only disappeared a generation ago. Its traces can still be seen in soft leather books, odd pieces of furniture, a grandfather clock, a tea set, and a compulsive deracination from place and class on the part of its few survivors. In writing about family responsibilities in relation to the story of the stripe, I fall between the stripes, the ambiguities of responsibility. My forbears are made historically visible in the actions and wealth of a family who never visited the plantations, but who relocated from the Netherlands to Britain as part of the free movement of modernity, and in pursuit of a larger profit. And, moreover, I have my own particular stripe to frame this interrogation of the hospitable reception for these migrants. My great grandfather died in 1921. His grandson recalls a family story that, to mark the death, the *Liverpool Echo* published its front page with a black stripe around the edge, in honor of the man who had done so much for their Cotton Exchange. His "applied foreign-ness," as we might call it, and communicative mobility marked Liverpool's brand as a cosmopolitan trading city with a difficult history, and a challenging future as cotton receded as a primary source of wealth.

To research place branding is to undertake an exercise in finding an intellectual path between academic disciplines. Even without the parochial byway of a family history, it is obvious that the path was also going to prove a political journey, between the Scylla and Charybdis of capitalist, and anticapitalist, certainties, loyalties, and logical trajectories. Writing in the same review about books that discuss new urban paradigms in Asia, Hal Foster charges Rem Koolhaus with "ambiguous moves," in so far as he critiques hypermodernity but also contributes to it through his architectural projects (16). Even before he signed up to state architecture for the People's Republic of China, Koolhaus was enmired in the problem of engagement and critique as a mutual trajectory:

> It has led him to oppose spectacle-architecture of the sort promoted by institutions such as the Guggenheim Museum, yet also to design a Guggenheim gallery in Las Vegas (albeit a non-spectacular one). This isn't a simple story of co-option: architecture must attend to the Groszstadt, if not surf it, and it is difficult to imagine a politics today that does not negotiate the market somehow. (Foster 2001: 16)

Koolhaus's spectacularism presents the problem of willful and profitable self-delusion, which came into much starker focus at the Beijing Olympics. Foster asks, "[T]o what ends are these insights and schemes put?

Is OMA/AMO [Koolhaus project frames] an avant garde without a project beyond innovative design?" (Foster 16). But isn't that why we invented trade, to make ourselves larger and bigger than the mini-parochialisms that sustain our basic relationships?

The Odyssean trick of tying oneself to a mast and enjoying the singing is perhaps as good as it gets in dealing with the challenge of not knowing quite what to think, while being required by one's curiosity to ask questions which cannot yet be adequately answered in received trajectories of practice or theory. But there is a strange Odyssean obstinacy in listening to all sides of a story and refusing to accept any one as better, or worse, than any other. Koolhaus plays to all points of view and eventually his voice rings hollow. So, in this exploration of hospitality and branding, and by depending on the stripe as a presiding metaphor, I am not espousing a nonexistent middle way, but rather a fascination with the griminess of human materiality. Koolhaus cannot be as grandiloquent as he wishes without being compromised. There are precedents for compromise, but there are no excuses, just decisions taken in context. Without knowing the details of engagement with the abolitionists or subsequent feelings about the abandoned slave trade (at a very late date in The Netherlands), it is not fair or possible to judge my great grandfather, but his cosmopolitan heroisms lie in innovation and being different, and not obviously in siding with the dispossessed against the embarrassment of wealth.

> Corporate identity—modelled on Church and Nobility—was initiated by the Railways: The Midland favoured Gothic, and so, in a less expensive way, did the Great Eastern. The Great Western remained its strong Gooch and Brunel self. Greek learning dominated the London and North Western. The Great Northern went in for a reliable homeliness rather than beauty. (John Betjeman, qtd. in Olins 1978: 20)

If railways give a Victorian slant to the age of branding, then material culture, taken quite literally, also provides the term *branding* with metaphorical companionship. *Stuff,* in its older usage, means "material, fabric or cloth." And, of course, stuff was at the heart of the British Empire's trade in goods, capital, and people; without it, railways may never have proved as necessary or as timely as they did.

In 1751, before the advent of a national rail system in England, a group of Mancunians (and other Lancastrians, London traders, and two Irish linen producers) protested to a committee of the House of Commons that the Dutch and French were taking their "checked and striped" linen trade away from them by trading direct to the colonies, and undercutting prices when they did so. Manchester felt particularly disadvantaged by the costs of the internal transport on the privately managed ship canal. The British trade fought back with a new duties system and, eventually, the advantages of industrial England—with railways as the mainstay of competitive goods travel from cotton mill to port. The Dutch, in the person of my forebears, then set up in Liverpool and reglobalized the mill-towns' trade in any case. The conditions and ownership of production and transportation were thus extremely complex, but the original place brand of the lobbyists, and not Liverpool, underwrote England's overall success in the cotton trade. In 2007, in Australia, where slaves were once named "convicts" and also wore stripes, the word for linen in haberdashery stores is still "Manchester."

In Michel Pastoureau's history, he observes temporal breaks between the stripe as an indicator of devilish wickedness or social estrangement, and stripes as marks of playful or determined indiscretion. In the first case, to wear the stripe was to be marked out as an outcast or an outrage. Fools and vagabonds were depicted in art as the striped loner walking against the crowd. Cistercian monks wore a striped cloak to make a point—about the thin line between mendicancy and madness, perhaps. Yet, the stripes of heraldic semiotics were also indicators of status, of birthright and nobility (or bastardry). Pastoureau prefers French examples, but there are Albion stripes: the striped stocking of the Wife of Bath—prolific abundant lover and the garters of Malvolio—Olivia's ill-starred and ill-favored lover. For Malvolio as much as for Robespierre, the stripe becomes a badge of the revolutionary, and a conceit of the bold and the glamorous. And, of course, the stripe was always the refuge of the English textile industry, where the striped sheet made possible a sneaky segue to color in the marketing strategies of the cotton and linen houses of Manchester.

CODA

Four years before I came across it in the context of branding, nations, and the flag, Terry Castles was reading the same Pastoureau book for a review piece commissioned by the *London Review of Books*. Her reading had been interrupted by September 11th, and she was no longer sure whether she could get back to it. She did, however, and she sums up the book's basic argument—that stripes were bad and now are protective, perhaps even patriotic—but she can't decide whether it matters anymore:

> Yeah, yeah, as they say in New York. It's a week later and I still can't make up my mind if it matters—or will matter for very long. There are stripes everywhere, of course: Old Glory and bunting all over the streets, big sad flags draping down from windows. Little bristly ones sticking up from people's car antennas. I live in a gay neighbourhood (near the Castro) and the dykes and queens turn out to be pretty patriotic. (We're all proud of Mark Bingham, the gay rugby player from San Francisco [. . .] who helped crash Flight 93 into the ground). [. . .] I feel like an effigy. Sirens go off outside, a lonely plane goes by I've been

wearing my usual old striped T shirt to sleep in, but it feels pretty fuck-
ing useless. (Castles 2001: 20–21)

Doris Lessing, the 2007 Nobel Laureate in Literature, made a stinging
comment on U.S. responses to 9/11, saying that American's experiences
were less "terrible"' than those inflicted cumulatively by the IRA in Britain
and Northern Ireland. Presumably, she might have said much the same
about 7/7 in London, but has not done so, because American naivety was
the focus of her scorn, rather than a competitive numbering of victims and
a measured assessment of world impact.[5] In the same week, the author
Martin Amis had a public falling-out with his nemesis, the Marxist literary critic Terry Eagleton, about terrorism, superiority, and Amis's "temp-
tations" to prejudice in the face of fundamentalism. These various sallies
from authors and academics across the boundaries of acceptable, indeed,
tasteful, political opinion, stemmed from the intellectual hearts of Britain, and were widely reported in television, and giveaway newspapers in
cosmopolitan London and Manchester. They could not, of course, have
come from anywhere else without being condemned as parochial. As these
flurries of outrage were underway, the Tate Modern was hosting a show
called "Shibboleth," by Doris Salcedo. "Shibboleth," or "The Crack," as it
was more popularly known in the city, comprises a long, deep crack in the
floor of the Turbine Hall. Described by the author as a meditation on postcolonial indecision, the Crack meanders like a volcanic fault line through
the main gallery of the city's great house of modern and conceptual art.
Visitors' reactions to it were amusing. Some were looking to see how it
was made, and whether it would be mended for the next show. Children
stretched their legs across it and skittered like spiders down the hall. But,
for all that it was both more and less exciting than its concept promised,
I agreed with the artist's vision. As a temporarily returned migrant to the
city, fresh off flight BA16 from Sydney, this Crack struck me as an ode to
indecision and equivocation. Not that there is anything wrong with, or
misplaced about, indecision, or even that it cannot be made whole—though
never perfect, since anything once cracked always risks breaking again—
but that the whole edifice of the cosmopolitan heartland is reassuringly
parochial, even at its most oblique.

NOTES

1. The text was reproduced in full as part of the "London Sugar and Slavery,"
   exhibition, 2007, Museum at Dacklands, London. Permission to quote from
   poem sought from agent.
2. See the website of the "Human Cargo" exhibition at the Plymouth Museum,
   <http://www.humancargo.co.uk/HC_ContemporaryArt.pdf> (accessed October 20, 2007).
3. See also the much later tract insisting that the "Futures" system in Cotton
   trading—by that point corrupted into a system for accumulation rather than

for maintaining stocks and prices—be retained (in the face of the national-ization projects of Attlee's postwar Labour administration). "The Case for the Liverpool Cotton Exchange," privately published by Aims of Industry, 1947 (London): "The proposal to abolish the Liverpool Cotton Exchange and to substitute for it bulk-buying of raw cotton by the Government threat-ens, if implemented, to be so disastrous that Aims of Industry has decided to make public the facts as widely as possible" (Frontispiece).

4. At a slightly later period (1880s–90s), Dutch traders in Ningbo, China's southern, commercially-oriented and wealthy port city, worked with local Chinese businessmen to connect the provinces to the ports by telegraph. This was despite explicit refusal from the Qing court to approve such a develop-ment (Zhou 2006).

5. Doris Lessing, republished in guardian.co.uk/uk/2007/oct/23/usa.world/ quoted in online media, *El Pais*, October 11, 2007. "September 11 wasn't that bad" (accessed January 30, 2008).

11 Cosmopolitanism with Roots

The Jewish Presence in Shanghai before the Communist Revolution and as Brand in the New Metropolis

Andrew Jakubowicz

INTRODUCTION

This chapter addresses the idea of cosmopolitanism (Turner 2006) in Shanghai as it has been manifest through the presences of Jewish communities during two periods of time, the decade from 1938 and the decade since 1995. These periods encompass a sharpened fragment of dislocated life that illuminates the contradictions of cosmopolitanism and its peculiar attachment to the symbolic meanings of Shanghai (Dong 2000). While Jews have never been a large part of Shanghai's population, their presence may well have been critical to that quality of its cosmopolitanism.

While Stalin once disparagingly referred to Jews as "rootless cosmopolitans," (Chernov 1949; Donkis 2003: 53) the Jewish communities that made Shanghai their home or haven during Shanghai's international period played an important role in bridging the West and the East. In the past twenty years, that history and the present development of Shanghai have come into a curious collision over the Jewish memory of Shanghai and Shanghai's memory of "its" Jews. The role of the major diasporic Jewish communities is therefore at the heart of a grounded, "rooted" yet hybrid cosmopolitanization of Shanghai. The layered sources of the Jewish presence, at one point making up 10% of the non-Chinese population of the city, point to the different casts of the implications of "Jew" in European and Asian politico-cultural lexicons. In the post-2000 redevelopment of the old Jewish "ghetto," these implications provide an entry into understanding the multilayered complexity of contemporary Shanghainese claims to modernity and cosmopolitanism, in a country whose leaders remain in a sense the heirs of Stalin.

SHANGHAI AND THE COSMOPOLITAN DEBATE

Shanghai exemplifies the alternative modernity that challenges Western pathways to development. Its contemporary brand screams cosmopolitanism, while holding fiercely to local power. Economic development bypasses democratic politics, grand visions of recomposition are imposed on layers of brutalized history, and the construction crane is the omnipresent avian symbol of the city. Shanghai expresses something quintessentially Chinese, that has yet ingested the dynamism of global capitalism.

In its mid-1930s apogee as the *entrepôt extraordinaire*, American geographer John Orchard (1936) celebrates Shanghai thus:

> Shanghai holds the commercial, financial, and industrial leadership of China. There is no rival, and none is likely to arise in the near future. In few countries of the world is there a city occupying a position of such relative national supremacy in the economic activities that are capable of record and measurement. [. . .] It is China's principal point of contact with the world. (1–2)

Three generations of war, revolution, turmoil, and transformation followed, in which the European and Asiatic influences were scrambled, expunged, incorporated, and then reworked into the new communism with the market face of Deng Xiaoping. As one commentator notes of the 1990s city:

> What made Shanghai into a cosmopolitan metropolis in cultural terms is difficult to define, for it has to do with both 'substance' and 'appearance'—with a whole fabric of life and style that serves to define its 'modern' quality. (Lee 2001: 87)

Shanghai is always historical, however. It contains the Ming Dynasty Yu Yuan gardens, now adjacent to a Starbucks coffee shop in Fang Bang Lu; but also, a museum in Xingye Lu holds the girls' school where the first congress of the Communist Party took place in 1921. Scattered through the city are remnants of other histories (see Figure 11.1)—the buildings of the European and Euro-Asiatic companies on the Bund; the 1930s modernist apartment blocks and hotels that housed both European and Chinese middle class residents; and, in a back street behind the Bund and in a passageway across from the infamous Ward Road Hongkou prison, the two remaining synagogues of what had once been the city's Jewish diaspora communities. There are further reminders of the Jewish communities that came in waves to the city from 1850—the mansions of Sephardic Mesopotamians such as the Sassoons and the Hardouns; Harbin and Tienstin Russians, with their apartment blocks, and mercantile stores; then the short-staying but important refugees from the Holocaust, from Germany, Austria, and Poland, whose passing is marked by hundred recovered gravestones now stacked in a Buddhist cemetery.

Today, Shanghai modernity is very wary of anything that might threaten the power of its ruling elites, yet creative, subversive, and very cosmopolitan, at its heart. Knight (2003) suggests that,

[a]gainst prejudices and provincialism, the cosmopolitan learns about diverse cultures in order to extend her moral sensibilities to others. [. . .C]osmopolitanism offers new opportunities for self-transformation. (Knight 641)

In his discussion of Borges, the Argentinean essayist and novelist Abbas (2000) posits that [i]n the modern era, which corresponded to the economic and political dominance of Western nations, cosmopolitanism by and large meant being versed in Western ways, and the vision of "one world" culture was only a sometimes unconscious, sometimes unconscionable, euphemism for "First World" culture. (771)

He continues,

The ideal of cosmopolitanism, to quote a much-discussed essay of Ulf Hannerz's (Hannerz 1990: 239), as "an orientation, a willingness to engage with the other [. . .] an intellectual and aesthetic stance of openness toward divergent cultural experiences" may be an admirable one, but it is sustainable only in metropolitan centers where movement and travel are undertaken with ease and where the encounter with other cultures is a matter of free choice, negotiated on favourable terms. (771)

Figure 11.1 Kofman Mansions Hunan lu (previously Ferguson Road), Shanghai 2000, courtesy Andrew Jakubowicz.

For Abbas, Shanghai's being as a space of "extrality" (the local abbreviation for the idea of extra territoriality, or the multiple zones of law that operated in the city under the colonial agreements) is its defining characteristic—as a cosmopolis it could only survive and prosper because of the indifference that was necessary for both Europeans and as Chinese in the face of such hugely discrepant lifestyles (amply represented in its film and literature; see Zhang 1999). Yet, the European presence allowed Western modernity to spread through the interstices of Chinese urban society.

JEWS AND THE MAKING OF SHANGHAI'S MODERNITY

The mudflats downstream from the Chinese city of Shanghai were wrested by the British from the decaying Qing dynasty at the end of the Opium Wars in 1842. At about the same time the last surviving remnants of the first Jewish communities of China, dating back to the end of the first Christian millennium, were washed away in the civil unrest that overtook thousands of Chinese towns. In Kaifeng in distant Henan province, the walls of the synagogue dating back to 1069 or so collapsed as the riverbanks were broached. By then its treasures, such as they were, had been taken by Christian missionaries to Canada and the United States of America (Goldstein 2000).

Along the banks of the Whampoo (Huangpu), the British Government and its European allies and competitors staked out their pieces of territory. Some of the first merchants to help them out in this task were Jews, originating from the Ottoman Empire heartlands of present-day Iraq, resident in India, with links to the opium-growing areas of northern India. The trade that would make Shanghai was based on drugs—incoming opium and outgoing tea—cotton, and silver, and the avenues they opened would throw together quite literally almost every culture under the sun (Mayer 1999). For a hundred years Jewish communities would be part of Shanghai's diversity up to the last remnants of the wartime refugees surviving into the Cultural Revolution (Jakubowicz 2008).

THE SEPHARDIS

By the time they fled Shanghai in the early 1940s for Hong Kong or the Caribbean, the most Oriental of Jewish communities had become the most British. The Sephardis (strictly a Spanish nomenclature, but later applied to any non-Ashkenazim) were never large in number, perhaps no more than a thousand. They were, however, a highly effective part of the mercantile class that developed in Shanghai. The leading lights—Hardoun, Sassoon, Ezras, Josephs, Abrahams, Kadourie—were critical players in both the economic and architectural development of the city. Caesarani (2002) talks of these Asiatic Port Jews as precursors to the emancipatory modernization of Jewry in Europe.

Sir Jacob Sassoon built the Neo-Hellenic 'Ohel Rachel' synagogue in 1924, a dual homage to his dead wife, Rachel, and his attachment to the Judeo-Christian Western aesthetic to which he aspired. The synagogue still stands the pillared end scrubbed clean, the end where the bimah once was now covered with a tangle of creepers and vines. Sir Victor Sassoon expanded the original family holdings in a string of apartment blocks, hotels, and in his own Tudoresque country house (now next to the Shanghai Zoo, but once adjacent to the golf course). The best-known Sassoon creations are the 1932 Embankment House, an elongated Art Deco block on Soochow Creek, and the renowned Peace Hotel (1929), originally the Cathay Hotel. The Cathay—with Sir Victor's bachelor apartment atop its green pyramid-roofed tower—was quintessentially what the cosmopolitanism of Shanghai was supposed to encompass.

The Kadourie family's ostentatious mansion in the west of the city is known as the Marble Hall and houses the Children's Palace. Hardoun, whose "concubine" was a Chinese woman, built an extraordinary Chinese garden and mansion, where he once hosted Sun Yat Sen. When Hardoun died in the 1920s, he was reputed to be the richest man in Asia. His palace was replaced in the 1950s by a gift from the Soviet Union, the super-Stalinist Shanghai exhibition center.

RUSSIANS

Russians starting coming to Shanghai in the 1880s, though the numbers rose after the alliance formed between the Tsar and the Dowager Empress in the wake of China's defeat by Japan in 1894. Russia's colony in Manchuria, built around the central city of Harbin, grew dramatically as the railway was built from Siberia to the coast. Russians drifted down to Shanghai, and after 1905 with the pogroms in Russia, many of these Russians were Jews from the western pale or demobbed troops left in the east after the defeat of the Russians by the Japanese. The revolution and the civil war spurred further immigration and among the broad Russian community in Shanghai by the end of the 1930s there were about 8,000 Jews (Goldstein 1993; Kranzler 1972/73; Krasno 1992; Ristaino 1990).

The Russian Jews came from two generations—older traders, merchants, and furriers, and younger formally educated professionals and business people. They brought many Eastern European cultural elements with them—a passion for classical music, a commitment to chess, a love of modern style, and for many, a politics influenced by the tensions of Europe—some were Leftists, others Zionists. They clothed the elegant

women of the city, they played in orchestras, they were central in building the Jewish Club in Bubbling Well Road, they developed a number of
the smaller apartment houses, and contributed to the building of new
synagogues, such as the modernist Beth Aharon in the French Concession and the orientalist Ohel Moishe in Hongkew (Hongkou in modern
pinyin spelling).

The Russians included both the multi-ethnic Jewish community with
its various institutions, and the politically divided (between White and
Red) Russian community. The young Jews from Harbin were as likely
to be playing chess or bridge at the Soviet Club as at the Jewish Club,
as likely to be following a secular politics as a revisionist Zionist one
(Moustafine 2002). They could be playing Tchaikovsky or dancing to the
big-band sound of Harbin-born Russian Serge Ormel at the Paramount
Ballroom.

The older leadership of the Russian community found a common agenda
with the Sephardic elders as the position for Jews in Europe became more
dangerous. In the wake of the Nazi rise to power, Kristallnacht and the
Anschluss, the Jews of Shanghai would have to work out how to receive and
manage the refugee Jews of Germany, Austria, and later Eastern Europe,
especially Poland.

THE GREAT INCOMING

From 1936 to 1940 over 25,000 German and Austrian Jews found refuge
in Shanghai, more than made it to Palestine (Guang 1995; Heppner 1993;
Kranzler 1976; Wakeman and Yeh 1992). They were overwhelmingly men,
though there were many families, and most came penniless from the Nazi
terror. Facilitated by Adolf Eichmann's office in Vienna for the Resettlement of Jews, many were released from Dachau and Buchenwald on condition that they left the Reich (Altman and Eber 2000). Traveling by Italian
ships from Genoa, prevented from disembarking en route at any British
port, accepted by the Japanese powers in Shanghai, they came ashore into
an uncertain future.

Sassoon emptied the lower floor of his Embankment House, and turned
it into temporary accommodation. Teams of new arrivals were made up
into work gangs by the Jewish community and with the agreement of the
Japanese went onto Chapei-side to clear rubble and build shelter, in an
area devastated by the war between Japanese and Chinese troops (Rutland 1987).

The refugees were a curious cross section—lawyers, doctors, artists,
teachers, scientists, engineers, musicians, and "waiters" by the dozen. They
established a school for refugee children, and took over the Ohel Moishe
synagogue. They set up businesses at the interstices of European society,
parleying technical skills into livelihoods.

THE FINAL SEGMENT

In late 1941, just before the Japanese takeover of all Shanghai, about a thousand Polish Jews were shipped into Shanghai from Japan, the remnants of the 4,000 Sugihara survivors (Levine 1996). This group—about half of whom were Chassidic yeshiva members (traditional orthodox rabbinical students and teachers) and the remainder Bundist activists and artists, and educated urban middle class Poles—spread through the city, in proximity to the Russians. The rabbinical scholars were given access to the Beth Aharon synagogue and turned it into a religious center for the survival of Eastern Jewish orthodoxy (Zuroff 1984). Indeed, the Mir Yeshiva was the only Eastern European Jewish religious community to survive the Holocaust virtually unscathed.

The more secular community established a soup kitchen, a credit union, and many other reflections of the society that was being destroyed in Europe. Some joined the Jewish club. Nearly every political group in Jewish Poland was present, as were fragments of other great Chassidic colleges of Byelorussia.

THE DESIGNATED AREA—"SHANGHAI GHETTO"

In 1943 the Japanese ordered all non-Chinese refugees to move to the Dee Lay Jao police district (Hongkew) in the Japanese-controlled sector, where many were already living (James 1994). The new arrivals, many from the French Concession with its rather nicer apartments and neighborhoods, had to find accommodation, secure a pass from the sadistic Japanese police commander, and secure an income. This "ghetto" was a forcing house of culture, political conflict, and collaboration, and in a climate of fear, hunger, overcrowding, and anxiety, the community sought to stay intact. There were coffee houses without coffee and afternoon teas without cakes. The hundreds of musicians vied with each other for a few hours' playing (especially if it meant a pass into the main city of Shanghai), while the doctors took turns to offer office hours.

The streets were always full, people walking and talking together, anything to escape their living conditions. Artists' and theatre groups, poetry readings, and political meetings all sought space and time. Newspapers and newsletters abounded, often cyclostyled onto used scraps of paper, or typed in carbons so faint they were like shadows, or on paper so thin it barely held together. The suicide rate rose—and refugee families who had been suffered the devastating typhus epidemic in mid-1942 were again exposed to disease and starvation. As the years in the ghetto lengthened and food became harder to get, the quality of life declined.

A relieving Japanese officer decided, in mid-1944, to take a census of the foreigners, not all of them Jews. This document, only unearthed at the end of the 1990s, reports on the names, ages, origins, addresses, and occupations of over 14,000 residents of the area (probably less than 70% of the total refugees living there; Armbrüster, Kohlstruck, and Mühlberger 2000). The overwhelming majority were classified as "Germans," though the locals included Indians, Danes, Finns, Poles, Hungarians, Romanians, and Bulgarians.

The war ended in Shanghai in late August, but not before American forces overflying their targets along the river bombed the ghetto in July 1945, killing over 40 residents.

By September 1945 the city was under Kuomintang control and American occupation. Chiang Kai Shek ordered all the refugees to leave China—allowing only the Sephardic and Russians among the Jews to remain. While negotiating for time, the Jewish refugees set out for yet another place that would have them—and the majority ended up in Israel, from where they could not be sent somewhere else. In Shanghai in 1949, the People's Liberation Army marched down Nanking Road, and the old (dis)order passed.

RECOVERING JEWISH SHANGHAI—SHANGHAILANDERS, CHABADS, AND THE NEW GENERATIONS

When China reopened relations with Israel in the early 1990s, the question of the Jews and Shanghai began to resurface. Jewish buildings had long been expropriated by the state—the Ohel Rachel was a storehouse for the Shanghai education ministry, and the adjacent Jewish school housed education-department offices. The Ohel Moishe had been taken over by the Tilanqiao district government for offices and housing, while Jewish cemeteries had been transferred to a new location in the west in the 1950s, and then desecrated and dispersed during the Cultural Revolution. Sassoon's villa had been the last hangout of the Gang of Four, and then privatized. The Ezra Marble Hall was a palace for the brightest and most creative children of the city.

Yet Jewish literature was already of interest in China, as it provided a way of studying American contemporary culture through the eyes of an "underclass" or oppressed minority (Xu Xin, Nanjing, 2002, personal interview with author). In the United States, the Shanghai police records, seized by the Office of Strategic Services (predecessor of the Central Intelligence Agency) in 1949, were found and released into the National Archives, where they became available to Western scholars (and were well used; Ristaino 1990, personal interview Ristaino 2004). An American thesis on the Jews, Japanese, and the Nazis in Shanghai, revealed the complicated interactions of political ideology, racisms, and community differences (Kranzler 1972/73). A Chinese political scientist, Pan Guang, completed a research degree examining the rise of Zionism in Shanghai among Jewish refugees, based on records held in the Shanghai archives. By the late 1990s

Guang was the director of the Shanghai Academy of Social Sciences Center for Jewish Studies, within the Institute for Eurasian Studies. He had organized an exhibition on the Jews of Shanghai, and produced a book based on the exhibition in English and Chinese (Guang 1995, personal interview Pan Guang 2000).

Throughout the 1990s Jewish diasporic interest grew. In the mid-1990s the Chabad movement, some of whose founders had spent the war years in Shanghai, sent a Lubavitch rabbi to establish a Chabad house to serve traveling Jews and Jewish temporary residents. He began a tradition of Friday night dinners, where after a religious service a shared meal would be taken among the various guests, each of whom would stand and tell the story of what brought them to Shanghai.

*Wider academic interest also took hold. Conferences were organized at Harvard (Goldstein 2000), in Germany (Malik 2000), in Nanjing by Professor Xu Xin in 2002, and in August 2005 in Shanghai by Professor Pan Guang. Various exhibitions have also been developed—in China, Canada, Germany, Austria, and Australia. In Shanghai the exhibitions have been linked to the politics of memory—those put forward by the Shanghai government and Pan Guang and held in the Ohel Rachel synagogue (one as part of the sixth anniversary of the end of the War in China in November 2005), perhaps competing for primacy with those run by the Ohel Moishe group (such as that in May 2004, organized by the Consulate General of Israel in Shanghai and curated by an Israeli scholar Yehudit Itmar, in cooperation with the Foreign Affairs Office, Hongkou District People's Government Shanghai, and the Center for Jewish Studies Shanghai portraying Jewish children during the Holocaust in Europe). In this context Shanghai politics played a role—the city versus the district, with the Israeli government as a key instigator of the events.

REMEMBERING THE GHETTO—MOVIES

One of the most potent triggers of interest outside China has been a stream of films made about Shanghai. Often prompted by survivors, the films contributed to one of the central themes of Chinese cosmopolitanism that only in China were Jews received, accepted, and saved. In China anti-Semitism did not exist. In China the stranger was welcomed and protected. It was not then so much that the Jews were a funnel of cosmopolitan modernity into China, but that China was already cosmopolitan *ab initio*, and therefore able to recognize a common humanity beyond the labels of European ideologies.

The first of these films—*Escape to the Rising Sun*, shot in April 1989—documented the return to Shanghai by fifteen survivors from Europe, retracing their steps. Most of the other films followed similar paths. The films' titles build a narrative—*A Place to Save Your Life* (1992), *Exile Shanghai* (1997), *Port of Last Resort* (1998), *Fleeing to*

Shanghai (2000), and *Shanghai Ghetto* (2002). *Fleeing to Shanghai*, made by Shanghai Television, was produced in Chinese and English versions, and shown on Shanghai television, thereby introducing this history and the themes of their cosmopolitan humanitarianism to the local population.

THE SYNAGOGUES

Despite the narrative of an *ab initio* humanitarian impulse in China, being Jewish is not an acceptable ongoing identity for Chinese nationals. Judaism is not a recognized religion in China; it does not fit Mao Zedong's model of a nationally legitimate body of belief, and Chinese nationals attending Jewish services are committing a criminal offence, a problem intensified by the recent Chinese government attacks on "cults" (i.e., unrecognized "religions" such as Falun Gong). Thus, perhaps, although "Jew" may indicate a nationality, an ethnicity, a culture, a religious faith, and an identity, in Shanghai its meaning is most clearly contested in the struggles over the two remaining synagogues, their ownership, and their uses.

In the mid-1990s, the Shanghai authorities began to notice an increasing pressure to recognize the Jewish history of the city. They had to clean up the front and inside of the Ohel Rachel in expectation of a visit by President Bill Clinton—in actuality it was Hillary and Madeleine Albright who turned up, and the synagogue had become a matter of international diplomacy. The synagogue building remains an unresolved question—the Chabad want it to be returned to Jewish control and reopened as a working Orthodox synagogue; the Shanghai government does not want to lose control; the Shanghai Academy would quite like it as a museum and fundraiser, and for it to be made available occasionally for Jewish ceremonies. But as Judaism is not recognized, it is difficult for any government body to license a Jewish religious building.

Around the corner from Ohel Moishe in Hoshan Park, the Hongkou District People's Government erected a memorial stone in 1999. The stone, in Hebrew, Chinese, and English, marked the first official visit to the area by returning American Shanghailanders. The stone reads,

The Designated Area for Stateless Refugees

From 1937 to 1941, thousands of Jews came to Shanghai fleeing from Nazi persecution. Japanese occupation authorities regarded them as "stateless refugees" and set up this designated area to restrict their residence and businesses. The designated area was bordered on the west by Gongping Road, on the east by Tongbei Road, on the south by Huiming road, and on the north by Zhoujiazui Road.

The Park is across Wayside Road from the former headquarters of the Jewish Joint committee, a key agency in funding the survival of the ghetto dwellers; the building has been renovated with funds from the legacy of an American former refugee, and now houses old people's accommodation. The Park provides a place for local residents to play mahjong, sit and talk, play cards, and for the children to play on a small fun park. It has become a terrain of contested meanings and competing potential uses.

OWNING AND PRESERVING MEMORY

By 2002, the Chabad movement was sufficiently well resourced to open a new center outside the downtown area, complemented in 2005 by its own synagogue. The center acts as the religious and social center—a new Shanghai Jewish focus. Building on that strength, the Chabad has become a major actor in the definition of Judaism's role in the future of the city. It has identified itself as the definitive Jewish voice in relation to religious matters—and the future of the Ohel Rachel, while also setting itself up as a competitor to the Israeli consulate, the other institutional body. For many Chinese government bodies, Israel is the governmental representative of the Jewish interest—and explaining that you can be Jewish and not be represented by either Israel or the Chabad can be quite an interesting exercise in cross-cultural communication.

One of the most critical roles the Chabad has sought is the preserver of Jewish memory—in particular, the protector of the gravestones of the Jewish dead. Part of the developing "Jew industry" of China has been the growth of tour guides with special knowledge of Jewish sites and stories. One such tour leader G., associated with the Israeli consulate in Shanghai, was contacted in 2000 by a member of a group she had led through Hongkou. He was calling from an antique store in the west of the city, where he had been offered by the owner what appeared to be a Jewish gravestone, engraved with Hebrew script. G. contacted freelance Israeli news cameraman Dvir Bar-Gal, and together they went to visit the store. The story that emerged was that the stones came from excavations in villages near the old airport, from pathways and ponds, and yards. These stones, it eventuated, had been given to the local people in the 1960s by Red Guards who had ransacked and destroyed "foreign devil" symbols, to wit the Jewish (and other European) cemeteries of Shanghai. The stones had been moved from the closed foreign cemeteries in the city to its outskirts during the early 1950s—some under the eye of the remaining Jewish communal bodies of the day.

Dvir began a campaign to find, recover, preserve, and commemorate the stones. He made a short film about his finds for Israeli TV and tried to raise funds for their preservation. He developed a somewhat taut relationship with the Chabad group, who believed they were the appropriate protectors of the spiritual residues. He began to track down the descendants of those named on the stones—about 80 or so have been recovered—and document their stories.

Many have gone to Shanghai to see the gravestones and have been interviewed by Dvir. In 2004, at his new gallery in an old factory complex on Soochow Creek, he developed the idea of a memorial park, and set up a competition for the best design. This move collided with a variety of other interventions that were designed to set "Jewish Shanghai" within the postmodernity of the city.

REDEVELOPING SHANGHAI

The redevelopment of Shanghai's physical structure has accelerated as new plans emerged for its transformation. At the Shanghai Urban Planning Exhibition Building in Ren Min (People's) Square, a huge scale model of the city in twenty-years' time fills one level. The Huangpu River is lined by walkways and parks. The seedy *shikumen* and *longtang* slums have been replaced by gardens and clusters of high rise apartments. Huge commercial centers displace crowded shop houses, and freeways and metros run where streets and alleys used to meander. The modernist dream of a global city is laid out and its edges seem to be far away. Every square kilometer of the huge expanse is landscaped, manicured, and packaged for the consumer lifestyle of China's future. Orchard's 1936 claim for the city's superiority can be echoed today, with the same overtones of amazed fascination.

Yet there are undertones of violence and resistance, as the plan is unfurled and its realities affect people's lives. No part of the city will be left untouched, and nowhere is more immediately open to the developers' bulldozers than the territory of the Hongkou's river front, the North Bund. Even so, the city has identified twelve preservation zones, one of them the core of Tilanqiao, where two elements are identified, "Huoshan Road Jewish Residential Area" and "Jews' Temple on Changyang Road."

THE NORTH BUND PROJECT

The demolition of the old buildings of Hongkou began in the late 1990s, when Dalny Road (Dailan Lu) was torn down to make the Hongkou/Pudong road and rail tunnel—a project plagued with problems such as flooding and embankment collapses. The North Bund plan—the riverside part of Hongkou—has been described by the government as "a masterpiece of the twenty-first century." The design competition held in 2002 proposed a modern business and residential district with skyscrapers, apartment blocks, cruise-ship docks, and even a huge Ferris wheel (modeled on the London Eye). The company behind the redevelopment is Shimao, owned by new billionaire Xu Rongmao, one of China's wealthiest entrepreneurs, and a key player in the new world of Pudong across the river. The project would remove the remnants of the old Jewish quarter, leaving perhaps only Ohel Moishe and the row houses of Houshan Lu (little Vienna).

Chris Choa, an American architect whose firm was one of the competition winners, argues for the preservation of more of the Hongkew story. He notes that much of the redevelopment will be left to private developers interested in making as much money as possible, with the "master plan" little more than a guide to the overall shape. Choa proposes a memorial site in the middle of Hongkou, using Hoshan Park as the site for the memorial gravestones uncovered by Bar-Gal (personal interview, Choa 2005).

CARVED HISTORY

The Carved History Project developed by Choa and Bar-Gal sought to focus attention on the contemporary relevance of the Jewish presence, and to reanimate the discussions about the placing of the gravestones and the future of the designated area heartland. The Israeli Consulate sponsored the exhibition that Bar-Gal developed at the ArtSea studio and gallery during November 2004.

Wang Jie, a journalist with the online *Shanghai Daily News*, described the project in detail: "'Carved History' is an artistic and conceptual exhibition where nine Western artists and architects have given free rein to their creative powers in designing the proposed memorial." "As a sponsor of this exhibition," she continues,

> we believe that the story of the Jewish community, especially in the period of World War II, is an important part of Shanghai's history, says Ilan Maor, Israeli consul general in Shanghai [. . .] In the current project, the artists and architects are not limited by details of location, size, materials or budget. However, [there are two requirements, one that] the recovered headstones [be] use[d] and [the other that] the location of the memorial site [. . .] be within the area once known as the "Shanghai Jewish Ghetto" in the Tilanqiao area of Hongkou District. [. . .] For example, James Brearley's "Floating Stones" suggests the formation of an inverted grave-mound [using the gravestones].
>
> The dialectic nature of burial-without-ground echoes the uneasy history of the Jewish immigrants of the 20th century in Shanghai. Floating enables freedom but, at the same time, creates disconnection and impermanence. Another proposal, entitled "Presence of Absence," is the creation of Corvin Matei. His memorial is based on the voids in the marble created when the Hebrew names of the dead are carved.
>
> Under Matei's plan, some important buildings in the area will be fully restored, while others will only be kept as roofs that once provided shelter for the refugees. Within this space the tombstones will be displayed along a "memory path" that winds through the site.
>
> Some plans for the memorial even in multimedia such as Tim Schwager's "Voices in Stone." A small speaker buried in the concrete will say, at

random, the name of a person and place of origin in different languages, including Chinese, Yiddish, Hebrew and English. (Wang 2004 n.p.)

By late 2005 the project had reached a stalemate, with no response received from either the Hongkou district Government or the Shanghai City. Instead, a new actor had appeared—Living Bridge.

According to its mission statement, the Canadian Living Bridge Corporation, whose offices are in Shanghai and Toronto

> focuses on strengthening ties between communities through development projects that foster understanding of cultures and their history. [...] Living Bridge endeavours to establish relationships between communities through experiential programming that is an integral part of the project. With [...] a focus on building a new economy for the project area, and creating a model for urban planning excellence, Living Bridge Corporation will always be at the forefront of sustainable modern urban renewal.

The only project listed on the Living Bridge website is the Shanghai one and it is described thus:

> A community is reborn. The Tilanqiao development project will incorporate the restoration of an historic Jewish community including pre-war residential housing, the Old Broadway Theatre and the Ohel Moishe Synagogue. The first and second phases of the project will also include a high rise office complex and hotel tower, high end indoor and outdoor shopping malls near the riverside cruise ship terminal and pleasure park zones, high and mid rise residential condominiums and a community/leisure zone that will include a library, cinema, museum and other cultural and entertainment facilities.
> [...]
> Living Bridge has been granted exclusive master developer rights [...]. Increasing interest in restoration projects by the Shanghai municipal government has resulted in the Tilanqiao area being declared one of only twelve heritage sites in Shanghai.[1]

In a *New York Times* feature of May 31, 2004, entitled "Salvaging Jewish Heritage in China, Block by Block," Sheridan Prasso wrote of the efforts of Chris Choa to save as much of the old ghetto as possible and described the establishment and aims of Living Bridge:

> [M]omentum is growing to preserve the entire neighborhood. An alternate [*sic*] plan has been drawn up by two Canadians, Ian Leventhal and Thomas M. Rado, who are Jewish. They formed a company called Living Bridge, which is trying to raise $450 million to preserve at least 50 ghetto buildings in a nine-block area. [...] Mr. Leventhal and Mr.

Rado, who are working with government-appointed preservation profes-
sors from a Shanghai university and a Toronto architect, made a presentation to district officials in Hongkou last Monday. If district officials can
be convinced of the financial viability of the Leventhal-Rado restoration
plan—which also calls for a boutique hotel, an extensive memorial park
and a car-free pedestrian zone—it would then go to the Shanghai city
government for consideration when they auction the area to developers.
(Prasso 2004 n.p.)

The plan to raise $450 million to preserve the neighborhood core and
turn the row houses and former Joint building into a boutique hotel complex seemed to have stalled in 2005 (Movius 2005). Living Bridge supposedly had agreed to mount an exhibition of Shanghai Jewish history at the
main city museum by the end of 2005, as part of its contribution to the
linking of cities with their cultures and histories—but this never happened;
only Pan Guang's recycled display boards from the late 1990s were put on
show again at Ohel Rachel.

Meanwhile the streets of Tilanqiao were being demolished at breakneck
speed, with little in the way of preservation in sight. Honshan Park remained
a quiet oasis surrounded by the sound of traffic and the pounding of pile
drivers. The many players circled each other, bent on their own visions and
interests. Now, Tongji University of Shanghai College of Architecture and
Urban Planning appears to be the advisor of choice to the Hongkou District
Government, and in September 2005 ran the Eleventh International Design
Seminar in Urban Culture and Landscape Renewal in Shanghai. Planners
attached to the College are undertaking the detailed preservation plan for the
Tilanqiao area, working from the broad guidelines of the Shanghai Munici-
pality, a design brief that encompasses the total redevelopment of the North
Bund by Shimao, with the tiny preservation area contained within it.

Shanghai does not have a great reputation for preserving its past. Review-
ing the whole process of urban preservation in the city, Italian urbanist
Salvatore Diglio (2006) concluded that "Shanghai is more committed to
economic growth than to preserving its historical and cultural heritage.
However the city is experiencing great policy dynamism, although it is still
mainly based on an approach concerning the protection of major historic
sites rather than area (or district) conservation, a concept that in China
doesn't seem to be yet fully conceived" (120).

JEWISH COSMOPOLITANISM IN
CONTEMPORARY SHANGHAI

If cosmopolitanism refers to a capacity to stand outside the local while
still recognizing its importance, to draw on values that are perceived to be
universal when confronted by those that are culturally constrained, and to

owe allegiance to a global community rather than to give uncritical loyalty to the nation state, then Shanghai is a quintessential site for the struggle between cosmopolitanism and localism.

The struggle over the Jewish presence in contemporary Shanghai illuminates the role of memory and memorializing in a city where the past exists to be swept away, and where the foreign is only ever to be appropriated into the local. The Jewish presences in Shanghai reflect its former possibilities as a multicultural city, a city of many spaces and places, where localities could link into a wider world that made sense to the people there, but nowhere else. Multiculturalism is not a key concept in the new Shanghai's self-image. The planning schemes genuflect to the physical residua of previous ties, but, as Ou-fan Lee notes, there are few contemporary Chinese—developers, officials, or dissidents—who would want to celebrate the colonial shame of its entry into modernity, or to give foreigners the purchase on the future they once had (Lee 2001).

The Shanghai that was cosmopolitan depended in part on the chaos that allowed it to be so—nothing was fully controlled or known, everywhere was shaky and fluid. There were many countervailing nodes of power. The Concession and Settlement and the Chinese city offered zones into which people could slip and move around, seeking a way of surviving, and even prospering, on the edge of the waves that flowed around them. The challenge that Shanghai faces in the future is to enable the ambiguities and complexities to continue, while at the same time respecting the many pasts that have moved through the city's spaces, pasts that have left very few traces but because of that, are so very precious.

NOTES

1. <http://www.livingbridge.net/> (accessed March 21, 2008).

12 A La Mode
The Cosmopolitan and the Provincial

Yi Zheng

This chapter addresses the constitutive relationship between the cosmopolitan (*yang*) and the provincial (*tu*) in the fashioning of a modern Chinese urbanity. It understands fashion change as "communicative" and "institutional" (Barthes 2006), thus intimately and broadly social: located in sartorial and other material details as well as changing ideas and practices of cultural urbanity. It examines these changes as they are figured in modern and contemporary Chinese city narratives in terms of the multidirectional

Figure 12.1 Chengdu, Sichuan 2008, a stylish tradition, courtesy Leicia Petersen.

dynamics of the cosmopolitan and the provincial, and demonstrates that a place-specific narrative is needed to account for the making of a grounded modern Chinese urbanity. Conventional time-centered stories tend to obliterate the spatial specificity and thus the very make-up of such urbanity because of their emphases on the coming-into-being of a modern urbanity as a monodirectional progress. Here, a place-specific consideration is used as a revisionist aesthetic and historical parameter within which to understand anew the cultural history of a fashionable Chinese modernity as well as modern Chinese narrative practices.

TIME, PLACE, AND FASHIONABLE MODERNITY

Fashion, the domain of change, seems the prerogative of the modern in its twentieth-century Chinese connotation.[1] Indeed, for all its cultural and historical ambiguities, fashion has "acquired positive meaning as the spectacle of the Modern" (Ko 1999: 144). In "Jazzing into Modernity," Dorothy Ko notes that the concept of fashion in its short Republican history was reconfigured from *shimao* (current mode) to *modeng* (modern).[2] However, the substitution from the French *à la mode* to the English "modern" does not indicate changing perceptions of the world map of fashion and fashionable places. As numerous accounts of Republican or Shanghai fashion make clear, Paris was the modern fashion source for the Chinese metropolis (Shi 2005). But the changing terminology does confirm the hegemony of the modern not only in sartorial trends, but also in narratives of cultural and social fashion in twentieth-century Chinese life. It accentuates the predominance of time in the story of the fashioning of a Chinese modernity.

Stories of trends and fashionable tastes in twentieth-century China often treat fashion as the marker of time. This tendency is reinforced in the late-twentieth century adaptation of fashion into *shishang* (trends and longings of the times). In the picture-memoir *minguo wanxiang: shishang* (The Republic Panorama: Fashion), a wistful re-invocation of real and imagined Republican bourgeois life, fashion in vogue (*liuxing shishang*) is equated with metropolitan progress in a tradition of constant change:

> Only in the metropolis can trends and fashions move as fast as the stars, and adhere to constant change. Only there can customs and new needs fuse into one and metamorphose into endless novel incarnations and in turn manifest themselves in the details of everyday life, and, then, spread far and wide into other places (Shi 2005: 6).[3]

The metropolis in this case is figured as the hotbed of modern progress, predicated on its aura of fluidity, its happy insouciance to old customs and tireless fascination with novelty. If the modern metropolis has a tradition, it is one of constant change, signposted by the whirlwinds of shifting fashion. It is a tradition that manifests a foreign-sourced cosmopolitanism where all that is left for the locals to do is to catch up in time. To be fashionable then is to be progressive.

In this retroactive tale, what defines fashion and fashionable modernity is urbanity, constant change, and timely progress. The other image that dominates the lovingly remembered Shanghai fashion scene is the proximity of the megametropolises of the epicenters of world civilization (*wenming*)/fashion marked not by space, but time:

> It only takes three to four months for what is most fashionable in Paris to be in vogue in Shanghai. [. . .] So are other things, like the timely new outfits from Japan, and the 'puffed quilt' style for women worn by the Hollywood stars [. . .] . (Shi 2005: 84)

What is fashionable is necessarily cosmopolitan, though the map of the world is presented only to be compressed to represent the movement of time. This compression of specific spatial locations along one progressive timeline, what I call "the verticalization of space and change," is characteristic of the changing fashion stories leading up to modernity. In the contemporary postreform reminiscences about the older modern urbanity it is exemplified by the glittering and fashionable possibilities of the treaty port megametropolis of the presocialist era. These possibilities are often figured as a lost dreamland ready to be picked up again in China's postsocialist bid to be rejoined with the globalizing world. One might call this a peculiar postsocialist Chinese retro fashion, redolent with brash contemporary politics. But this retroaction is nonetheless a logical continuation of the once fashionable story of modern progress.

Against the grain of these stories that chart modern Chinese urbanity as temporal progress, there are other city narratives that highlight place not only as scene of action, but also as constitutive of modern cultural and social fashion. In these, processes of modernity are often complicated and spatialized as concurrent vignettes rather than sequential scenes. And the materiality of cosmopolitanism is perceived as more than fancy goods, even in accounts where fashion still dominates. Finnane (2003) certainly centralizes the significance of place in framing the "fashionable impulses" of a particular city in that not so easily delineable process of becoming modern. Here a history of fashion that is understood by reference to "place" can still be used to support a temporal schema, that is, as history. Finnane's placing of this periodization in the sartorial practices of Yangzhou problematizes modernity's lineal progression. For example, if indeed fashion in China is by and large the domain of the modern period, its conceptual beginning is much earlier, and has multiple sources. Finnane (2003) explains,

> By the late seventeenth century, if not earlier [. . .] "Suzhou style" and "Yangzhou style" (*Su shi* and *Yang shi*) emerged as parallel, notionally

contrasting, but probably mutually influential modes of dress. Educated men in China began to bemoan the instability manifest in the rise of "contemporary styles" (*shiyang*) of clothing and its unhappy consequences for social order. (Finnane: 401)

And from around 1795, "there was an observable decline in the urban economy as the salt trade entered an era of crisis," (404) but according to chronicles of the time, this was not accompanied by any diminishing interest in fashion or other forms of novelty and pleasure seeking in the city (Finnane 2003: 394–96). In this chapter, fashion changes occur in particular locales for multiple reasons, among which contingency is as significant as social and economic trends. However, what is more interesting in Finnane's emplaced account of fashionable modernity is her characterization of the presence of the cosmopolitan in shaping the local sartorial trends. This is presented not so much as modern progress, but as the presence of a "world context" (Finnane 2003: 392). The object, then, in following place-specific changes in modern Chinese urban fashion, including sartorial details, would be to seek the meanings of this presence of the world context in local places.

A LA MODE: THE COSMOPOLITAN AND THE PROVINCIAL

The cosmopolitan and its other, the provincial—understood as the bounded local place—are usually thought of as a contrasting couplet. Like Raymond Williams' country and city, they are central organizing principles in structuring understandings of "fundamental ways of life," and they often stand for a much wider structure of sensibility than what is entailed in our physical environs (Williams 1973: 1). In Keith's understanding, Williams' insinuation of the country and city into a way of thinking about everyday life is always about something more than just a descriptive vocabulary. Keith (2005) writes that "this opposition invoked sets of social relations and power relations that were crystallized in specific buildings, aesthetics, characters and moralities" (26). Williams's characterization of these structures of sensibility with their attendant urban and rural values is deeply culturally and historically rooted. It can nonetheless be borrowed to understand the stock imageries of the contrasting modern/cosmopolitan/urban and the outmoded/backwaters/rural in the usual stories of the Chinese modern, which are just as deeply rooted. The smaller cities, including the not-so-small provincial centers, are often vaguely delegated back in time into the rural as cultural location in these depictions. The cosmopolitan and the provincial thus delineated are emphatically associated with modern values. In the sense of fashion as stylistic configuration, while the metropolis is seen insouciantly seeking the endless progress of cosmopolitan novelty, the provinces and the country are forever stuck in nonchange, or worse, slow and bad imitation. The fashionable impulses of the provincial in this context seem an oxymoron; those who dare to wear them on their sleeves are cast as impostors aping foreign manners (*jiayangguizi*). The cosmopolitan and the provincial in these associations are temporal rather than spatial constructions.

Cosmopolitanism has always been figured as an ideal against fear and distrust of the other. This is certainly the case in Anthony Appiah's (2006) celebration of a metric of human scale, in which love of and comfort with the other is simply necessary and good ethics in a world of strangers. By this logic the colonial adventures of Richard Burton are as admirable as the ex-colonized African's migration to the metropolis.[4] Appiah's cosmopolitan citizen is of one world and many, a portrait in line with, but extending beyond, both its classic Greek and modern Kantian origin. It has moved from the man who traverses the Greek cosmos, and then the "universal" and "eternal peace"—if one can interpret eternal peace as a general well-being—to the pluralist of "one world and many." "One world and many" is therefore more heterogeneous than the Greek islands, and worldlier and more humanly possible than eternal peace. In this way it is a more historically grounded and realistic, moral-ethical calculus. The other recent model is Homi Bhabha's reframing of the problem of the cosmopolitan through a language of geographical scale. And according to Keith it is based on a notion of "affiliative hybridization," which appeals to a very different politics of location, such as "the unknowable nature of the city habitus [and] the ecological certainties of a finite globe" (Keith 128). What is to Keith a frame of multiple perspectives within an uncertain register is, to me, Bhabha's most significant cosmopolitan formulation. His language of geography is built on, rather than dismissive or transcendent of, places. His cosmopolitan vision is grounded in a spatial consciousness.

> [For] a radical cosmopolitan concern can only articulate itself by conceiving the rapidly accelerating and expanding world as somehow "incomplete," narrower than the horizon of human totality, in contention with the modernist myth of linear progress elsewhere. (Bhabha 2003: pt.1, para. 8)

In current discussions of cosmopolitanism, however, the metropolitan centers are its central if not exclusive referent. They either speak of the "diversity of routes of arrival and roots of origin of the populations of today's cities" or point "towards a different way of seeing the city, an acknowledgement of the heterogeneity of contemporary social reality." Cosmopolitanism is often envisioned as an ethical project that aims to resolve the moral questions that arise from the attempt to reconcile various differences in the context of contemporary global cities (Keith 2005: 39).

However, heterogeneity of origins, routes of arrival, modes of life, and cultural preferences can be understood as characteristic of many kinds of urban formations and are therefore not attributes peculiar to the contemporary megametropolis. Furthermore, cosmopolitanism as we inherit it today is an historical category. The process of Appiah's one world and many extends back more than two centuries, as do the modern Chinese stories of fashion and urbanity. And as a historical possibility, one that can serve as the foundation for any contemporary ethical choice, its location has to be extended. The presence of the world has been felt in many places other than the megametropolis of the former world empires, as is attested to by both historical and fictional accounts. In fact, the traversing of different worlds, whether by guile, force, or happy volition, is the very stuff that makes up the genealogy of the modern world. In the process of modernization, cosmopolitanism became no longer simply an ethical but a future ideal; it became an adventure and a romance (like the story of Richard Burton). As an historical possibility and practice, it is grounded in its particular routes and locations. In some parts of the world, notably the home places of the "others" of the colonial or imperial European powers, cosmopolitanism is experienced as the "world" coming to the local places, converging with the extant "heterogeneity of origins, routes of arrival, modes of life and cultural preferences" of the local inhabitants. And in this sense it is bound with its other—the local-bounded place and locale-based perceptions. In other words, to understand cosmopolitanism historically and in place, one has to juxtapose it with categories that emplace—define it in terms of place and scale—such as the provincial.

In the context of the development of a modern Chinese urbanity, cosmopolitanism is best understood as the presence of one world and many. In terms of cultural and social fashion in these urban formations, it is indicated by the historical linguistic popularity of the word *yang* (the oceanic, that which comes from overseas) since the mid-nineteenth century (Feng 2001). In fact, the gradual popularity of the associations and connotations of *yang* became the best approximation of the grounded cosmopolitanism that developed in China's protracted, often traumatic modernization process. Although as a historically denoted term and concept *yang* keeps oscillating in its emotive connotation and value judgment—from cosmopolitan longing to morally derisive exclusion—it is still the one term that is most popularly used in what might be called an everyday modern Chinese urbanity and its imaginative representation. The provincial, on the other hand, is usually defined not only as that which belongs to or comes from the provinces, but as that which is unsophisticated and unwilling to accept new ideas or ways of life. The equivalents in Chinese language are *waishengde, difangde, xiangjiande* as well as *xiangqide, cuyiede, pianxiade*. In terms of style, the provincial is at best associated with a certain plain primitive charm, or the plain bad taste of country bumpkins. It is therefore the opposite of *yang* in fashion—*tu* (of and belonging to earth, countryside, unsophisticated, parochial). As contrasting stylistic and cultural conceptual configurations, *yang* gradually went beyond its connotation of mere foreign exotica to stand for the trendy, timely, and modern progressive, whereas *tu* became something not only too local in place, but also backwards in time.

However, these associations seem to have little to do with the actual historical and contemporary importance of Chinese provinces and the province-based political economy. Franz Michael, for example, has established that regionalism has been one of the most important phenomena in Chinese imperial history (Michael 1971).[5] Goodman's studies of political and social changes in provincial China, on the other hand, are significant for understanding twentieth-century and contemporary China (Goodman 1997).[6] In his reflection on "The Province, the Nation, and the World," Levenson (1967) delineated the intricate relationships between these three concepts as mutually constitutive rather than diagonally opposing. For him, rather than a transcendental moral program, they are historically changing categories, which have specific temporal and spatial connotations. The cosmopolitan strain in twentieth-century China, sometimes appearing as nationalism itself and sometimes against it in Levenson's delineation, is bound with its other, the provincial, both literally—as the inevitable locus of the local part to the national or cosmopolitan whole—and figuratively as the imagined whole's stagnant past. The provincial, both as political economic locus and its cultural sentimental imaginary, is therefore essential in recounting the modern Chinese story, including narratives of its fashionable urbanity.

CITY NOVELS AND LOCAL COSMOPOLITANISM

It is useful to think of modern Chinese urbanity as characterized by the presence of the cosmopolitan—the world as context. That is, ideas, things, and people from the world beyond China (*yang*) having a significant presence in local places. The world I am referring to here is Appiah's one world and many, sometimes vaguely denoted in the transitional Chinese language as the West Ocean (*xiyang*), the East Ocean (*dongyang*) and the South Ocean (*nanyang*). As numerous stories of city life and fashion demonstrate, what is present in any particular place at the various modernizing junctures are intersections of different and coexisting worlds. The provincial is thus a constitutive part of the world as context in the story of a fashionable Chinese modernity, rather than its antithesis. Following this lead, Finnane's (2003) tale of Yangzhou cosmopolitan/local fashion and Zamperini's (2003) account of fashion and identity in late Qing Shanghai use city memoirs and city novels as revealing particulars of local, but at the same time temporal, sartorial practices. Zamperini argues that most premodern Chinese fiction writers took pains to provide their readers with detailed descriptions of their characters' clothes because they believed in the power of clothes to reveal moral orientation and cultivation, in addition to social status, gender, and class. And, what is most interesting in the early modern city novels that came out of the late Qing period is the tension between these microcosmic and the macrocosmic ways of identifying. As Zamperini notes, "Clothes start marking the time of the body and of the society in which it operates. For the first time in Chinese fiction, dresses reveal the time and the space in which the characters move" (Zamperini 303).

Zamperini's argument for the importance of sartorial description in Chinese fiction both insightfully delineates a tradition and notes the incipient moment of change. But city novels as loci for social and cultural fashion, including the fictional and sartorial change, can be understood even more fundamentally in their generic construction. The descriptive details in the urban setting not only reveal character development in historical context, but also firmly locate changes in place. Detailed descriptions of scene and the vignette dramatizations of characters' relationships are most often the key components of these novels. The stories present change in location, rather than focusing on the allegorical *Bildungsroman* of a burgeoning nation, which emphasizes change in time. A focus on description, from the sartorial to other material or sentimental signs of a fashionable urbanity, can thus lead to a rethinking of the modern novel as genre as well as location for a multilayered Chinese cultural and affective modernity.

"Light, Heat and Power!" is the famous opening gambit for showcasing the startling urbanity of Shanghai in Mao Dun's *ziye* (Midnight), first published in 1931. Old Mr. Wu, a bona fide member of the provincial gentry running away from peasant riots to his capitalist son's mansion in the French Concessions, is confronted on his first entry into Shanghai with the sound and fury of the nightless metropolis:

> What is most startling, however, are the extraordinarily large-sized neon-light advertisements high on all foreign looking buildings. They blare out scarlet beams and green beams, fiery and phosphorescent: Light, Heat and Power! (Mao 1986, 1)[7]

But what really scares Old Mr. Wu to death (literally, even the recitation of the Confucian classic *taishang ganyingpian* (Treatise on Response and Retribution), a timeless practice for moral guidance, did not revive him) is a sartorial detail. To his detriment, Old Wu sees the naked-looking thigh (actually clad in transparent silk stocking) of a woman sitting on a rickshaw, sticking out of the high-cut slits of her satiny *cheongsam*. The perilous urbanity/modernity here embodied in the metropolis is not narrated in the development of Old Wu's character. In fact, the narrative of Old Wu ends when he dies before the dawn of next day. What remain in the reader's mind and stand for the lethal modernity/urbanity of a "morbidly prosperous"[8] metropolis are the spatialized descriptive details of the cityscape and its startlingly clad resident female bodies, and their deadly effect on the old and provincial. This generic specificity, that is, the importance of the spatial descriptive, is also borne out by Mu Shiying's "New Sensationalism" in its capturing of his most beloved and most loathed night scene in Shanghai:

"The Great Evening Post!" The paper boy opened his blue mouth, with its blue teeth and blue-tipped tongue. Opposite, tilted towards it is the blue neon-lit high-heeled pump. "The Great Evening Post!" Suddenly he acquired a red-mouth, from which a tongue stuck out, and from the wine bottle opposite wine is pouring out. Red street, green street, blue street, purple street. [. . .] Oh, the metropolis decked out with such contrasting-hued cosmetics! (Mu 1933: 71)

A bit awkwardly, Mu seeks to record his urban sensations with what he conceives as fresh visual images. He is keen to show off what he has learnt from the cinematic art—itself part of the fashionable cultural urbanity— the juxtaposition of nonsequential, parallel scenes in montage. One can argue that this is simply a classic example of the New Sensationalist School, in which the eschewing of sequential narrative is expected. However, Mao Dun is a textbook social-realist. *Ziye*, like most of his other novels, aims to represent the most typical, therefore the truest, aspects of his society and times. But, as demonstrated in the example of the opening scene, Mao Dun's representative realism is to be found as much, if not more, in his description as in the structure of his narrative. The truest and most typical are represented here in the demonstration of the visual sensual details of an urban-ity/modernity that is as much the web-like setting as part of the unfolding of the story. In other words, the different kinds of modernity/urbanity of the characters and events are dramatized and made real in descriptions of clothes, architecture and streetscapes, and in scenes of multilayered human interaction. This means one can extend the usual definition of novelistic realism from representing progression in time, to demonstrating the typi-cal, detailed- and locale-based presence of one world and many. Modern novels, then, especially those that proclaim a self-conscious realism, not only lend themselves to the most proper form of the "national allegorical" (Jameson 1986), but, more important, are the most vivid and emplaced demonstrations of the coming-into-being of one world and many.[9] The lat-ter is the process and consequence of what can be called our shared moder-nity. If in Mao Dun's metropolitan perception the cosmopolitan and the provincial are diagonally opposed—they kill each other—in Mu Shiying's visual capturing of Shanghai as his home city, the cosmopolitan is localized: his neonlights of wine and high heels are the local scene par excellence.

Li Jieren's multivolume historical city trilogy *da bo* (Li 1997a, 1997b, 1997c, first pub. 1937)—or *The Great Waves*—might serve as a better example of the modern Chinese novel as the spatial-descriptive; that is, as vignettes that produce emplaced modern urbanity and offer an understand-ing of the interplay between the cosmopolitan and the provincial in local places. For, although Li tried in later years to join the "nation and narra-tion" and reshape his ambitious and sprawling *oeuvre* into the progres-sive and historical mode, the volumes remain hopelessly "naturalistic" and locale bound (S. Li 1986: 207–49). The minutiae of the provincial city life refuse to settle themselves into the local colors of a national temporal whole. They take over as the main players in the unfolding of a non-progressive, often disjointed and emplaced process of change—the binding of one world. *The Great Waves* is also a case in point because it professes, like Flaubert's *Madame Bovary* (1857/2005), to be a study of provincial manners at particular historical junctures. To look at the minutiae of the waves of change in social and cultural fashion in Li's provincial "city novel" (Hanan 1998) is to embark on a number of things. First, it joins a complex set of narratives that reach far beyond the tension between tradition and modernity in narrating modern China and Chinese fashion (Edwards 2007). Li's scenes of the great foreboding waves in the gentry and plebeian lives of the provincial city showcase an impressive cultural complexity in sartorial details as well as other material and sentimental signs of urbanity. And they undo the conventional account that posits fashion trends in China variously as the desire for modernity or the echo of tradition. Li's *naturalism*—a critical term often applied negatively to his compulsion to describe lives and times in great detail—is vindicated in vignettes of the *fin de siècle* whirlwinds of gentry activism and plebeian movements in the provincial city of Chengdu. It is highlighted in the minutiae of unpredictable sea-change in local lives and perceptions. Fashion shifts in clothes, cityscape, and social (in particular, gender) relations become central as signs of a provincial modernity that is not necessarily progressive, but is nonetheless cosmopolitan. These shifts dramatize the material and sentimental presence of different worlds as the context for the emergence of such modern urbanity. The constitutive presence of the cosmopolitan (*yang*) and the provincial (*tu*) can thus serve as "structures of attention" (S. H. Donald 2006) in examining Li's provincial historical vision enacted and demonstrated in multiple-spatial descriptive "eat drink man woman" (*yinsi nannu*) plus clothing scenarios of local urban life.

S. H. Donald (2006) defines "structures of attention," through Williams and Crary, as ways to understand city dwellers' and sojourners' affective as well as structural relations to their environs in the production and consumption of the idea of the city; as organizations of perception and feeling (65–67). She provides useful analytical focal points for a reading Li's city novel. One should not only look at how Li structures our attention—what he wants us to see—but also what we notice, that is, the scenes and things in the "city life" carefully choreographed to catch our attention. In this sense, it is significant that Li begins his *Great Waves* with the ripples in the dead pond of a small town. The first volume of the sprawling novel, called *sishui weilan* (Ripples in the Dead Pond, 1997c), was first published in 1935. It is set in Tianhui, a small country town outside Chengdu in the last decades of the nineteenth century. The reader's first encounter with the presence of what might be called cosmopolitan fashion is in the ingenious sartorial activities of an unusual and unusually charming, woman. She is a woman who, with her extraordinary feminine capability and peculiar location, straddles town and country, and moves with the same ease and cheeky audacity amongst the peasants, the gentry, the city plebeians, and the foreign mission, and is thus often the harbinger of tidings between the different worlds.

Deng Yaogu has small bound feet, and embroiders her own lotus shoes. But this seems not to have hindered her from going places with, as well as without, husbands. One consequence of her frequent traversing is unequivocally demonstrated in her clothes. When asked how she manages to pin her headscarf so prettily, she shakes her head and laughs out loud:

> Miss, if I tell you, you will laugh at me. [. . .] This is what I saw during the Winter Month two years ago, when I went with Boy Jin's current Father Gu to do the Foreign Winter festival. There was a foreign woman who wore it like this. [. . .] Do you think it looks good? (Li 1997b: 12)

This ability to take advantage of different worlds makes Deng exceedingly stylish in the eyes of the city-gentry-boy narrator:

> [T]he cuffs of her lotus-pink purple wide-legged trousers are bound with one wide strip of black foreign satin, and then trimmed again with light greenish-blue braided lace. I could not tell what is the color and material of her padded jacket, as it is covered by a layer of clean scallion white unlined outer jacket made of foreign cotton cloth, trimmed at both shoulder and cuff with wide black bands. On it she also wears a royal blue cloth apron. On the necklines of both her inner and outer garments fashionable low collars are sewn, revealing a long section of her neck, though not very white, but looks extremely soft, fine textured and satiny. (Li 1997b: 13)

With the episode of Deng, whose country-town, tu-yang exploits make her a modern adventuress, Li's ripples in a dead pond dramatize *avant la lettre* the presence of the world as material and sentimental signs of a provincial modern awakening. The traversal of different worlds as the inspiration for change is first illustrated in Deng's imaginative "aping" of foreign fashion. The significance of her sartorial ingenuity lays not so much in her boldness to adopt foreign fashion—the result is a locally recognizable attractive fusion into her late Qing outfit, as in her practice of fashion—something that is recognizable by both country-born adventuress and urban-gentry youth because of her spatial mobility. It is an act that makes the cosmopolitan local. In Li's depiction, Deng becomes a proto-modern type: a semiconscious participant in the trends of the times. This is not because of her progressive consciousness, for she is not shown to have any, but because of her spatial mobility and transgression. This sometimes incongruous but always significant mixing of worlds is demonstrated more emphatically in the cityscape and urban-gentry life, as the novel moves from small town to the provincial capital of Chengdu.

In the provincial capital, the Master of the Hao Mansion, Hao Dasan, like many of his local official-gentry brethren, is only third-generation Sichuanese. This is typical of the *fin de siècle* half-official, half-gentry class in Chengdu. Like some of them, he owns acres of fertile land in the surrounding counties, and numerous shops as well as real estate in the city. Though he is reputed to be well-read (his officialdom was bought after he passed the county examination), it is also known that he does not understand the New Learning (*xinxue*), which is beginning to be in vogue in the provinces. Nevertheless,

> not understanding New Learning does not interfere with Hao Dasan's dressing and eating routine, especially since he already has the prospects of being a waiting-list prefecture magistrate. There is really no need for him to follow the trend of New Learning and be taken as a Rebel. Thus he can still calmly and leisurely follow the old rules and habits left over by his grandfather, and methodically, comfortably live his own life. (Li 1997b, 178–79)

But then again, in the methodically and leisurely comfortable Hao Mansion, "[t]hough their life style follows the old and the customary, it is nonetheless fused with many a novelty, indeed in the material sense." They have purchased, for example, a bronze-shelved and colored-glass topped lamp that burns foreign kerosene, and learnt from the professional foreign lamp salesmen how to light it properly. In fact, they have replaced, at a great cost, the lighting in the whole estate with foreign kerosene lamps of various shapes and colors. They have also taken great pleasure in having their photographs taken, also at great cost, and it is to their delight that Chengdu finally has its own resident photographers. All in all,

> [i]n the Hao Mansion these cosmo-foreign (*yang*) things are really not few. As to the multi-colored glazed glass windowpanes, the full-length looking-glass with the red sandalwood pearl-inlaid stand, they are obtained long ago through Grandpa's hands. The most recent and useful, in fact the whole household has grown dependent on them, are the very rare toothbrushes, toothpaste, foreign cloth towels, foreign soap, perfumes and so on, small things. How come that foreigners who look so thick and stupid can make these homely things so very well, that once you touch them, you can never live without them? (Li 1997b: 179–80)

Love of otherworldly things is not necessarily accompanied by love of other worlds, but it does force certain admiration from the provincial hearts and minds. At least it shows these worlds are very much present in the everyday provincial life, at a great cost, both economically and affectively. This duplicity in reaction is further set up in Hao and his friend's discussion of the Boxers, foreigners, and the imperial affairs at the capital and in the provinces at the end of the volume. In general, Hao and his local gentry-official chums prefer the Boxers to the foreigners because of their pragmatic imperial allegiance (on hearing the Dowager Regent's declared support for them) and dissatisfaction with the rising competing power for land and wealth from local converts (to Christianity). They did not show any innate parochial distaste for things and people alien, but on the whole their attitudes are those of a distant audience to a spectacular show. Both the foreigners and the Boxers seem to belong to worlds, which though impinging, are nevertheless still distant, geographically as well as affectively. Interestingly though, they seem as fascinated by the foreign worlds as they are by the magic of the Boxers. For instance, at the height of the Boxer Rebellion, Dasan and his friend He Huanzhong have a chat:

> Hao Dasan does not know how many countries the foreigners have, nor how many of them are there, so he asks He Huanzhong, who was once in Magistrate Yu's retinue and had been to Shanghai. And thus has some knowledge of the New Learning. (Li 1997a: 186)

Mr. He recounted the number of foreign countries he knew, mostly those that the Magistrate had business dealings with or were visible in Shanghai. Hao suddenly remembered the United States of America, where his foreign kerosene came from. The conversation then turns from gleeful applauding of the Boxers' heroic deeds to anxieties about the sources of their everyday delights. Hao worries out loud:

> If they do break into the Beijing embassies, I wonder if the foreigners will ever come again. It'd be a real worry if they won't. All our nice *yang* goods, where would they come from then? (Li 1997b: 186)

The dubious love for foreign goods, which shows the ambiguity of the provincial gentry's reaction to the presence of other worlds in the midst of their familiar environs, is part of Li's careful structuring of attention. It reminds us that the cosmopolitan has come to the heart of the local provincial at a time when the age-old Confucian ideal of its imperial cosmos—all under heaven—is dramatically and traumatically coming apart. The unraveling and reforming of this end-of-the-world world are demonstrated by the material and affective comfort and duplicity with the provincial city's cosmopolitan elements on the part of the gentry. In Li's description it is not so much the fledgling nation–state, but the wide world, that is its context. The citified gentry, whose presence, together with that of the urban merchants, craftsmen, and plebeians (Li's city story covers them all), already signaling the heterogeneity of origins, different routes of travel and modes of arrival of the urbanites of this *fin de siècle* world, are neither conservatives nor progressives of this history. As Li goes on to narrate it over several decades, these city dwellers, from gentry men to plebeian women, continue to be the heroes and heroines, villains and losers, of this gradual becoming of a modern Chinese urbanity. They are jugglers—opportunists—in a process of slowly fusing other worlds with their own, punctured alternately with enthusiastic embraces, revolutions, and rebellions, in their daily juggling of a simultaneous cosmopolitan and provincial existence. For Li, the modern Chinese story is indeed the story of changing places. It is the coming-into-being of one world and many at the very heart of the provinces.

Understood in this way, the nonlineal locale-based city narratives are the most representative modern Chinese stories of urbanity. While they do not hurry along to propel history to its "end," which is a historical perception and narrative practice that sweeps away the multiple players and especially the textures and structures of life and feelings of history, they demonstrate the complicated constituents of change and process. In this context, the cosmopolitan and the provincial always implicate and condition each other. The cosmopolitan, therefore, should indeed be understood as the world context of local urban transformations in fashion, cultural perception, and practice. And the coming-to-be of the modern provincial is the process of becoming one world and many in the bounded local place.

NOTES

1. On dress and Republican modernity, see Finnane (1999: 119–23); Huang (1999: 133–40); Ko (1999: 141–53); and, on dressing the modern Socialist body, V. Wilson (1999: 167–86); Chen (2003: 361–93).
2. Peter Carroll, however, tells us that *shimao* emerged from the late nineteenth-century Shanghai brothel demi-monde as a new coinage for "fashion/popular"' to describe the burgeoning, often hybrid Chinese-foreign consumer culture of the treaty port. It is therefore a case of true cosmopolitan hybridization rather than direct linguistic cultural translation (Carroll 2003: 443–74).
3. This and all other translations from the Chinese are my own.
4. In Appiah's (auto)biography, Burton not only travelled, but was adept at understanding other people's cultures. He was such a wonderful reader and translator of the civilization of others that the fact that he had begun from the colonizing end seems irrelevant. One might take this with some irony, though Appiah does not seem to intend it. This is one point of discomfort for the author in accessing Appiah's otherwise fine thesis.
5. For Michael, this is largely due to the dynamic role played by the gentry between the state and the autonomy of the sphere of the Confucian social order. The dynamics between the gentry, the imperial state, and the relative autonomy of the sphere of the Confucian social order can be seen played out as the complications that underwrite part of the social, cultural and sartorial fashion changes in Li Jieren's (1997b) historical city novel

The Great Waves (da bo), on which my discussion will focus in the third part of this essay.
6. I would also like to thank Professor Goodman for providing me the essential sources for the study of provincialism.
7. The last three words are in English in the original.
8. A catchphrase used in Socialist China to describe Shanghai modernity before it became "progressive" with the change of tide in the postreform era.
9. The term *emplaced* is used here to mean located in the most specific settings and embodied in nameable details of people and things.

Part IV
Coda

13 Cosmopolitanism, Branding, and the Public Realm

Jeff Malpas

The Anholt City Brands Index rated Sydney, in December 2005, as the third strongest city "brand" in the world (Anholt 2005).[1] Let me begin, then, with some images of Sydney from that same time. Here is a description from reporter Tony Eastley on the national morning news show AM on Monday December 12th:

> The racial events that erupted at Cronulla in Sydney's south at the weekend continued overnight, with police cars attacked in one suburb and dozens of private vehicles smashed in another. At Woolaware, near Cronulla, a man was stabbed by a gang of youths. He's in hospital in a serious condition. What have been simmering, but relatively minor racial problems at one of Sydney's beaches blew out of control yesterday at Cronulla. Large numbers of mainly young people had gathered to, in their words, reclaim Cronulla beach from gangs of youths, mainly of Lebanese decent. There were dozens of arrests as police tried to maintain control of an increasingly drunken mob. Anyone of Middle Eastern appearance became a potential target. Several people were set upon and bashed. (Eastley 2005)

The events at Cronulla, which spilled over into surrounding suburbs, shocked people across the country, leading to a heated debate about racism in Australian society, including the part played by talkback radio in the lead-up to the riots, the influence of the gang culture of Sydney's southern beaches, and the possible role of Prime Minister John Howard in encouraging an atmosphere of division and intolerance. For many people, the events were a flashback to the xenophobic politics of the 1990s associated with the short-lived One Nation Party led by Pauline Hanson, but in the contemporary climate they also resonated with anxiety over Islamic fundamentalism and the threat of terrorism.

The Cronulla riots stand in marked contrast to the image of Sydney, projected through the 2000 Olympics in particular, as a cosmopolitan and multicultural metropolis, a city built around its beautiful harbor, its Opera House and Bridge, and, of course, its beaches. It was the reclamation of those beaches that was to become a recurring theme in interviews with participants in the riots of December 11th and 12th. The riots in Cronulla also contrasted with images of a month or so earlier, in November of 2005, when Sydney was the venue for Australia's qualification for the 2006 soccer World Cup. Australia's victory over Uruguay saw a huge outburst of national pride, particularly among ethnic communities for whom football is a central obsession. The Australian flag that figured so prominently in the celebrations of the victory against Uruguay, and that appeared all around Sydney the following day, was also prominent in the Cronulla riots. What was perhaps most shocking to many people was the way in which those inflicting the violence did so while also brandishing the Australian flag (see Fig. 13.1).

How are we to interpret the fact that the events at Cronulla happened at a time when we are supposedly more cosmopolitan than ever before,

Figure 13.1 Selling Australia in Cronulla 2007, courtesy Andrew Jakubowicz.

and in a city that is supposedly one of the most cosmopolitan and the most multicultural? What does it mean for Sydney, for its identity, its image, its "brand"—a brand carefully cultivated by the presentation of the city during the 2000 summer Olympics. Moreover, inasmuch as the tensions that appear seem to have become a feature of many communities around the world—the Cronulla riots bear comparison, for instance, with the riots in Paris in October and November of 2005, only a matter of weeks before the events in Cronulla—so the issues at stake are not restricted solely to an Australian or even Asian context, but have a significance for cities everywhere.

There are, of course, a set of prior questions here. What do we mean by "cosmopolitanism," and what is at issue in the idea of a city "brand"? I have to admit to having arrived at a somewhat skeptical stance with regard to both of these ideas: skeptical because it seems to me that the discourse of cosmopolitanism has itself become so attenuated and broad that it is often no longer clear what it means, or else, when it *is* made clear, the concept appears in a highly problematic light; skeptical because the idea of the branding of cities seems to me to depend on a number of dubious assumptions about the globalized nature of our world and about the character of the city as such.

To take the second of these points first, while the ideology of city branding may appear ubiquitous and, in the eyes of some, inevitable, that ideology implies a conception of the city as, to a greater or lesser extent, a commodity to be marketed and advertised. Whatever the reality of city life, the branding of cities implies an understanding of the nature of the city as an homogenous entity whose identity can indeed be encapsulated and subsumed under a single "brand" or image. The events in Cronulla—and these provide just one recent, and particularly propinquitous, example— may be taken to show the way in which the city's heterogeneity may undermine attempts to commodify it, thus the gap that readily opens between the brand and the reality. Moreover, they may also demonstrate the way in which, no matter how economically important one might deem the branding and marketing of cities, such branding also runs counter to, even while it draws upon, the tight relationship between identity and place.

As I indicated earlier, the branding of cities also stands within a contemporary discourse that often invokes the idea of the "cosmopolitan," but is seldom explicit as to what that idea implies. *Cosmopolitanism* should be distinguished from *multiculturalism,* despite the fact that the two are often associated and sometimes treated as more or less equivalent. Multiculturalism is a very recent notion that refers to a willingness, often enshrined in government policy, to embrace a diversity of ethnicities within a single national or civic community. Cosmopolitanism is both older and philosophically more complex. It referred originally to the idea of a mode of political engagement that looks beyond particular local and parochial allegiances to the universal—to a form of "world citizenship." By contrast,

and while it is seldom made explicit, the sense of cosmopolitanism associated with the branding of cities is closely connected with the phenomenon
of globalization, and the supposedly increased mobility of capital and of
population that is a part of this phenomenon. Such cosmopolitanism is
based not so much on any notion of universal or world citizenship, but
rather on a conception of the free-floating investor or consumer who has
no primary affiliation other than to the optimization of investment return
or lifestyle satisfaction, irrespective of where that may be achieved. The
idea of the branding of cities can thus be seen as tied to what is effectively
a "consumerist" form of cosmopolitanism that is some distance removed
from the original sense of the term. (Then again, it might be argued that
it inadvertently connects with some of the more unpleasant and politically
problematic uses of the term—the idea, for instance, of the rootless and
money-making Jew who was such a common figure in the normalized anti-
Semitism of early twentieth-century Europe.)

Yet although, on the one hand, the idea of city-branding is indeed linked
to this sort of consumerist cosmopolitanism, and so to the conception of
the individual as having no independent affiliation to any place in particular beyond the financial and lifestyle affordances of that place, the language
and imagery associated with city brands also seeks to establish the brand
in terms of its own uniqueness. This gives rise to a very specific sort of
tension, which derives in part from the character of branding as such—the
tension between the commodification that branding implies, and the way
in which the construction of the brand nevertheless aims to project a sense
of uniqueness, individuality, distinctness, and differentiation. In the case of
the branding of cities, however, the tension at issue is more specific to the
way in which the branding of cities draws on much of the same imagery
and language that otherwise contribute to a sense not only of the identity of
a city, but also of the identity of its inhabitants. The power of a city brand
thus derives from that which gives individuals a sense of belonging to,
and identification with, a particular city—and yet, of course, such branding also presupposes a conception of the individual as having no primary
attachment of that sort at all, at least none that could not be over-ridden by
a better combination of opportunities and attractions.

The branding of cities may thereby be seen to instantiate a tension
between a form of cosmopolitanism *and* a form of what we may call "parochialism." On such an account, cosmopolitanism refers to the prioritization
of a global, universalist perspective in which local, regional, and national
boundaries are of only secondary (if any) significance, while parochialism,
by contrast, involves prioritizing a perspective based in some specific locale.
Parochialism, it may be argued, is what we saw in Cronulla. Such a contrast between parochialism and cosmopolitanism is, however, a little too
simple, since cosmopolitanism itself exhibits something of the same tension
between the cosmopolitan and the parochial within it. One way this is
manifest is in the presence within cosmopolitanism, at least in its modern

forms, of two tendencies, one emphasizing heterogeneity and difference, the other emphasizing homogeneity and uniformity. It is, of course, the latter tendency that is associated with the globalizing perspective of much cosmopolitan thinking, but such thinking, it may be argued, itself issues from a desire to enable and to protect diversity and difference from the emphasis on heterogeneity. Thus the existence of uniform structures at a global level (systems of international law, for instance, directed at protection of human rights) that are not restricted by local or national boundaries can be seen as protecting or even enabling the possibility of a diversity of different practices at more localized levels. In this manner, one may take the two tendencies at issue here as actually two faces of the same project—the opening-up of a global perspective that is not tied to any particular locality, region, or nation is taken to be the best and only way to protect the differentiation that is itself associated with the local, the regional, and the national.

Yet just as the ideology of branding operates against the very concepts of identity and attachment upon which it may draw, in the same way the cosmopolitan emphasis on the global and the universal, on the homogenous and generic, causes problems for the preservation of the local and the regional, the heterogeneous, and the different. The reason for this is simple: globalized structures and approaches, even when aiming to support a level of localized diversity, will always threaten to undermine such diversity simply because of the way they do indeed accord the perspective of the uniform and the global priority over the specific, the local, or the regional. To take an example from the economic sphere, the ideology of free trade, which has itself been associated with the increasing emergence of globalized manufacturing and marketing, but which has sometimes also been promoted as a way of opening up world trade, has tended to lead to an homogenization, rather than diversification, in production methods and processes, in sales and promotion techniques and modes of organization, and in the nature of the products manufactured.

If cosmopolitanism is understood as giving one "perspective" priority over others—the global or the universal over the local or parochial—then it is hard to avoid the conclusion that it must always tend towards the uniform and away from the differentiated. It is thus that the common association of cosmopolitanism with globalization can be seen to be partially correct, even though it represents a somewhat inaccurate appropriation of the idea of the cosmopolitan given its historical associations. There is a way, however, of thinking about the cosmopolitan that does not take it as prioritizing any one perspective above others, and in particular, as not prioritizing a global perspective. The solution is simply to treat cosmopolitanism as not entailing any perspective, whether global or local, as such. Yet before I take this further, there is another, related issue that deserves consideration.

Inasmuch as cosmopolitanism is seen as implying a dissociation from the particularities of locality or region, of city or nation, then cosmopolitanism seems to face a basic difficulty: cosmopolitanism arises as a way of engaging in the world—we might see it, therefore, as having an essential ethical or political dimension—that is not predicated on any particular attachment, but actually eschews such attachment. Yet it is only our concrete locatedness in the world—what existentialist thinkers have referred to as our "thrownness" or "facticity" (Malpas 2006: 51–52)—that gives content to the ethical and political decisions we must make, and that enables us to be oriented in the world in such a way that decisions can matter to us, and can, indeed, be demanded of us. The idea of an engaged stance that is not concretely situated is not the idea of an engaged stance at all. To put this in terms of the language of place, and the attachment to place, it is simply our locatedness in the particularity of place, of a particular "situation," that is the basis for decision and for action (Malpas 1999). If cosmopolitanism is indeed to constitute a way of engaging in the world, then it cannot be understood as entailing any dislocation from place, any dissociation from the particularity of our locality, region, or whatever. The question is whether cosmopolitanism can be reconfigured in a way that accords with this requirement.

If one holds to cosmopolitanism as consisting in the holding a certain globalist perspective, then it will be difficult to achieve the kind of reconfiguration that seems called for here. But, as I suggested earlier, it may be that the mistake lays in the idea of cosmopolitanism as itself consisting in a particular perspective in the first place—a "global" perspective as opposed to a "local" or "parochial" one. One might argue, of course, whether the idea of a "global perspective" (like philosopher Thomas Nagel's "view from nowhere": see Nagel 1986) is at all feasible to begin with. However, leaving that aside, there is a way of thinking about the cosmopolitan that need not involve setting the global against the local here.

In its original sense, cosmopolitanism involves the idea of a mode of citizenship that is directed towards the world as a whole; which is not to say that it may not also be articulated through the particularities of one's own place within that world. Indeed, it seems that we could reconceptualize the idea of the cosmopolitan as consisting in the assertion of one's engagement in the city as the basis for one's engagement in the world. In other words, our worldly engagement might emerge from our more particular civic engagement. The difference between this and some other versions of cosmopolitanism is that it makes our own involvement in the local and the regional first as that which enables and directs our engagement with the global. It also marks out the space of the city as the space in which real engagement with others has to take place. The city, and not the globalized "world," turns out to be the primary place of ethical and political engagement.

This reconfigured sense of the cosmopolitan clearly stands in contrast to the globalized "cosmopolitanism" that might otherwise be taken to be associated with, among other contemporary phenomena, the ideology of the city brand; it also stands in marked contrast to the idea of the city as itself a brand. If one looks to the Anholt City Brands Index 2005, that placed Sydney third in the list of 50 city brands (London and Paris came first and second), one finds that its index is based on the following six factors: presence (a city's international status and standing); place (people's perceptions about a city's physical aspect); potential (the economic and higher educational opportunities that a city is believed to offer visitors, businesses and immigrants); pulse (the appeal of a vibrant urban lifestyle); people (respondents' impressions of the inhabitants, community, and safety); and prerequisites (people's perceptions of their basic requirements of a city, i.e., affordable accommodation, schools, hospitals, etc.; Anholt 2005). The language and mode of presentation of the City Brand Index is clearly not that of the city as a place of belonging or attachment, or of the city as a site for political engagement, but rather of the city as indeed constituted in terms of the lifestyle and image that is associated with it.

> Yes, cities have always been brands, in the truest sense of the word. Paris is romance, Milan is style, and New York is energy. These are the brands of cities and they are inextricably tied to the histories and destinies of all these places (Anholt City Brnds Index 2005).

In the ideology of the city brand the city ceases to be a place and becomes, instead, an abstracted image, a disembodied desire, a generic "myth."

In the 1960s, urban theorist Kevin Lynch explored the way in which people come to see the cities in which they live. He argued that people look to find legible images of their cities, built on the interaction between "self and place," that not only contribute to their own emotional stability, but also enable their capacity to act within the city (see Lynch 1984, for his reflections on his original, 1960 *Image of the City*). He argued that people look to find legible images of their cities, built on their interaction with their urban environments that not only contribute to their own emotional stability, but also enable their capacity to act within the city (see Lynch 1984). The idea of the city as brand is the idea of a very different sort of image from that suggested by Lynch. Whereas Lynch's idea of the city image is based on the individual's own engagement with a particular cityscape, and depends upon specific modes of interaction between individuals and urban places, the city brand involves an image of the city that may well be completely removed from any actual engagement with the city as such—an image that often depends heavily on visual and narrative representations of the city that have a broad, rather than individual appeal, and that are often severed from particular and concrete modes of attachment or activity.

Here the image of the city as brand turns out to be a very different type of image, quite apart from its difference in content, from the image of the city that might serve to play a role in, and even to express the actual attachment of individual residents to, the city in which they live and to which they belong. Indeed, since the idea of the city brand may be derived as much, if not more, from the perceptions of nonresidents as from those of residents, the city as brand is even further removed from the city as a place in which one actually lives (for an alternative argument, see S. H. Donald and Gammack, 2007).

What connection might there be between the third strongest city brand, Sydney, and the rioting that took place in Cronulla in December 2005? Or between the second strongest brand, Paris, and the racial violence and rioting that forced the closure of so many streets there earlier in the same year? The Cronulla riots foreground the issue of our attachment to the places in which we live, and demonstrate the way in which that attachment can itself be a source of violence, division, and dislocation. Such attachment is nevertheless at the heart of the life of any city; it is what the city depends on, as well as that which can threaten its disruption. The idea of the city as brand seems not to touch such issues at all, but stands strangely apart from it.

The city is that in which we live, and through which our lives are often articulated and shaped, and yet, as expressed in the ideology of the city brand, it is little different from the relationship we have with any other commodity—that we are citizens of this city is little different from the fact that we consume this variety of soft drink or that make of sports shoe. The globalized cosmopolitanism that we may take to be associated with such branding is similarly a cosmopolitanism that no longer has any connection with the political, or, one might argue, with the world—a cosmopolitanism of the commoditized image, of citizenship as mere consumption, of place as mere representation. Such globalized cosmopolitanism effaces the character of the city, not as some global "brand," but rather as the space in which differences as well as commonalities appear in concrete form, and in which the specificity of our own placed attachment enables an engagement that goes beyond that particular location. As Hannah Arendt writes:

> The reality of the public realm relies on the simultaneous perspectives and aspects in which the common world presents itself and for which no common measurement or denominator can ever be devised. For though the common world is the common meeting ground of all, those who are present have different locations in it, and the location of one can no more coincide with the location of another than the location of two objects, being seen and heard by others derive their significance from the fact that everybody sees and hears from a different perspective. [...] Only where things can be seen by many in a variety of aspects without changing their identity, so that those who are gathered around them know they see sameness in utter diversity, can worldly reality truly and reliably appear (Arendt 1958: 57).

The public realm of which Arendt speaks is above all a civic space. It is also a cosmopolitan space, in the truest sense, but it is not the space merely of a generic "image" or "brand." It is a space of multiple images and representations, a space of complex and shifting relations. Above all it is a space of concrete and singular appearance, in which what appears, even if always in plural forms and aspects, are the very entities and events from which representation and image arise and to which they must always refer back. It is a space in which we are enabled to find and re-find ourselves, others, and the world.

The concreteness and singularity of the entity and the event (what we might also think of as its "placed" character) is what enables our own communication and community across the differences constituted in the multiplicity of their appearances, and it is this concreteness and singularity (this "placedness") that returns us from the potentially isolating abstraction of the representation (and so also of the brand). The way in which representations, including image and brand, stand in relation to the concrete and the singular is how representations gain their content and significance; but it is also through our relatedness to and embeddedness in the realm of the concrete and the singular—our relatedness to the entities and events among which we are ourselves located—that the possibility of commonality or community with others, and so the possibility of the cosmopolitan and the civic, first arises. Without that public realm there is no space in which the encounter with self or other can occur, neither is there even a space in which the brand—nor any other representation—can appear or exercise its effects. The cosmopolitan, then, and the civic along with it, is essentially dependent upon the possibility of a space and a place to which the brand, the image, and the representation refer us back, but from which they also threaten to take us away. The idea of the city brand embodies ideas of both our attachment to place, and the identities those places carry with them, but it also obscures the character of place, and our relationship to place, as always more complex and differentiated than can be encompassed by any brand or image. The danger that the brand carries with it, then, is something like the danger that was felt on Sydney's southern beaches in December of 2005. It is the danger that the places we inhabit, the public spaces in which self and community are articulated, will be reduced to homogenized and commoditized images—as the brand "Australia" was evident at Cronulla—in which there is no longer any clear sense of the possibility or need for the negotiation of difference and the ongoing working out of commonality. There is always the danger, in other words, that the cosmopolitanism of the public realm to which Arendt refers us might be overtaken and obscured by the cosmopolitanism of the globalized image that is the brand.

NOTES

1. Anholt City Brands Index, http://www.citybrandsindex.com/ accessed December 20, 2005 and September 24, 2008. Sydney was listed as "no 1" in the 2007 report.

Filmography

28 Days Later (Danny Boyle, 2002)

Abre los Ojos (Alejandro Amenàbar, 1997)

Accatone (Pier Paolo Pasolini, 1961)

Alfie (Lewis Gilbert, 1966)

An American in Paris (Vincente Minnelli, 1951)

April in Paris (David Butler, 1952)

The Beach (Danny Boyle, 2000)

Bellissima (Luchino Visconti, 1951)

Ben Hur (William Wyler, 1959)

Bicycle Thieves (Vittorio De Sica, 1948)

Bon Voyage! (James Neilson, 1962)

The Conversation (Francis Ford Coppola, 1975)

Coronation Street (ITU, UK, 1960–present)

Darling (John Schlesinger, 1965)

Eastenders (BBC.TU, UK, 1985–present)

Escape to Shanghai [*Flucht nach Schanghai*] (Dietmar Schulz, 2005)

Escape to the Rising Sun [*Survivre à Shanghai*] (Diane Perelsztejn, 1990)

Exile Shanghai (Ulrike Ottinger, 1997)

The Family Way (Ray Boulting, 1966)

Fleeing to Shanghai (director unknown, Shanghai Television, 2000)

Funny Face (Stanley Donen, 1957)

Gentlemen Prefer Blondes (Howard Hawks, 1953)

Germany Year Zero (Roberto Rossellini, 1947)

Gidget Goes to Rome (Paul Wendkos, 1963)

Grandi magazzini (Mario Camerini, 1939)

The Happy Road (Gene Kelly, 1957)

Il deserto rosso (Michelangelo Antonioni, 1964)

In the French Style (Robert Parrish, 1963)

Jacquot de Nantes (Agnès Varda, 1991)

A Kind of Loving (John Schlesinger, 1962)

La Reine blanche (Jean-Loup Hubert, 1991)

Last Tango in Paris (Bernardo Bertolucci, 1972)

The Last Time I Saw Paris (Richard Brooks, 1955)

Le Quai des brumes (Marcel Carné, 1938)

Les Parapluies de Cherbourg (Jacques Demy, 1964)

Lola (Jacques Demy, 1961)

London (Patrick Keiller, 1994)

Love in the Afternoon (Billy Wilder, 1957)

Lovely to Look At (Mervyn LeRoy, 1952)

Ma and Pa Kettle on Vacation (Charles Lamont, 1953)

Manhatta (Charles Sheeler and Paul Strand, 1920)

Metropolis (Fritz Lang, 1927)

A New Kind of Love (Melville Shavelson, 1963)

Nights of Cabiria (Federico Fellini, 1957)

Omega Man (Boris Sagal, 1971)

Paisà (Roberto Rossellini, 1946)

Paris Holiday (Gerd Oswald, 1958)

Paris When It Sizzles (Richard Quine, 1964)

The Pervert's Guide to Cinema (presented by Slavoj Žižek, director Sophie Fiennes; Channel Four, 2006)

The Pink Panther (Blake Edwards, 1963)

A Place to Save Your Life (Karen Shopsowitz, 1992)

Port of Last Resort (Joan Grossman and Paul Rosdy, 1998)

Quo Vadis (Mervyn LeRoy, 1951)

Rabid (David Cronenberg, 1977)

Roman Holiday (William Wyler, 1953)

Rome Adventure (Delmer Daves, 1962)

Rome Open City (Roberto Rossellini, 1945)

Scipio Africanus (Carmine Gallone, 1937)

Seven Hills of Rome (Roy Rowland, 1958)

Shanghai Ghetto (Dana Janklowicz-Mann and Amir Mann, 2002)

Silk Stockings (Rouben Mamoulian, 1957).

Sur le passage de quelques personnes à travers une assez courte unité de temps (Guy Debord, 1959)

Three Coins in the Fountain (Jean Negulesco, 1954)

Trainspotting (Danny Boyle, 1996)

Une Chambre en ville (Jacques Demy, 1982)

Vanilla Sky (Cameron Crowe, 2001)

What's New Pussycat? (Clive Donner, 1965)

Wings of Desire (Wim Wenders, 1987)

Zazie dans le Métro (Louis Malle, 1960)

Bibliography

Abbas, A. "Cosmopolitan De-scriptions: Shanghai and Hong Kong." *Public Culture* 12 (2000): 769–86.

Ackroyd, P. *London: The Biography*. London: Vintage, 2001.

The Aims of Industry. *The Case for the Liverpool Cotton Exchange*. London (no pub.). 1947.

Alberoni, F. *Consumi e società*. Bologna: Il Mulino, 1964.

Alberoni, F., and G. Baglioni, G. *L'integrazione dell'immigrato nella società industriale*. Bologna: Il Mulino, 1965.

Altman, A., and I. Eber. "Flight to Shanghai, 1938–1940: The Larger Setting." *Yad-Vashem Studies* 28 (2000): 51–86. <http://www31.yadvashem.org/odot_pdf/>.

Amiel, M. "Bernardo Bertolucci: Au cinéma le temps se glisse entre les chose et les gens. . . ." *Cinéma*, 172, January (1973): 60–63.

Amin, A. "Ethnicity and the Multicultural City: Living with Diversity." *Environment and Planning A*, 34 (2002): 959–80.

Anderson, K. J. *Vancouver's Chinatown: Racial Discourse in Canada, 1875–1980*. Montreal: McGill-Queen's UP, 1991.

Ang, I. "Migrations of Chineseness: Ethnicity in the Postmodern World." *Mots Pluriels*, 7 (1998). <http://www.artsuwa.edu.au/MotsPluriels/MP798ia.html>.

Anholt, S. (ed.) Place Branding and Piblic Democracy. London: Bell and Howell. (2004–present).

———. *Brand New Justice: the Upside of Global Branding*, Oxford: Butterworth Heinemann, 2003.

Anholt City Brands Index *How the World Views Its Cities*. 2005.<http://www.citybrandsindex.com>.

Les Anneaux de la mémoire. Les Anneaux de la mémoire: itinéraires de l'exposition, Nantes: Association des Anneaux de la mémoire, 1993.

Appiah, K. *Cosmopolitanism: Ethics in a World of Strangers*. New York: Norton, 2006.

Aragon, L. *Le Paysan de Paris*. Paris: Gallimard, 2004 [First published in 1926].

Archibugi, D., and D. Held., eds. *Cosmopolitan Democracy: An Agenda for a New World Order*. Cambridge: Polity, 1995.

Arendt, H. *The Human Condition*. Chicago: U of Chicago P, .

Armbrüster, G., M. Kohlstruck, and S. Mühlberger. *Exil Shanghai, 1938–1947; Jüdisches Leben in der Emigration*. Berlin: Hentrich & Hentrich, 2000.

Arvidsson, A. *Brands: Meaning and Value in Media Culture*. London: Routledge, 2006.

Ayrault, J.-M. "Nantes à la rencontre du monde." *Nantes Passion* 28 (1992): 3.

———. "Une Statue commémorera l'abolition de l'esclavage." *Nantes Passion* 85 (1998): 7.

Baedeker, K. *Paris and Environs with Routes from London to Paris: Handbook for Travellers*, 15th rev. ed. Leipzig: Baedeker, 1904.

Balibar, E. "Strangers as Enemies: Further Reflections on the Aporias of Transnational Citizenship." *Globalization Working Paper 06/4*. Hamilton, ON: Institute on Globalization and the Human Condition, 2006. <http://globalization.mcmaster.ca/wps/balibar.pdf>.

Barker, J. *Wordsworth: A Life*. London: Viking, 2000.

Barthes, R. *The Language of Fashion*. Ed. A. Stafford and M. Carter, Trans. A. Stafford. Sydney: Power, 2006.

Bauman, Z. "Making and Unmaking of Strangers." *Thesis Eleven*, 43(1) (1995): 1–16.<http://www.the.sagepub.com/cgi/reprint/43/1/1?ck=nck>.

Bazin, A. *What is Cinema, Vol. 1*. Trans. by H. Gray, Berkeley: U of California P, 1971. [First published in 1967].

Beck, U. "The Cosmopolitan Society and Its Enemies." *Theory, Culture and Society* 19(1/2) (2002): 17–44.

———. *The Cosmopolitan Vision*. Cambridge: Polity, 2006.

———. "A New Cosmopolitanism is in the Air." *Signandsight.com*, 20 November, (2007). <http://www.signandsight.com/features/1603.html>.

———. "Nation–State Politics can only Fail the Problems of the Modern World." *Guardian*, 15 January, (2008). <http://www/guardian.co.uk/uk/2008/jan/15/>.

Bell, D., and M. Jayne. *City of Quarters: Urban Villages in the Contemporary City*. Aldershot: Ashgate, 2004.

Belleret, R. "Vivre à Nantes: une ville ouverte aux ailleurs." *Le Monde*, October 20, (1999).

Benedictus, L. "Every Race, Colour, Nation and Religion on Earth." *Guardian*, January, 21, (2005). <http://www.guardian.co.uk/uk/2005/jan/21/britishidentity.race>.

Benjamin, W. *The Arcades Project*. Trans. H. Eiland and K. McGlaughlin. Cambridge, MA: Harvard UP, 1999.

Benton, G. "Chinatown UK v. Colonial Hong Kong: An Early Exercise in Transnational Militancy and Manipulation, 1967–1969." *Ethnic and Racial Studies*, 8(2) (2005): 331–47.

Berman, M. *All That Is Solid Melts into Air: The Experience of Modernity*. London: Verso, 1983.

Bhabha, H. "Culture's In-Between" *Questions of Cultural Identity*. Ed. S. Hall and P. du Gay. London: Sage, 1996. 53–60.

———. "Minority Culture and Creative Anxiety." Keynote address the the Re-inventing Britain Conference, British Council, 2003. <http://www.britishcouncil.org/studies/reinventing_britain/bhabha_1htm>.

Binnie, J., et al. Eds. *Cosmopolitan Urbanism*. London: Routledge, 2006.

Bogdanor, V. Ed. *Joined-Up Government*, Oxford: Oxford UP, 2005.

Bozkurt, O. "Wired for Work: Highly-Skilled Employment and Global Mobility in Mobile Telecommunications Multinationals." *The Human Face of Global Mobility*. Ed. M. Smith and A. Favell. New Brunswick, NJ: Transaction, 2006. 211–43.

Bragin, J. 'A Conversation with Bernardo Bertolucci', *Film Quarterly*, 20(1) (1966): 39–44.

Breton, A. *Nadja*. Paris: NRF, 1928.

Bridge, G. *Reason in the City of Difference: Pragmatism, Communicative Action and Contemporary Urbanism*. London: Routledge, 2005.

British Council. *Britain's Design Industry: the Design Workshop of the World*. London: British Council, 1998.

British Council Creative Industries Unit. *Creative Industries*. London: British Council, 2004.

Brooks, A., and R. Kushner "Cultural Districts and Urban Development." *International Journal of Arts and Management*, 3(2) (2001): 4–15.

Brown, A., J. O'Connor, and S. Cohen. "Local Music Policies within a Global Music Industry: Cultural Quarters in Manchester and Sheffield." *Geoforum*, 31(4) (2000): 437–51.

Brugge, D., and M. Tai. "Use of Small-Area Data to Support a Community Agenda in Boston Chinatown." *Local Environment*, 7(2) (2002): 203–19.

Caesarani, D. Ed. *Port Jews: Jewish Communities in Cosmopolitan Maritime Trading Centres, 1550–1950*. London: Frank Cass, 2002.

Çağlar, A. "Verordnete Rebellion: Deutsch-türkischer Rap und türkischer Pop in Berlin." *Globalkolorit: Multikulturalismus und Populärkultur*. Ed. R. Mayer and M. Terkessidis. St Andrä/Wördern: Hannibal, 1998. 41–56.

Calhoun, C. "The Class Consciousness of Frequent Travelers: Toward a Critique of Actually Existing Cosmopolitanism." *South Atlantic Quarterly*, 101(4) (2002): 869–97.

———. *Nations Matter: Culture, History and the Cosmopolitan Dream*. London: Routledge, 2007.

Calzolari, V. "Il volto della città americana." *Urbanistica*, 32, December (1960): 13–19.

Campani, G., F. Carchedi, and A. Tassinari. Eds. *L'immigrazione silenziosa: La comunità cinese in Italia*. Torino: Fondazione Agnelli, 1994.

Canter, D. *The Psychology of Place*. London: Architectural Press, 1977.

Carroll, P. "Refashioning Suzhou: Dress, Commodification, and Modernity." *positions: east asia cultures critique*, 11(2) (2003): 443–78.

Castles, T. "11 September: Some LRB Writers Reflect on the Reasons and Consequences." *London Review of Books*, 23(19) (2001): 20–21.

Celant, G. Ed. *The Italian Metamorphosis, 1943–1968*. New York: Guggenheim Museum Publications, 1994.

Chan, C. et al. *The UK Chinese People: Diversity & Unmet Needs*. Nottingham: Division of Social Work, Social Policy & Human Services, Nottingham Trent University, 2004.

Chan W. "A Gift of a Pagoda, the Presence of a Prominent Citizen and the Possibilities of Hospitality." *Environment and Planning D*, 23(1) (2005): 11–28.

———. "Planning Birmingham as a Cosmopolitan City: Recovering the Depths of its Diversity." *Cosmopolitan Urbanism*. Ed. J. Binnie et al. London: Routledge, 2006. 204–19.

Chen, T. "Proletarian White and Working Bodies in Mao's China." *positions: east asia cultures critique*, 11(2) (2003): 361–93.

Chernov, F. "Bourgeois Cosmopolitanism and its reactionary role," Bol'shevilz: Theoretical and Political Magazine of the Central Committee of the ACP(B), Issue #5, 15 March 1949, 30–41. Accessed 7 September 2008. http://www.cyberussr.com/rus/chernov-cosmo-e.html.

Cheronnet, L. *Paris tel qu'il fut: 104 photographies anciennes*. Paris: Tel, 1951. [Foreword dated 1943].

Chinese in Britain Forum [CiBF]. "Success for our Children, Missed Opportunities for our Community" Conference theme. London: CiBF, 2007.

Chinese Community Centre [CCC]. *Chinese People in the UK*, London: Chinese Community Centre, 2005. <http://www.ccc.org.uk/>.

The Chinese Exclusion Act, 1892, passed U.S. Congeress May 6, 1882. U.S. Congress. Washington, USA.

Christiansen, F. *Chinatown, Europe: An Exploration of Overseas Chinese Identity in the 1990s*. London: Routledge, 2003.

Cochrane, A., and A. Jonas. "Re-Imagining Berlin: World City, National Capital or Ordinary Place?" *European Urban and Regional Studies*, 6(2): (1999) 145–64.

Collyer, M. *The Algerian Community in Britain*. London: King's College, ICAR Country Guide, 2004. <http://www.icar.org>.
———. "When Do Social Networks Fail to Explain Migration? Accounting for the Movement of Algerian Asylum-Seekers to the UK." *Journal of Ethnic and Migration Studies*, 31(4) (2005): 699–718.
Coombes, A. "Travelling Tales: Narrative and History in the Work of Joy Gregory." *Continental Drift: Europe Approaching the Millennium*. Ed. M. Sand and A. McNeill. Munich: Prestel, 1998. 99–101.
Coop, J., and S. Taylor. *Bulls and Bears: Cartoons of Members and Ring Traders of the Liverpool Cotton Exchange*. Liverpool, 1908.
Cowley, J. "The Politics of Belonging: Some Theoretical Considerations." *The Politics of Belonging: Migrants and Minorities in Contemporary Europe*. Ed. A. Geddes and A. Favell. Aldershot: Ashgate, 1999. 15–41.
Craddock, S. "Embodying Place: Pathologizing Chinese and Chinatown in Nineteenth-Century San Francisco." *Antipode* 31(4) (1999): 351"71.
Crary, J. "Spectacle, Attention, Counter-Memory." *October 50* (1989): 96–107.
Creative Industries Taskforce. *Creative Industries: Mapping Document*. London: Department for Culture, Media and Sport, 1998.
Curthoys, A. "An Uneasy Conversation: the Multicultural and the Indigenous," in Docker, J. and G. Fischer (eds.) *Race, Colour and Indentity in Australia and New Zealand*, Sydney: UNSW Press, 21–36.
Dayan, D. and E. Katz. *Media Events: The Love Broadcasting of History*. Cambridge: Harvard University Press, 1992.
de Beauvoir, S. *Breton or Poetry*. Trans. and Ed. H. Parshley. London: Everyman Library, 1993.
de Certeau, M. *The Practice of Everyday Life*. Trans. S. Rendell. Berkeley: U of California P, 1988. [Translation first published in 1984].
Deleuze, G. *Cinema 1: The Movement-Image*. Trans. H. Tomlinson and B. Habberjam. London: Continuum, 2005.
Demos. (London Think Tank). "Manchester is Favourite with 'New Bohemians.'" Media Release, May, 26. 2003. London. <http://www.demos.co.uk/media/press-releases/bohobritain>.
"Dernier tango à Paris." *Le Monde*, December 15 (1972), 15.
Derrida, J. *On Cosmopolitanism and Forgiveness*. London: Routledge, 2001.
'Dicky Sam.' *Liverpool and Slavery: An Historical Account of the Liverpool-African Slave Trade*. Liverpool: Bowker, 1884.
Diglio, S. "Urban Development and Historic Heritage Protection in Shanghai." *Web Journal on Cultural Patrimony*, 1, (2006). <http://www.webjournal.unior.it/Articoli.php?idVolume=17>.
Donald, J. *Imagining the Modern City*. London: Athlone, 1999.
———. "Internationalisation, Diversity and the Humanities Curriculum: Cosmopolitanism and Multiculturalism Revisited." *Journal of Philosophy of Education*, 41 (3) (2007): 289–308.
Donald, S. H. "The Idea of Hong Kong: Structures of Attention in the City of Life." *Urban Space and Cityscapes: Perspectives from Modern and Contemporary Culture*. Ed. C. Lindner. London: Routledge, 2006. 63–74.
Donald, S. H., and J. Gammack. *Tourism and the Branded City: Film and Identity on the Pacific Rim*. Aldershot: Ashgate, 2007.
Dong, S. *Shanghai: the Rise and Fall of a Decadent City, 1842–1949*. New York: HarperCollins, 2000.
Donski, L. *Forms of Hatred: The Troubled Imagination in Modern Philosophy and Literature*, Amersterdam: Rodapi, 2003.
Dorrian, M. "Cityscape with Ferris Wheel: Chicago, 1893." *Urban Space and Cityscapes: Perspectives from Modern and Contemporary Culture*. Ed. C. Lindner. New York: Routledge, 2006, 17–37.

Dyer, R. *White.* London: Routledge, 1997.
Eade, J. *Placing London: From Imperial Capital to Global City.* Oxford: Berghahn, 2000.
Ealham, C. "An Imagined Geography: Ideology, Urban Space, and Protest in the Creation of Barcelona's 'Chinatown,' c. 1835–1936." *International Review of Social History* 50 (2005): 373–97.
Eastley, T. *AM,* Australian Broadcasting Commission radio broadcast, 12 December 12, 2005. Print version available at <http://www.abc.net.au/am/content/2005/s1528707.htm>.
Edwards, L. "Dressing for Power: Scholars' Robes, School Uniforms and Military Attire in China." *The Politics of Dress in Asia and the Americas.* Ed. M. Roces and L. Edwards. Brighton: Sussex Academic Press, 2007, 42–64.
Eliot, T. S. "The Waste Land." *Selected Poems.* London: Faber & Faber, 1961. (Original published 1922).
Elsaesser, T. *Metropolis.* London: BFI, 2000.
Emmer, P. *The Dutch Slave Trade: 1500–1850.* Oxford: Berghahn, 2006.
Evans, G., and J. Foord. "Rich Mix Cities: From Multicultural Experience to Cosmopolitan Engagement." *Journal of European Ethnology,* 34(2) (2004): 71–84.
Feng, W. "*Yi, Yang, Xi, Wai* and Other Terms: the Transition from 'Barbarian' to 'Foreigner' in Nineteenth-Century China." *New Terms for New Ideas: Western Knowledge and Lexical Change in Late Imperial China.* Ed. M. Lackner, I. Amelung and J. Kurtz. Leiden: Brill, 2001. 95–124.
Farina P. et al. *Cina a Milano: Famiglie, ambienti e lavori della popolazione cinese a Milano.* Milan: Segesta, 1997.
Favell, A. "London as Eurocity: French Free Movers in the Economic Capital of Europe." *The Human Face of Global Mobility.* Ed. M. Smith and A. Favell. New Brunswick, NJ: Transaction, 2006. 247–74.
FinFuture. *Business Plan, 2006/7—For Partners and Stakeholders.* London: FinFuture, 2006.
Finnane, A. "Military Culture and Chinese Dress in the Early Twentieth Century." *China Chic: East Meets West.* Ed. V. Steele and J. Major. New Haven: Yale UP, 1999. 119–31.
———. "Yangzhou's 'Modernity': Fashion and Consumption in the Early Nineteenth Century." *positions: east asia cultures critique,* 11 (2003): 395–425.
Flaubert, G. *Par les champs et par les grèves.* Paris: Encre, 1979 [Original published in 1886].
———. *Madame Bovary.* Trans. M. Overstall, M. Bowie, and M. Mauldon. Oxford: Oxford UP, 2005. [Original published 1857].
Florida, R. *The Rise of the Creative Class, and How It's Transforming Work, Leisure, Community and Everyday Life.* New York: Basic Books, 2005.
Forman, M. "'Represent': Race, Space and Place in Rap Music." *Popular Music,* 19(1) (2000): 65–90.
Fortier, A.-M. "Too Close for Comfort: Loving thy Neighbour and the Management of Multicultural Intimacies." *Environment and Planning D,* 25 (2007): 104–19.
Foster, H. "Bigness" [A review of the *Harvard Guide to Shopping* and *Great Leap Forward.* Ed. by Rem Koolhaas et al.], *London Review of Books,* 23, November (2001): 13–16.
Frei, K. *Wer sich maskiert, wird integriert: Der Karneval der Kulturen in Berlin.* Berlin: Schiler, 2003.
Freud, S. "The 'Uncanny.'" *Writings on Art and Literature.* Trans. by J. Strachey. Ed. W. Hamacher and D. Wellbery. Palo Alto: Stanford UP, 1997. (Original published in 1919), 193–233.
Fried, R. *Planning the Eternal City: Roman Politics and Planning since World War II.* New Haven: Yale UP, 1973.

"Front de Seine: Secteur Beaugrenelle." *Architecture d'aujourd'hui,* June–July (1968): 90 [A special issue on Paris].

Garland, A. *The Beach.* New York: Rutherford Books, 1997.

Germain, A., and M. RadiceM. "Cosmopolitanism by Default: Public Sociability in Montreal." *Cosmopolitan Urbanism.* Ed. J. Binnie et al. London: Routledge, 2006. 112–39.

Gilroy, P. *After Empire: Melancholia or Convivial Culture?* Abingdon: Routledge, 2004.

Giroire, P. "Monument contre l'abolition de l'esclavage." *Ouest-France,* 25 May: 2004.

Goldstein, J. "Shanghai Consular Records about Jewish Refugees." *Society for Historians of American Foreign Relations. Newsletter* 24: (1993) 19–23.

———. *The Jews of China: a Sourcebook and Resource Guide, Vol. 2.* Armonk, NY: Sharpe, 2000.

Goodman, D. Ed.*China's Provinces in Reform: Class, Community and Political Culture.* London: Routledge, 1997.

Gras, P. "L'après-friche portuaire entre imaginaire, mémoire et culture." *Urbanisme* 341 (2005): 36–38.

Greater London Authority [GLA]. *London—The World in a City: An Analysis of the 2001 Census Results, London.* Greater London Authority Data Management and Analysis Group Briefing 2005/6. London: GLA, 2005.

Greater London Council, Industry and Employment Branch. *London Industrial Strategy: The Cultural Industries.* London: Greater London Council, 1985.

Gregory, J. "Memory and Skin." *Continental Drift: Europe Approaching the Millennium.* Ed. M. L. Sand and A. McNeill. Munich: Prestel, 1998. 101–13.

Grillo, R. "An Excess of Alterity? Debating Difference in a Multicultural Society." *Ethnic and Racial Studies,* 30 (2007): 979–98.

Guang, P. *Youtai Ren Zai Shanghai: The Jews in Shanghai.* Shanghai: Shanghai Pictorial, 1995.

Gudjonsson, H. "Nation Branding." *Place Branding,* 1 (2005): 283–298.

Guyvarc'h, D. "Nantes au XIXe et au XXe siècles; du port vécu au port rêvé." *La Ville maritime: temps, espace et représentations.* Ed. F. Roudaut, Brest: Université de Bretagne Occidentale, 1996, 75–84.

———. *La Construction d'une ville: Nantes (1914–1992).* Villeneuve d'Ascq: Septentrion, 1997.

———. "Les troubles de la mémoire nantaise." *Cahiers des Anneaux de la Mémoire,* 1(1999): 127–39.

Hall, S. "Divided City: the Crisis of London." *Open Democracy,* October 28 (2004). <http://www.opendemocracy.net/content/articles/PDF/2191.pdf>.

Hamilton, C., and A. Scullion. "The Effectiveness of the Scottish Arts Council's Links & Partnerships with other Agencies." Unpublished report for Glasgow University, 2002.

Hamnett, C. *Unequal City: London in the Global Arena.* London: Routledge, 2003.

Hanan, P. "*Fengyue Meng* and the Courtesan Novel." *Harvard Journal of Asiatic Studies,* 58 (1998): 345–72.

Hannerz, U. "Cosmopolitans and Locals in World Culture." *Global Culture: Nationalism, Globalization and Modernity.* Ed. M. Featherstone. London: Sage, 1990, 237–252.

Harvey, D. "From Managerialism to Entrepreneurialism: The Transformation in Urban Governance in Late Capitalism." *Geografiska Annaler B,* 71(1) (1989): 3–17.

Hatziprokopiou, P. "Locating Difference in the Cosmopolis: Spaces of 'Ordinary' and 'Branded' Diversity and the Place of London's Chinatown." Paper presented at workshop entitled "Class and Place: Cosmopolitan Perspectives on a 'Grounded' Sensorium." UTS, Sydney, June 2007.

Häussermann, H., and C. Colomb. "The New Berlin: Marketing the City of Dreams." *Cities and Visitors: Regulating People, Markets, and City Space.* Ed. L. Hoffman et al. Oxford: Blackwell, 2003. 200–18.

Hemelryk, P. *Forty Years' Reminiscences of the Cotton Market: The American War Time and After.* Liverpool, 1916.

Heppner, E. *Shanghai Refuge: A Memoir of the World War II Jewish Ghetto* Lincoln: U of Nebraska P, 1993.

Hiebert, D. "Cosmopolitanism at the Local Level: the Development of Transnational Neighbourhoods." *Conceiving Cosmopolitanism: Theory, Context and Practice.* Ed. S. Vertovec and R. Cohen. Oxford: Oxford UP, 2002. 209–23.

Hobsbawm, E. "Foreword" *Art and Power, Europe under the Dictators, 1930–1945.* Ed. D. Ades et al. London: Thames & Hudson, 1995. [A Hayward Gallery exhibition catalogue].

Holmes, C. *John Bull's Island: Immigration and British Society, 1871–1971.* Basingstoke: Macmillan, 1988.

Holmes, C. "Cosmopolitan London." *London, the Promised Land?: The Migrant Experience in a Capital City.* Ed. A. Kershen. Aldershot: Avebury, 1997. 10–37.

Home Office. *Asylum Statistics.* London: Home Office, 2007.

Hornby, Hemelryk Cotton Brokers. *Telegraphic Cipher Code for Cotton.* Liverpool and London, 1884.

———. *Private Telegraphic Code.* London, 1924.

Hornsby, C. Ed.*The Impact of Italy: The Grand Tour and Beyond.* London: British School at Rome, 2000.

How the World Views Its Cities, 2nd ed. 2006. <http://www.citybrandsindex. com>.

Huang, M. "A Woman Has So Many Parts to Her Body." *China Chic: East Meets West.* Ed. V. Steele and J. Major. New Haven: Yale UP, 1999. 133–40.

Hutnyk, J. "The Dialectics of European Hip Hop." *South Asian Popular Culture,* 3(1) (2005): 17–32.

International Organization for Migration [IOM]. *Chinese migrants in Central and Eastern Europe: the cases of Czech Republic, Hungary and Romania.* Geneva: IOM, 1995..

"Italia a New York." *Domus,* 298, September (1954): 3–10.

Iveson, K. "Strangers in the Cosmopolis." *Cosmopolitan Urbanism.* Ed. J. Binnie et al. London: Routledge, 2006. 70–86.

Jacobs, B. *Fractured Cities: Capitalism, Community and Empowerment in Britain and America.* London: Routledge, 1992.

Jakubowicz, A. "Remembering and Recovering Shanghai: Seven Jewish Families Reconnect in Cyberspace." *Save As . . . : Digital Memories.* Ed. J. Garde-Hansen and A. Reading. London: Palgrave Macmillan, forthcoming, 2009.

James, R. *Escape to Shanghai: A Jewish Community in China.* New York: Free Press, 1994.

Jameson, F. "Third-World Literature in the Era of Multinational Capital." *Social Text* 15 (1986): 65–88.

———. *Signatures of the Visible.* London: Routledge, 2007.

Jensen, R. *Marketing Modernism in Fin de Siècle Europe.* Princeton, NJ: Princeton UP, 1994.

Joppke, C. "The Retreat of Multiculturalism in the Liberal State: Theory and Policy." *British Journal of Sociology,* 55 (2004): 237–57.

Jowell, T. *Government and the Value of Culture,* London: Department for Culture, Media and Sport, 2004. <http://www.culture.gov.uk/NL/rdonlyres/ DE2ECA49–7F3D-46BF-9D11-A3AD80BF54D6/0/valueofculture.pdf>.

Kant, I. *Project for a Perpetual Peace: A Philosophical Essay.* Printed for S. Couch-man for Vernor and Hood, 1796. Digitized at Oxford University, Bodleian Library, 2007.

Kaufman, E. "The Rise of Cosmopolitanism in the Twentieth-Century West: A Comparative Historical Perspective in the United States and European Union." *Global Society,* 17 (2003): 359–83.

Kavaratzis, M. "From City Marketing to City Branding: Towards a Theoretical Framework for Developing City Brands." *Place Branding* 1(1) (2004): 58–73.

Kearney, R. *Strangers, Gods and Monsters: Ideas of Otherness.* London: Rout-ledge, 2003.

Keith, M. *After the Cosmopolitan? Multicultural Cities and the Future of Racism.* London: Routledge, 2005.

Kennedy, P. "Making Global Society: Friendship Networks among Transnational Pro-fessionals in the Building Design Industry." *Global Networks,* 4 (2004): 157–80.

———. "The Subversive Element in Interpersonal Relations—Cultural Border Crossings and Third Spaces: Skilled Migrants at Work and Play in the Global System." *Globalizations,* 4 (2007): 355–66.

Kershen, A. *London, the Promised Land? The Migrant Experience in a Capital City.* Aldershot: Ashgate, 1997.

Kerverdo, R. Letter to the Editor, *Presse-Océan,* April 26 (2004).

Khanna, P. "The Empire Strikes Back." *Guardian,* February 2 (2008): 27–28.

———. Second World Empires and Influence in the New Global Order, New York: Random House 2008a.

King, R., and E. Ruiz-Gelices. "International Student Migration and the European 'Year Abroad': Effects on European Identity and Subsequent Migration Behav-iour." *International Journal of Population Geography,* 9 (2003): 229–52.

Knecht, M., and L. Soysal. Eds. *Plausible Vielfalt: Wie der Karneval der Kulturen denkt, lernt und Kultur macht,* Berlin: Panama, 2005.

Knight, D. "Shanghai Cosmopolitan: Class, Gender and Cultural Citizenship in Weihui's *Shanghai Babe." Journal of Contemporary China* 12 (2003): 639–53.

Ko, D. "Jazzing into Modernity: High Heels, Platforms and Lotus Shoes." *China Chic: East Meets West.* Ed. V. Steele and J. Major. New Haven: Yale UP, 1999. 141–53.

Kofman, E. "Figures of the Cosmopolitan: Privileged Nationals and National Outsiders." *Innovation: The European Journal of Social Science Research* 18 (2005a): 83–97.

———. "Migration, Citizenship and the Reassertion of the Nation-State in Europe." *Citizenship Studies* 9(2005b): 453–67.

Kosnick, K. *Migrant Media: Turkish Broadcasting and Multicultural Politics in Berlin.* Bloomington: Indiana UP, 2007.

Kracauer, S. *Theory of Film: The Redemption of Physical Reality.* Princeton, NJ: Princeton UP, 1997. [Original published 1960].

Kranzler, D. "The Jewish Refugee Community of Shanghai, 1938–1945." *Wiener Library Bulletin (Great Britain)* 26(3/4) (1972/73): 28–37.

———. *Japanese, Nazis and Jews: The Jewish Refugee Community of Shanghai, 1938–1945.* New York: Yeshiva UP, 1976.

Krasno, R. *Strangers Always: A Jewish Family in Wartime Shanghai.* Berkeley: Pacific View Press, 1992.

Krätke, S. "City of Talents? Berlin's Regional Economy, Socio-Spatial Fabric and 'Worst Practice' Urban Governance." *International Journal of Urban and Regional Research,* 28 (2004): 511–29.

Kristeva, J. *Strangers to Ourselves.* Trans. L. Roudiez. London: Harvester Wheat-sheaft, 1991.

Kwong, P. "Manufacturing Ethnicity." *Critique of Anthropology,* 17 (1997): 365–87.

Kymlicka, W. *Multicultural Citizenship: A Liberal Theory of Minority Rights.* Oxford: Oxford UP, 1995.

Lam, T., and C. Martin. "Settlement of Vietnamese Refugees in London, Official Policy and Refugee Responses." Social Science Research Report. London: South Bank University, 1997.

Lambert, G. Ed. *Les Ponts de Paris*, Paris: Action artistique de la ville de Paris, 1999.

Landry, C. *The Creative City: A Toolkit for Urban Innovators.* Stroud: Comedia, 2000.

Lash, S., and J. Urry. *Economies of Signs and Space.* London: Sage, 1994.

Lastrucci, M. "De la difficulté de rappeler la traité." *Cahiers des Anneaux de la mémoire*, 1 (1999): 141–68.

Lau, S. *Chinatown Britain.* London: Chinatown Online, 2002.

Lavenex, S. "The Competition State and Multilateral Liberalization of Highly Skilled Migrants." *The Human Face of Global Mobility.* Ed. M. Smith and A. Favell. New Brunswick, NJ: Transaction, 2006. 29–54.

Lee, L O.-F. "Shanghai Modern: Reflections on Urban Culture in China in the 1930s." *Alternative Modernities* 2nd ed. Ed. D. P. Gaonkar. Durham, NC: Duke University Press, 2001. 86–122.

Lee, M., et al. "Chinese Migrant Women and Families in Britain." *Women's Studies International Forum*, 25 (2002): 607–18.

Lefebvre, H. (1996) *Writings on Cities.* Trans. and Ed. E. Kofman and E. Lebas. Oxford: Blackwell, 1996.

———. *Critique of Everyday Life.* Vol. 2. New York: Verso, 2008.

Lelièvre, P. *Nantes au 18ième siècle, urbanisme et architecture.* Paris: Picard, 1988.

Le Marec, Y. "Esclavage: 'le mauvais projet fait à Wodiczko.'" *Ouest-France*, April 23 (2004).

Leontidou, L. "Five Narratives of the Mediterranean City." *The Mediterranean: Environment and Society.* Ed. R. King, L. Proudfoot, and B. Smith. London: Arnold, 1997, 181–93.

Levenson, J. "The Province, the Nation, and the World: the Problem of Chinese Identity." *Approaches to Modern Chinese History.* Ed. A. Feuerwerker, R. Murphey, and M. C. Wright. Berkeley: U of California P, 1967. 268–88.

Levine, H. *In Search of Sugihara: The Elusive Japanese Diplomat Who Risked his Life to Rescue 10,000 Jews from the Holocaust.* Glencoe: Free Press, 1996.

Li, J. R. *Baofeng yuqian* [Before the Tempest]. Beijing: People's Literature Press, 1997a.

———. *Da bo* [The Great Waves]. Beijing: People's Literature Press, 1997b.

———. *Sishui weilan* [Ripples in the Dead Pond]. Beijing: People's Literature Press, 1997c.

Li, S. *Li Jieren de shenghuo he gongzuo* [The Life and Work of Li Jieren]. Sichuan Academy of Social Sciences Press, 1986.

Lin, X. "Chinese Students in London: Experiences and Needs." Unpublished MA dissertation. London: Middlesex University, 2007.

London Chinatown Chinese Association [LCCA]. *London Chinatown Souvenir Magazine.* London: LCCA, 1985.

London Development Agency. *The Mayor's Commission on the Creative Industries: Improving Links in Creative Production Chains.* <http://www.creative-london.org.uk>.

London Eye Press Pack. (2007). <http://www.ba-londoneye.com/pdf/press_pack.pdf>.

Lynch, K. "Reconsidering the Image of the City." *Cities of the Mind: Images and Themes of the City in the Social Sciences.* Ed. L. Rodwin and R. Holister. New York: Plenum, 1984. 151–161.

Malik, R. Ed. *From Kaifeng . . . to Shanghai: Jews in China* Nettetal, Germany: Steyler, 2000.

Malpas, J. *Place and Experience: A Philosophical Topography.* Cambridge: Cambridge UP, 1999.

———. *Heidegger's Topology: Being, Place, World.* Cambridge, MA: MIT P, 2006.

Mandel, R. "Second-Generation Non-Citizens: Children of the Turkish Migrant Diaspora in Germany." *Children and the Politics of Culture.* Ed. S. Stephens. Princeton, NJ: Princeton UP, 1995. 265–81.

Mao, D. *Ziye* [Midnight]. Beijing: People's Literature Press, 1986.

Markova, E., and R. Black. *East European Migration and Community Cohesion.* York: Rowntree Foundation, 2007. <http://www.jrf.org.org.uk/bookshop/ebooks/2053-migration-community-cohesion.pdf>.

May, J. "The Chinese in Britain, 1860–1914." *Immigrants and Minorities in British Society.* Ed. C. Holmes. London: Allen & Unwin, 1978. 111–124.

Mayer, M. "Bagdadi Jewish Merchants in Shanghai and the Opium Trade." *Jewish Culture and History* 2(1) (1999): 58–71.

Michael, F. "Regionalism in Nineteenth-Century China." *Modern China: An Interpretive Anthology.* Ed. J. Levenson. New York: Macmillan, 1971. 34–52.

Molz, J., and S. Gibson, S. Eds. *Mobilizing Hospitality: The Ethics of Social Relations in a Mobile World.* Aldershot: Ashgate, 2007.

Montgomery, J. "Cultural Quarters as Mechanisms for Urban Regeneration." 2003. <http://www.planning.sa.gov.au/congress/pdf/Papers/Montgomery.pdf>.

Morris, M. "On the Future of Parochialism: Globalisation, *Young and Dangerous IV*, and Cinema Studies in Tuen Mun." *Film History and National Cinema, Studies in Irish Film II.* Ed. J. Hill and K. Rockett. Dublin: Four Courts, 2005. 17–36.

Mouffe, C. *The Democratic Paradox.* London: Verso, 2000.

Moustafine, M. *Secrets and Spies: the Harbin files,* Sydney: Random House, 2002.

Movius, L. "Trying to the Relive the Past: Restoring Shanghai's Old Jewish Neighborhood Won't be Easy." *Asian Wall Street Journal,* March 18–20, 2005. <http://www.movius.us/articles/AWSJ-tilanqiao.html>.

Mu, S. Y. *Wuge ren zai yezonghui li, gongmu* [Five Figures of the Nightclub, Public Cemetery]. Shanghai: Xiandai shuju, 1933.

Museums Association. *Bulletin,* 352. London: Museums Association, 1996.

Nagel, T. *The View From Nowhere.* Oxford, Oxford UP, 1986.

Nava, M. *Visceral Cosmopolitanism: Gender, Culture and the Normalization of Difference.* Oxford: Berg, 2007.

Nederveen Pieterse, J. *Ethnicities and Global Multiculture: Pants for an Octopus.* Plymouth: Rowman and Littlefield, 2007.

Northwest Regional Development Agency. *England's North West: the Strategy towards 2020.* Northwest Regional Development Agency, 1999.

North West Universities Association Culture Committee. *The Contribution of Higher Education to Cultural Life in the North West.* North West Universities Association, 2004.

Nussbaum, M. *Cultivating Humanity: A Classical Defence of Reform in Liberal Education.* Cambridge, MA: Harvard UP, 1997.

O'Connor, J. *The Definition of the Cultural Industries.* Manchester Institute of Popular Culture, 1999. <http://mmu.ac.uk/h-ss/mip/iciss/home2.htm>.

Observations on The Bill Introduced Last Session by Mr Wilberforce for the More Effectually Preventing the Unlawful Importation of Slaves. And the Holding of Free Persons in Slavery in the British Colonies. London: Richardson, Cornhill, 1816.

Olins, W. *The Corporate Personality: an Inquiry into the Nature of Corporate Identity.* London: Design Council, 1978.

O'Malley, B. "An Offer You Can't Refuse." *The Education Guardian*, December 5 (2006): 1.

ONS-Office for National Statistics (2008), Neighborhood Statistics Online, (London), available at http://www.neighborhood.statistics.gov.uk/dissemination/.

Orchard, J. "Shanghai." *The Geographical Review*, 26 (1936).

Pan American World Airways. "Pan American World Airways Will Resume Clipper Service between United States and France." *New York Times*, 14 January 14 (1946).

Papastergiadis, N. *The Turbulence of Migration: Globalisation: Deterritorialisation and Hybridity.* Cambridge: Polity, 2000.

Pastoureau, M. *The Devil's Cloth: A History of Stripes.* New York: Washington Square P, 2003.

Péron, P. Letter to the Editor. *Ouest-France*, October 16 (2004).

Pétré-Grenouilleau, O. *Nantes au temps du traite des noirs.* Paris: Hachette, 1998.

Pick, J., and M. Anderton. *Building Jerusalem: Art, Industry and the British Millennium.* Amsterdam: Harwood Academic, 1999.

Pieke, F. N. *Community and Identity in the New Chinese Migration Order.* Compas Working Paper. Oxford: Compas, 2005.

Pieyre de Mandiargues, A. "Le Passage Pommeraye." *Le Musée noir*, Paris: Laffont, 1946, 63–83.

Ponti, G. "Favola americana." *Domus*, 272, July-August (1952): 6–10.

Prasso, S. "Salvaging Jewish Heritage in China, Block by Block." *New York Times*, May 31 (2004) .

Rath, J. "The Transformation of Ethnic Neighbourhoods into Places of Leisure and Consumption." *CCIS Working Paper Series, 144*, San Diego: Center for Comparative Immigration Studies (CCIS), University of California, 2007.

Recchi, E. "From Migrants to Movers: Citizenship and Mobility in the European Union." *The Human Face of Global Mobility.* Ed. M. Smith and A. Favell. New Brunswick, NJ: Transaction, 2006. 53–77.

Reed, M. *Wordsworth: The Chronology of the Middle Years, 1800–1815.* Cambridge, MA: Harvard UP, 1975.

Ristaino, M. "White Russian and Jewish Refugees in Shanghai, 1920–44, as Recorded in the Shanghai Municipal Police Files, National Archives, Washington, D.C." *Republican China*, 16 (1990): 51–72.

Rogers, E., and A. Rossi. 'Un monumento per New York', *Casabella*, 223, January(1959): 3–11.

Roodhouse, S. "Have Cultural Industries a Role to Play in Regional Regeneration and a Nation's Wealth." *The International Journal of Applied Management*, 4(1) (2003): 180–216.

———. "The New Global Growth Industry: Definitional Problems in the Creative Industries—A Practical Approach." *Counting Culture? Practical Challenges for the Museum and Heritage Sector.* Ed. S. Roodhouse and C. Kelly. London: Greenwich UP, 2004. 13–31.

Roodhouse, S., and M. Roodhouse. "Cultural Intervention in British Urban Regeneration since 1945." Proceedings of International Arts and Cultural Management Association Fourth Biennial Conference, San Francisco, 1997.

Ross, K. *Fast Cars, Clean Bodies: Decolonization and the Reordering of French Culture.* Cambridge, MA: MIT P, 1995.

Rotherham Metropolitan Borough."Celebrating our Past Together, Developing our Distinctiveness Together, Creating our Future Together: A Cultural Strategy." Rotherham2000.

Royle, N. *The Uncanny.* Manchester: Manchester UP, 2003.

214   Bibliography

Ruby, C. "Nantes: mémorial à l'esclavage." *Urbanisme*, 341 (2005): 8.
Rudd, K. "Apology to Australia's Indigenous Peoples," Australia Parliament House, canberra, 2008, http://www.aph.gov.au/house/Rudd_Speech.pdf. Accessed 21 September 2008.
Ruggiero, V. "Fear and Change in the City." *City*, 7(1) (2003): 45–55.
Rumsford, C. Ed. *Cosmopolitanism and Europe.* Liverpool: Liverpool UP, 2006.
Rutland, S. "'Waiting Room Shanghai': Australian Reactions to the Plight of the Jews in Shanghai after the Second World War." *Leo Baeck Institute: Year Book (Great Britain),* 32 (1987): 407–33.
Ryan, L. et al. "Recent Polish Migrants in London: Social Networks, Transience and Settlement." [A report for study RES-000–22–1552, funded by the Economic and Social Research Council] London: Social Policy Research Centre, Middlesex University, 2007.
Sadler, S. *The Situationist City.* Cambridge, MA: MIT P, 1999.
Sandercock, L. *Cosmopolis II: Mongrel Cities of the 21st Century.* London: Continuum, 2003.
Sassen, S. *The Global City: New York, London, Tokyo.* Princeton: Princeton UP, 1991.
———. *Cities in a World Economy.* Thousand Oaks, CA: Pine Forge, 2000.
———. *Cities in a World Economy.* 3rd ed. Thousand Oaks, CA: Pine Forge, 2006.
Save Chinatown Campaign. *Save Chinatown* [A campaigning leaflet]. London: Save Chinatown Campaign. 2005.
Sawyer, M. "Manchester is the Beating Cultural Heart of Britain." *Observer, Review,* July 1 (2007).
Sen, A. *Identity and Violence: The Illusion of Destiny.* New York: Allen and Lane, 2006.
Sennett, R. *The Use of Disorder.* New York: Knopf, 1970.
———. "Cosmopolitanism and the Social Experience of Cities" *Conceiving Cosmopolitanism: Theory, Context and Practice.* Ed. S. Vertovec and R. Cohen. Oxford: Oxford UP, 2002. 42–47.
———. *Respect. The Formation of Character in an Age of Inequality.* London: Penguin, 2004.
Sepulveda, L., S. Syrett, and F. Lyon "New Ethnic Minority Business Communities in Britain: Challenges of Diversity and Informality." SPRC Working Paper Series, 1, London: Middlesex University, 2008.
Shaw, P., and K. Allen. "Continuing Professional Development for the Creative Industries: A Review of Provision in the Higher Education Sector." Report to HEFCE, London Arts Council of England and Design Council, 2001.
Shaw, S., S. Bagwell, and J. Karmowska. "Ethnoscapes as Spectacle: Reimaging Multicultural Districts as New Destinations for Leisure and Consumption." *Urban Studies,* 41(2004): 1983–2000.
Shi, Y. Ed. *Minguo wanxiang: shishang* [The Republic Panorama: Fashion]. Beijing: Solidarity, 2005.
Simmel, G. "The Metropolis and Mental Life." *The Sociology of Geog Simmel.* Ed. K. Wolff. New York: Free Press, 1950a. 409–24.
———. "The Stranger." *The Sociology of Geog Simmel.* Ed. K. Wolff. New York: Free Press, 1950b. 402–8.
Skrbis, Z, G. Kendall, and I. Woodward. "Locating Cosmopolitanism: Between Humanist Ideal and Grounded Social Category." *Theory, Culture and Society,* 21 (2004): 115–36.
Skrbis, Z., and I. Woodward, I. "The Ambivalence of Ordinary Cosmopolitanism: Investigating the Limits of Cosmopolitan Openness." *Sociological Review,* 55 (2007): 731–47.

Smart, A., and J. Smart. "Urbanization and the Global Perspective." *Annual Review of Anthropology*, 32 (2003): 263–85.

Soja, E. *Postmetropolis: Critical Studies of Cities and Regions*. Oxford: Blackwell, 2000.

Solesbury, W. *Evidence Based Policy: Whence it Came and Where it's Going*. Working Paper 1. London: ESRC Centre for Evidence Based Policy and Practice, 2001.

Song, M. "When the 'Global Chain' Does Not Lead to Satisfaction All Round: a Comment on the Morecambe Bay Tragedy." *Feminist Review*, 77 (2004): 137–40.

Soysal, L. *Projects of Culture: An Ethnographic Episode in the Life of Migrant Youth in Berlin*. Cambridge: Harvard UP, 1999.

———. "Rap, Hiphop, Kreuzberg: Scripts of/for Migrant Youth Culture in the WorldCity Berlin." *New German Critique*, 92 (2004): 62–81.

Stein, R. *The French Slave Trade in the Eighteenth Century: An Old Regime Business*. Madison: U of Wisconsin P, 1979.

Storkey, M., and R. Lewis. "London: a True Cosmopolis." *Ethnicity in the 1991 Census, Vol 3, Social Geography and Ethnicity in Britain: Geographical Spread, Spatial Concentration and Internal Migration*. Ed. Peter Ratcliffe. London: HMSO, 1996. 201–25.

Szerszynski, B., and J. Urry. "Visuality, Mobility and the Cosmopolitan: Inhabiting the World from Afar." *British Journal of Sociology*, 57(1) (2006): 113–31.

Tan, K. *Justice without Borders: Cosmopolitanism, Nationalism and Patriotism*. Cambridge: Cambridge UP, 2004.

Tardieu, J. *La Véritable Histoire du soldat inconnu*. Paris: Futuropolis/Gallimard, 1974.

Taylor, C. *Multiculturalism and "The Politics of Recognition."* Princeton: Princeton UP, 1992.

Tsing, A. "The Global Situation." *Cultural Anthropology*, 15 (2000): 327"60.

Turner, B. "Classical Sociology and Cosmopolitanism: a Critical Defence of the Social." *British Journal of Sociology*, 57(1) (2006): 133–55.

———. "The Enclave Society: Towards a Sociology of Immobility." *European Journal of Social Theory*, 10 (2007): 287–303.

Turner, C. *Marketing Modernism between the Two World Wars*. Amherst: U of Massachusetts P, 2003.

"Un nuovo grattacielo a New York." *Domus*, 358, September (1959): 1–3.

Urbanistica June 27, (1959a)[A special issue on Rome].

Urbanistica October 28–29 (1959b) [A special issue on Rome].

Urry, J. *Sociology beyond Societies*. London: Routledge, 2000.

Vaiou, D., and A. Kalandides. (2009). "Cities of 'Others': Access, Contact and Participation in Everyday Public Spaces." *Geographica Helvetica*.

van der Veer, P. "Colonial Cosmopolitanism." *Conceiving Cosmopolitanism: Theory, Context and Practice*. Ed. S. Vertovec and R. Cohen. Oxford: Oxford UP, 2002. 165–79.

Vertovec, S. "Super-diversity and its Implications." *Ethnic and Racial Studies*, 30 (2007): 1024–54.

Vertovec, S., and R. Cohen. Eds. *Conceiving Comsopolitanism: Theory, Context and Practice*. Oxford: Oxford UP, 2002.

Wakeman, Jr., F., and W. Yeh. *Shanghai Sojourners*. Berkeley: Institute of East Asian Studies, U of California P, 1992.

Waldinger, R., and D. Fitzgerald "Transnationalism in Question." *American Journal of Sociology*, 109 (2004): 1177–95.

Walzer, M. *On Toleration*. New Haven: Yale UP, 1997.

Wang, J. "Holocaust Recalled." *ShanghaiDaily.com*. October 26, 2004. <http://ShanghaiDaily.com/article/?id=116862&type=feature>.

Ward, S. *Selling Places: The Marketing and Promotion of Towns and Cities, 1850–2000*. London: Spon, 1998.

Werbner, P. "Vernacular Cosmopolitanism." *Theory, Culture and Society: Special Issue on Problematizing Global Knowledge*, 23 (2006): 496–98.

Werbner, P., and T. Modood. Eds. *Debating Cultural Hybridity: Multi-Cultural Identities and the Politics of Anti-Racism*. London: Zed Books, 1997.

Whitman, W. *Leaves of Grass*. (1855).

Wilkins, M. "When and Why Brand Names in Food and Drink?" *Adding Value: Brands and Marketing in Food and Drink*. Ed. G. Jones and N. Morgan. London: Routledge, 1994. 15–40.

Williams, R. *The Country and the City*. London: Chatto and Windus, 1973.

———. *Culture*. London: Fontana Paperbacks, 1981.

Williams, R. *Dream Worlds: Mass Consumption in Late Nineteenth-Century France*. Berkeley: U of California P, 1982.

Wilson, D. "Fuzhou Flower Shops of East Broadway: 'Heat and Noise' and the Fashioning of New Traditions." *Journal of Ethnic and Migration Studies* 32 (2005): 291–308.

Wilson, V. "Dress and the Cultural Revolution." *China Chic: East Meets West*. Ed. V. Steele and J. Major. New Haven: Yale UP, 1999. 167–86.

Wordsworth, D. *The Grasmere and Alfoxden Journals*. Oxford: Oxford UP, 2002.

Wordsworth, W. "Composed Upon Westminster Bridge, Sept. 3, 1802." *Poems in Two Volumes, Vol. 1*. London: Longman, Hurst, Rees and Orme, 1807. 118.

Yeoh, S., and K. Willis "Singaporean and British Transmigrants in China and the Cultural Politics of 'Contact Zones.'" *Journal of Ethnic and Migration Studies*, 31 (2005): 269–85.

Young, C., M. Diep, and S. Drabble. "Living with Difference? The 'Cosmopolitan' and Urban Reimaging in Manchester, UK." *Urban Studies*, 43 (2006): 1687–714.

Yuval-Davis, N. "Belonging and the Politics of Belonging." *Patterns of Prejudice*, 40(3) (2006): 26–54.

Zamperini, P. "On their Dress they Wore a Body: Fashion and Identity in Late Qing Shanghai." *positions: east asia cultures critique*, 11 (2003): 301–30.

Zhang, Y. *Cinema and Urban Culture in Shanghai, 1922–1943*. Stanford: Stanford UP, 1999

Zhou Y. *Historicizing Online Politics: The Telegraph, the Internet and Political Participation in China*. Stanford: Stanford UP, 2006.

Zhou, Y., and Y. Tseng., "Regrounding the 'Ungrounded Empires': Localization as the Geographical Catalyst for Transnationalism." *Global Networks: A Journal of Transnational Affairs*, 1 (2001): 131–54.

Žižek, S. *Enjoy Your Symptom! Jacques Lacan in Hollywood and Out*. London: Routledge, 2001.

Zubaida, S. "Middle Eastern Experiences of Cosmopolitanism." *Conceiving Cosmopolitanism: Theory, Context and Practice*. Ed. S. Vertovec and R. Cohen. Oxford: Oxford UP, 2002. 32–41.

Zuroff, E. "Rescue via the Far East: The Attempt to Save Polish Rabbis and Yeshivah Students, 1939–41." *Simon Wiesenthal Center Annual*, 1 (1984): 153–83.

Contributors

Alessio d'Angelo is a research fellow at Middlesex University. He has worked on a number of research projects with universities and research institutions in the United Kingdom and Italy, mainly focusing on migration and ethnic minorities. As a volunteer and a consultant, he has also worked with third sector and BME community organizations in both London and Rome. His current research interests include integration and "identity" issues, community organizations, social capital and social networks, statistics and data mapping for the social sciences. His recent publications include: *Kurdish Community Organisations in London: A Social Network Analysis* (2008), *Refugee Rights in Europe: Policies and Practice of Integration* (2005), edited with A. Ricci, and several contributions to the annual *Dossier Statistico Immigrazione*, IDOS, Italy.

Stephanie Hemelryk Donald is professor of Chinese Media Studies at the University of Sydney, where she researches the politics of media culture, and the intersection of social history and visual media. Her *Public Secrets, Public Spaces* (2000) analyses the relationship between political change, civil society, and film in the 1980s and early 1990s in China. *Little Friends* (2005) discusses postrevolutionary filmmakers and children's socialization. *Tourism and the Branded City: Film and Identity on the Pacific Rim* (2007) takes an interdisciplinary view of urban histories and visual identity. *The State of China Atlas* (3rd ed. 2009), *Media in China* (co-edited with Michael Keane, 2001) and *Picturing Power* (co-edited with Harriet Evans, 1999) are well-used texts in tertiary courses on China and visual media. Current research looks at middle class emergence in the PRC, mobile-phone use among young people, and the aesthetics of the poster in China.

Panos Hatziprokopiou is research fellow at the Social Policy Research Centre, Middlesex University. He has conducted research on aspects of migration to Greece and Britain, and on migrants from Albania, Bulgaria, and the former Soviet Union, and is currently involved in a major AHRC project on London's Chinatown. His main interests are in the dynamics of immigrants' settlement, the interplay between migration and social change in urban contexts, and questions relating to diaspora, diversity, and difference in the city. He is author of several articles and the book *Globalisation and Contemporary Immigration to Southern European Cities: Social Exclusion and Incorporation of Immigrants in Thessaloniki* (2006).

Andrew Jakubowicz is professor of Sociology, the coordinating director of the Centre for Cosmopolitan Civil Societies at the University of Technology, Sydney, and Secretary of the NGO Institute for Cultural Diversity. His parents, refugees from the Holocaust, escaped to Australia via Japan and China, thus giving him a lifelong curiosity about culture, risk, and survival. His research on China and its Jewish histories has produced the website "The Menorah of Fang Bang Lu" as well as articles and a television documentary. He was a board member of the Special Broadcasting Service from 1984 to 1986, and has served on the Australia Council's Community Cultural Development Board and Arts for a Multicultural Australia Advisory Committee. His online project "Making Multicultural Australia in the Twenty-First Century" won Australia's Best Secondary Website Award for 2005. He has taught in Europe, Asia, and the Americas.

Paul Kennedy is reader in Sociology in the Department of Sociology at Manchester Metropolitan University. In 2000 he helped to found the Global Studies Association in 2000 and has since worked on its committee in various roles. He has published books on African capitalism and development and is the co-author with Robin Cohen of Global Sociology, now in its second edition. He has co-edited three further books, two concerned with globalization themes. Recent research interests have focused on transnational professionals and skilled migrants and the transformatory possibilities for individuals and societies of living abroad. Specific studies in this area have included work on professionals in the global design/building industry, postgraduate EU migrants in Manchester, and the social networks of Brazilians living in the United Kingdom.

Catherine Kevin completed her PhD at the University of Sydney and is currently a lecturer in Australian History at Flinders University, Adelaide, South Australia. Her key research interests are histories of Australian reproductive medicine, reproductive politics, and Italian immigration to Australia. Works in progress include a monograph entitled *Great Expectations: A Political History of Pregnancy in Australia (since 1945)* and the editing of a collection of essays called *Feminism and the Body, Interdisciplinary Perspectives*. Recent publications include "Subjects for Citizenship: Pregnancy and the Australian Nation, 1945–2000"; "Forming Families on the Reproductive Frontier"; "Maternity and Freedom: Australian Feminist Encounters with the Reproductive Body"; and A History of Italian Settlement in New South Wales (1999), co-authored with Roslyn Pesman.

Eleonore Kofman is professor of Gender, Migration, and Citizenship and co-director of the Social Policy Research Centre at Middlesex University. Her research interests are in gender and migration in Europe, especially family and skilled migrations; cosmopolitanism, multiculturalism, and migration; and feminist political geography. She is co-author of *Gender and International Migration in Europe: Employment, Welfare and Politics* (2000) and co-editor of *Mapping Women, Making Politics: Feminist Perspectives on Political Geography* (2004), *Henri Lefebvre: Selected Writings* (2003) and *Globalization: Theory and Practice* (3rd ed. 2008).

Kira Kosnick is junior professor of Cultural Anthropology and European Ethnology at Frankfurt University. After earning her PhD in Cultural Anthropology from the New School for Social Research, New York, in 2003, she worked as a postdoctoral research fellow and lecturer in Britain, before moving to Germany in 2006. Her work deals with migrant media practices and cultural transformations in European urban spaces, with a particular focus on transnational migration between Turkey and Germany. Her most recent book is *Migrant Media: Turkish Broadcasting and Multicultural Politics in Berlin* (2007).

Xiujing Liang was born in China and has worked in universities and other research organizations in China and Denmark as well as in Britain. Her main research interests are in migration and ethnicity, overseas Chinese in United Kingdom and Europe. Her PhD thesis, "Exploring the Ethnic Identity of Overseas Chinese Community Leaders in Europe," was completed at Aalborg University in Denmark in 2002. She is now working as a research fellow on the research project "Cityscapes of Diaspora: Images and Realities of London's Chinatown," funded by the Arts and Humanities Research Council based at Middlesex University.

Christoph Lindner is professor and chair of English Literature at the University of Amsterdam and Research Affiliate at the University of London Institute in Paris. His main scholarly interests are in the interdisciplinary study of urban space and cultural production, especially architecture, film, literature, and photography. He is the author of *Fictions of Commodity Culture: From the Victorian to the Postmodern* (2003) and editor of *Urban Space and Cityscape: Perspectives from Modern and Contemporary Culture* (2006). Forthcoming book projects include *Imagining New York City: Literature, Urbanism and the Visual Arts* and an edition of essays, *Globalization, Violence, and the Visual Culture of Cities*.

Jeff Malpas is professor of Philosophy and ARC Australian Professorial Fellow at the University of Tasmania. He is also distinguished visiting professor at LaTrobe University. The author of many books and articles on a range of philosophical topics, especially on issues of place and space, his most recent book is *Heidegger's Topology* (2006).

Bill Marshall is professor of Comparative Literary and Cultural Studies at the University of Stirling, Scotland, having previously worked at the Universities of Glasgow and Southampton. He has written widely in the field of French and Francophone cultural studies, especially on cinema. His authored books include *Victor Serge: The Uses of Dissent* (1992), *Guy Hocquenghem* (1996), *Quebec National Cinema* (2001), *André Téchiné* (2007) and the forthcoming *The French Atlantic: Travels in Culture and History* (2008). He has also edited *Musicals: Hollywood and Beyond* (2000), *Montreal-Glasgow* (2005), and a three-volume encyclopedia, *France and the Americas* (2005).

Nicola Montagna is research fellow in the Social Policy Research Centre at Middlesex University. He has worked on a number of research projects in the United Kingdom and Italy, focusing in particular on skilled migration and new migrants. As a consultant, he has worked with local authorities and third-sector organizations in Italy on social policy issues, conducting research as well as consultancy activities. He has published extensively on a number of themes including migration, social policy, voluntary organizations, and social movements in both Italy and Britain.

Simon Roodhouse is professor in Creative Industries at the University of the Arts, London, adjunct professor of Creative Industries, University of Technology, Sydney, and director of Safe Hands (Management) Ltd, a strategic consultancy engaged in education and cultural industries. Previously he had been adjunct professor at CIRAC, Queensland University of Technology, Brisbane, Australia; visiting professor Creative Industries at the University of Bolton, and the University of Central England. He is the author of *Cultural Quarters: Principles and Practice* (2006) and established with the University of the Arts, London, the *Creative Industries Journal*. In addition, he was the chief executive of the University Vocational Awards Council, a consortium of HEIs and FECs dedicated to championing higher level vocational learning.

Rosemary Sales is professor of Social Policy at Middlesex University and joint-director of the Social Policy Research Centre. Her current research interests are in immigration theory and policy and in new migration flows. She has been involved in a number of research projects on these themes both at a European level and focusing on London. As well as research projects on Chinese migration to London, recent projects have examined migratory strategies of recent Polish migrants in London and skilled migration and migrant integration in Europe. Recent publications include *Understanding Immigration and Refugee Policy: Contradictions and Continuities* (2007) and *Growing up with Risk* (2007) edited with B. Thom and J. Pearce.

Mark Shiel is senior lecturer in the Department of Film Studies at King's College, London. He is the author of *Italian Neorealism: Rebuilding the Cinematic City* (2006) and co-editor of *Screening the City* (2003) and *Cinema and the City: Film and Urban Societies in a Global Context* (2001). His recent publications include "Banal and Magnificent Space in Electra Glide in Blue (1973), or An Allegory of the Nixon Era," Cinema Journal (Winter 2007), and "Hollywood, the New Left, and FTA," in Frank Krutnik et al. (eds), *"Un-American" Hollywood: Politics and Film in the Blacklist Era* (2007). He has been a Leverhulme Trust Research Fellow, a visiting scholar in the Department of Film, TV, and Digital Media at UCLA, and Davis Center Fellow at the Shelby Cullom Davis Center for Historical Studies at Princeton University.

Yi Zheng is a research fellow at the Institute for International Studies, UTS. She received her PhD from the University of Pittsburgh, has been Agora Fellow at the Advanced Studies Institute of Berlin, Germany; a senior fellow at the Advanced Studies Institute of Budapest, Hungary; a postdoctoral fellow at the Porter Institute for Comparative Poetics; and a lecturer in the Department of East Asian Studies, Tel Aviv University. Her recent publications include: "Cultural Tours and Spiritual Home: Yu Qiuyu and the Cultural Essays of 1990s China," *Portal* (January 2007); "The Figuration of a Sublime Origin: Guo Moruo's Qu Yuan," *Modern Chinese Literature and Culture* (Spring, 2004); "Personalized Writing and Chinese Feminist Criticism in the 'Post'-New Era," *Tulsa Studies in Women's Literature* (2004) and *Traveling Facts* (ed. with C. Baillie and E. Dunn, 2004); and "Cultural Traditions and Contemporaneity: the Case of the New Confucianist Debate," in W. Lepenies (ed.), *Entangled Histories and Negotiated Universals* (2003). Her monograph *The Modern Transformation of a Sublime Aesthetics: from Edmund Burke to Guo Moruo* is forthcoming, as is "A Taste of Class—the Manuals for Becoming Woman," in *positions: east asia culture critique*, with Stephanie H. Donald).

Index

For Product Safety Concerns and Information please contact our EU
representative GPSR@taylorandfrancis.com Taylor & Francis Verlag GmbH,
Kaufingerstraße 24, 80331 München, Germany

Printed and bound by CPI Group (UK) Ltd, Croydon, CR0 4YY
08/05/2025
01864319-0001